RETRIBUTION OR REALITY?

Retribution or Reality?

A Short Theological Introduction to the Book of Job

MICHAEL S. MOORE

PICKWICK *Publications* • Eugene, Oregon

RETRIBUTION OR REALITY?
A Short Theological Introduction to the Book of Job

Pickwick Publications
An Imprint of Wipf and Stock Publishers
199 W. 8th Ave., Suite 3
Eugene, OR 97401

www.wipfandstock.com

PAPERBACK ISBN: 978-1-7252-5461-9
HARDCOVER ISBN: 978-1-7252-5460-2
EBOOK ISBN: 978-1-7252-5462-6

Cataloguing-in-Publication data:

Names: Moore, Michael S., author.

Title: Retribution or reality? : a short theological introduction to the book of Job / Michael S. Moore.

Description: Eugene, OR: Pickwick Publications, 2023. | Includes bibliographical references and index.

Identifiers: ISBN 978-1-6667-0733-5 (paperback). | ISBN 978-1-6667-0734-2 (hardcover). | ISBN 978-1-6667-0735-9 (ebook).

Subjects: LCSH: Bible. Job—Criticism, interpretation, etc.

Classification: BS1415.2 M66 2023 (print). | BS1415.2 (ebook).

Contents

List of Abbreviations | *vii*

1 Introductory Remarks | 1

2 The Prosecutor's Question | 8
Seven Questions | 12
Heavenly Council | 20
The Keyword | 25
Economic Usage | 25
Non-Economic Usage | 27
Theological Reflection | 29
Prosecutor's Whereabouts | 30
Defendant's Piety | 31
Defendant's Motives | 31
Judge's Permission | 32
Spousal Advice | 33
Summary | 34

3 The Counselors' Questions | 36
Eliphaz | 39
Bildad | 52
Zophar | 57
Elihu | 61
Summary | 68

4 The Compensation/Retribution Motif in ANE Wisdom | 71
Egyptian Texts | 71
The Tale of the Eloquent Peasant | 72
The Dialogue of Ipu-Wer with the Lord of All | 80
Dialogue of a Man with His Soul | 83

Mesopotamian Texts | 84
The Babylonian Theodicy | 84
The Poem of the Pious Sufferer | 91
Summary | 97

5 The Compensation/Retribution Motif in Early Joban Tradition | 98
Targum Job | 100
TgJob Prologue | 100
TgJob Dialogues | 102
Summary | 106
Testament of Job | 106
Job and Satan | 109
Job and His Wife | 111
Job and the Three Kings | 114
Summary | 115

6 Concluding Remarks | 117
Job and His Pain | 119
Job's Spouse and "Friends" on His Pain | 123
Why Does Job's Spouse Presume That Cursing God Is Theologically Appropriate? | 123
Why Do Job's "Friends" Presume That Retributional Censure Is Theologically Appropriate? | 124

Bibliography | 127
Subject Index | 161
Author Index | 164

Abbreviations

The abbreviations below complement those listed in the SBL Handbook of Style

′	symbol indicating reverse side (e.g., 8′ refers to line 8 on tablet's reverse side)
1QpHab	The Habakkuk Commentary from Qumran Cave 1
1QS	The Scroll of the Rule from Qumran Cave 1
2En	2 Enoch
2ms	2nd masculine singular
ÄAT	Ägypten und Altes Testament
AB	Anchor Bible
ABD	*Anchor Bible Dictionary*. Edited by David Noel Freedman. 6 vols. New York: Doubleday, 1992
ABL	*Assyrian and Babylonian Letters.* Edited by Robert F. Harper. Chicago: University of Chicago Press, 1892–1914
ABR	*Australian Biblical Review*
AcBib	Academia Biblica
ad loc.	*"to the place"* (Lat.)
AEL	*Ancient Egyptian Literature.* Edited by Miriam Lichtheim. 3 vols. Berkeley: University of California Press, 1973
AfO	*Archiv für Orientforschung*

AGH	*Die akkadische Gebetsserie "Handerhebung."* Edited by Erich Ebeling. Berlin: Akademie-Verlag, 1953.
AHw	*Akkadisches Handwörterbuch.* Edited by Wolfram von Soden. Wiesbaden: Harrassowitz, 1965–81
AIL	Ancient Israel and Its Literature
A.J.	*Antiquities of the Jews*, by Titus Flavius Josephus
AJEC	Ancient Judaism and Early Christianity
AJSL	*American Journal of Semitic Languages*
AJSR	*Association of Jewish Studies Review*
Akk	Akkadian
ANE	Ancient Near East(ern)
ANET	*Ancient Near Eastern Texts Relating to the Old Testament.* Edited by James A. Pritchard. 3rd ed. Princeton: Princeton University Press, 1969
AOAT	Alter Orient und Altes Testament
APAW	*Abhandlungen der Preussischen Akademie der Wissenschaften*
Arab	Arabic
Aram	Aramaic
ArBib	Aramaic Bible
ARM	*Archives royales de Mari*
ATD	Das Alte Testament Deutsch
Atr	*Atraḫasis*
ATR	*Anglican Theological Review*
AYBRL	Anchor Yale Bible Reference Library
b.	Talmud Bavli
BAM	*Babylonisch-assyrische Medicin in Texten und Untersuchungen.* Edited by Franz Köcher. Berlin: de Gruyter, 1963
BBK	*Berliner Beiträge zur Keilinschriftforschung*
BBR	*Bulletin for Biblical Research*
BBRel	*Beiträge der babylonischen Religion. Ritualtafeln.* Edited by Heinrich Zimmern. Leipzig: Hinrichs, 1899

BDB	*A Hebrew and English Lexicon of the Old Testament*, by Francis Brown, S. R. Driver and Charles A. Briggs. 2nd ed. Oxford: Clarendon, 1953
BEATAJ	Beiträge zur Erforschung des Alten Testaments und des antiken Judentum
BETL	Bibliotheca Ephemeridum Theologicarum Lovaniensium
BFC	La Bible en français courant
Bib	*Biblica*
BibInt	*Biblical Interpretation*
BIFAO	*Bulletin de l'institut français d'archéologie orientale*
BibOr	Biblica et Orientalia
BiJuSt	Biblical and Judaic Studies
BIN	*Babylonian Inscriptions in the Collection of J. B. Nies*
BJSoc	*British Journal of Sociology*
BK	Biblische Kommentar
BL	*Historische Grammatik der hebräischen Sprache.* By Hans Bauer and Pontus Leander. 1922. Reprint, Hildesheim: Olms, 1981
BM	British Museum
BN	*Biblische Notizen*
BO	*Bibliotheca Orientalis*
BSac	*Bibliotheca Sacra*
BT	*Babylonian Theodicy*
BTB	*Biblical Theology Bulletin*
BWANT	Beiträge zur Wissenschaft vom Alten und Neuen Testament
BWL	*Babylonian Wisdom Literature*, by W. G. Lambert. Oxford: Clarendon, 1960.
BZ	*Biblische Zeitschrift*
BZABR	Beihefte zur Zeitschrift für Altorientalische und Biblische Rechtsgeschichte
BZAW	Beihefte zur Zeitschrift für die Alttestamentliche Wissenschaft
c.	*circa* ("approximately" Lat.)

Cam	*Caminhando*
CAD	*Chicago Assyrian Dictionary*
CANE	*Civilizations of the Ancient Near East.* 4 vols. Edited by Jack M. Sasson. New York: Scribner, 1995
CAT	*The Cuneiform Alphabetic Texts from Ugarit, Ras Ibn Hani and Other Places.* Edited by Manfried Dietrich, Oswald Loretz, and Joaquín Sanmartín. Münster: Ugarit-Verlag, 1995
CAT	Commentaire de l'Ancien Testament
CBQ	*Catholic Biblical Quarterly*
CBQMS	*Catholic Biblical Quarterly Monograph Series*
CEV	Contemporary English Version
CGJCR	*Childhood: A Global Journal of Child Research*
CH	*Codex Hammurabi*
CHANE	Culture and History of the Ancient Near East
CHB	*Cambridge History of the Bible.* Edited by P. R. Ackroyd and C. F. Evans. Cambridge: Cambridge University Press, 1970
CKS	*Complaints of Khakheperre-sonb*
ClAnt	*Classical Antiquity*
CMHE	*Canaanite Myth and Hebrew Epic*, by Frank Moore Cross. Cambridge: Harvard University Press, 1973
COS	*Context of Scripture.* Edited by William W. Hallo and K. Lawson Younger. Leiden: Brill, 1997
CRV	Contemporary Russian Version
CRC	Chemical Rubber Company (a subsidiary of Taylor & Francis)
CSB	Christian Standard Bible
CT	Cuneiform texts from Babylonian tablets
CT	*The Egyptian Coffin Texts*
D	"deity" (*Sum dingir*)
DA	*Deir `Allā Texts*
DCLS	Deuterocanonical and Cognate Literature Studies
DDD	*Dictionary of Deities and Demons in the Bible.* Edited by Karel van der Toorn et al. Leiden: Brill, 1999

DH	Deuteronomistic History
DI	*Descent of Ištar*
DILA	*Dialogue of Ipu-Wer with the Lord of All*
DME	*Dictionary of Middle Egyptian*. Edited by Raymond O. Faulkner. Oxford: Griffith Institute, 1962
DMS	*Dialogue of a Man with His Soul*
DOTW	*Dictionary of the Old Testament: Wisdom, Poetry, and Writings*. Edited by Tremper Longman III and Peter Enns. Downers Grove, IL: InterVarsity, 2008
DSBS	Daily Study Bible Series
DT	*Disappearance of Telipinu*
DTTM	*Dictionary of Targumim, Talmud, and Midrashic Literature*. Edited by M. Jastrow. London: Luzac, 1903.
DULAT	*Dictionary of the Ugaritic Language in the Alphabetic Tradition*. Edited by Gregorio del Olmo Lete and Joaquín Sanmartín. Translated by Wilfred G. E. Watson. Leiden: Brill, 2003
EA	*Die El Amarna Tafeln*. Edited by J. A. Knudtzon. 1915. Reprint, Aalen: Zeller, 1964
EBC	Earth Bible Commentary
EBD	*Egyptian Book of the Dead*
ECB	*Eerdmans Commentary on the Bible*. Edited by James D. G. Dunn and John W. Rogerson. Grand Rapids: Eerdmans, 2003.
EdF	Erträge der Forschung
EDSS	*Encyclopedia of the Dead Sea Scrolls*. Edited by Lawrence Schiffman and James VanderKam. New York: Oxford University Press, 2000
Ee	*Enūma eliš*
EE	*Executive Educator*
EEPA	*Education Evaluation and Policy Analysis*
Eg	Egyptian
e.g.	*exempli gratia* ("for example," Lat.)
EH	*Educational Horizons*
EHJ	*Encyclopedia of the Historical Jesus*. Edited by Craig A. Evans. New York: Routledge, 2008

EL	*Educational Leadership*
ER	*The Encyclopedia of Religion*. Edited by Lindsay Jones. 2nd ed. 15 vols. New York: Macmillan, 2005
Erra	*Erra Epic*
EstBib	*Estudios Biblicos*
ET	English translation
et al.	*et alia* ("and others," Lat.)
et passim	"and throughout" (Lat.)
EW	*Education Week*
EWAW	*Encyclopedia of Women in the Ancient World*, by Joyce E. Salisbury. Santa Barbara, CA: ABC-CLIO, 2001
ex nihilo	"out of nothing" (Lat.)
ExpTim	*Expository Times*
FAT	Forschungen zum Alten Testament
FB	Forschung zur Bibel
FH	Folio Histoire
FOTL	Forms of the Old Testament Literature
FS	Festschrift
GE	*Gilgamesh Epic*
GHK	Göttinger Handkommentar
Gk	Greek
GKC	*Gesenius' Hebrew Grammar*. Edited and enlarged by E. Kautzsch and A. E. Cowley. Oxford: Clarendon, 1910
GN	geographical name
GNT	Greek New Testament
HAL	*Hebräisches und Aramäisches Lexicon zum Alten Testament*. Edited by Ludwig Koehler and Walter Baumgartner. Leiden: Brill, 1967
HAT	Handbuch zum Alten Testament
HBC	*Harper's Bible Commentary*. Edited by James Luther Mays et al. San Francisco: Harper and Row, 1988
HBM	Hebrew Bible Monographs
Heb	Hebrew
HdO	Handbuch der Orientalistik

HEWS	*Historical Encyclopedia of World Slavery.* Edited by Junius P. Rodriguez. Santa Barbara, CA: ABC-CLIO, 1997
HKAT	Handkommentar zum Alten Testament
HSM	Harvard Semitic Monographs
HSS	Harvard Semitic Studies
HTS	Harvard Theological Studies
HUCA	*Hebrew Union College Annual*
IB	*Interpreter's Bible*
ibid.	*ibidem* ("the same place," Lat.)
ID	*Inanna's Descent*
IDB	*Interpreter's Dictionary of the Bible*
i.e.	*id est* ("that is," Lat.)
Int	*Interpretation*
ipv	imperative
ISV	International Standard Version
JAEI	*Journal of Ancient Egyptian Interconnections*
JAOS	*Journal of the American Oriental Society*
JBE	*Journal of Business Ethics*
JCS	*Journal of Cuneiform Studies*
JEA	*Journal of Egyptian Archaeology*
JEOL	*Jaarbericht van het Vooraziatisch-Egyptisch genootschap "Ex Oriente Lux"*
JETS	*Journal of the Evangelical Theological Society*
JJS	*Journal of Jewish Studies*
JL	Jeremiah's Laments
JNES	*Journal of Near Eastern Studies*
Joüon	*A Grammar of Biblical Hebrew*, by P. Joüon. Translated and revised by T. Muraoka. Rome: Pontifical Biblical Institute, 1991
JQS	*Journal of Qur'anic Studies*
JR	*Journal of Religion*
JRAS	*Journal of the Royal Asiatic Society*
JSJ	*Journal for the Study of Judaism*

JSJSup	Journal for the Study of Judaism Supplements
JSOT	*Journal for the Study of the Old Testament*
JSOTSup	Journal for the Study of the Old Testament Supplements
JSSR	*Journal for the Scientific Study of Religion*
Jub.	Jubilees
JYA	*Journal of Youth and Adolescence*
K.	Tablets in the Kouyunjik collection of the British Museum
KAI	*Kanaanäische und aramäische Inschriften*. Edited by H. Donner and W. Röllig. Wiesbaden: Harrassowitz, 1969–
KAR	*Keilschrifttexte aus Assur religiösen Inhalt*. Edited by Erich Ebeling. Leipzig: Hinrichs, 1923
KAT	Kommentar zum Alten Testament
KBo	*Keilschrifttexte aus Boğazköy*. Leipzig: Hinrichs, 1916–1923
KHAT	Kurzgefasstes Exegetisches Handbuch zum Alten Testament
KUB	*Keilschrifturkunden aus Boğazköy*. Berlin: Akademie, 1921–
LÄ	*Lexikon der Ägyptologie*. Edited by Wolfgang Helck et al. Wiesbaden: Harrassowitz, 1975–86
LAB	*Liber Antiquitatem Biblicarum*, by Ps.-Philo
LBS	Library of Biblical Studies
Lane	Lane, Edward W. *An Arabic-English Lexicon*. London: Williams and Norgate. 1863. Reprint, Beirut: Librairie du Liban, 1980
Lat.	Latin
LHBOTS	Library of Hebrew Bible/Old Testament Studies
LKU	*Literarische Keilschrifttexte aus Uruk*. Edited by A. Falkenstein. Berlin: Staatliche Museen, 1931.
LNTS	Library of New Testament Studies
LSG	Louis Segond Bible

LSJ	*A Greek-English Lexicon*. Compiled by Henry George Liddell and Robert Scott. Revised and Augmented by Henry Stuart Jones. Oxford: Clarendon, 1996.
Lud	*Ludlul bēl nēmeqi*
LUT	Revidierte Luther Bibel
m.	Mishnah
MÄS	Münchner Ägyptologische Studien
MBCBSup	Mnemosyne, Bibliotheca Classica Batava Supplementum
MHUJ	*Mittelungsblätter der hebräischen Universität Jerusalem*
ms.	manuscript
MSL	*Materialien zum sumerischen Lexicon.* Edited by B. Landsberger et al. Roma: Pontificium Institutum Biblicum, 1937–2004
MT	Masoretic text
NA	Neo-Assyrian
NAS	New American Standard
NB	Neo-Babylonian
N.B.	*Nota bene* ("note well," Lat.)
NCBC	New Collegeville Bible Commentary
NIBCOT	New International Biblical Commentary, Old Testament Series
NICOT	New International Commentary on the Old Testament
NLT	New Living Translation
NovTSup	Supplements to Novum Testamentum
NSBT	New Studies in Biblical Theology
OB	Old Babylonian
OBO	Orbis Biblicus et Orientalis
Od.	*The Odyssey* (Homer)
ODI	*The Oxford Dictionary of Islam*. Edited by John L. Esposito. Oxford: Oxford University Press, 2003
OG	Old Greek (LXX)
OIP	Oriental Institute Publications
OLA	Orientalia Lovaniensia Analecta
ORA	Orientalische Religionen in der Antike

OT	Old Testament
OTE	*Old Testament Essays*
OTL	Old Testament Library
OTP	*Old Testament Pseudepigrapha*. Edited by James H. Charlesworth. 2 vols. Garden City, NY: Doubleday, 1983
OWC	Oxford World's Classics
pace	"with all due respect" (Lat.)
PBS	Publications of the Babylonian Section, University Museum, University of Pennsylvania
pl.	plural
PN	proper name
Praep. ev.	*Praeparatio Evangelica*, by Eusebius
PRSt	*Perspectives in Religious Studies*
PTR	*Princeton Theological Review*
PTS	Patristische Texten und Studien
PVTG	Pseudepigrapha Veteris Testamenti Graece
R.	Rabbi
raison d'être	"reason for being" (French)
RB	*Revue biblique*
RBL	*Review of Biblical Literature*
RDEGG	*Routledge Dictionary of Egyptian Gods and Goddesses*, by George Hart. London: Routledge, 2005
REAMR	*Routledge Encyclopedia of Ancient Mediterranean Religions*. Edited by Eric Orlin. London: Routledge, 2016.
ResQ	*Restoration Quarterly*
RHPR	*Revue de l'histoire et de philosophie religeuses*
RHR	*Revue d'histoire des religions*
RIPE	*Review of International Political Economy*
RPT	Religion in Philosophy and Theology
RRT	*Reviews in Religion and Theology*
RTP	*Revue de théologie et de philosophie*
RSO	Russian Synodal Orthodox Version
RTS	Rostocker Theologische Studien

SAA	State Archives of Assyria
SAACT	State Archives of Assyria Cuneiform Texts
SAALT	State Archives of Assyria Literary Texts
SAAS	State Archives of Assyria Studies
SAIS	Studies in Aramaic Interpretation of Scripture
SAK	*Studien zur Altägyptischen Kultur*
SBL	Society of Biblical Literature
SBLANEM	Society of Biblical Literature Ancient Near East Monographs
SBLDS	Society of Biblical Literature Dissertation Series
SBLSS	Society of Biblical Literature Symposium Studies
SC	Sources chrétiennes
Sem	*Semeia*
sg.	singular
SJOT	*Scandinavian Journal of Theology*
SNTSMS	Studiorum Novi Testamenti Societas Monograph Series
SOR	Studies in Oriental Religions
SOTSMS	Society for Old Testament Studies Monograph Series
SP	Sacra Pagina
SPHS	Scholars Press Homage Series
SPOT	Studies on Personalities of the Old Testament
StBibLit	Studies in Biblical Literature
Sum	Sumerian
Šur	*Šurpu*
Syr	Syriac
t.	Tosefta
TA	Transactional Analysis
Tanak	The Hebrew Bible (Old Testament)
TCL	*Textes cunéiformes du Louvre*
TDNT	*Theological Dictionary of the New Testament*
TDOT	*Theological Dictionary of the Old Testament*
TEP	*Tale of the Eloquent Peasant*
TgDeut	Targum Deuteronomy (Ps.-Jonathan)

TgJob	Targum of Job
ThA	Theologische Arbeiten
Theo	Theodotion (d. 200 CE)
THOTC	Two Horizons Old Testament Commentary
TJob	Testament of Job
TLOT	Theological Lexicon of the Old Testament
TLZ	*Theologische Literaturzeitung*
Tn	*Die Inschriften Tukulti-Ninurkas I. und seine Nachfolge.* Translated and edited by Ernst Weidner. *AfO* 12. Graz: Weidner, 1959
TOB	Traduction oecuménique de la Bible
TOTC	Tyndale Old Testament Commentaries
TR	*Theological Review*
TRu	*Theologische Rundschau*
TThSt	Trierer theologische Studien
TynBul	*Tyndale Bulletin*
UBCS	Understanding the Bible Commentary Series
UF	*Ugarit Forschungen*
Ug	Ugaritic
UJER	*Universal Journal of Educational Research*
UNP	*Ugaritic Narrative Poetry.* Edited by Simon B. Parker. WAW 9. Atlanta: Scholars, 1997
V	Vatican
VG	*Grundriss der Vergleichende Grammatik der semitischen Sprachen*, by C. Brockelmann. Berlin: Reuther and Reichard, 1908–13
via	"by means of" (Lat.)
viz.	*videre licet* ("it is permitted to see," Lat.)
vss	versions
VT	*Vetus Testamentum*
VTSup	Supplements to Vetus Testamentum
WAW	Writings from the Ancient World
WAWSup	Writings from the Ancient World Supplements
WBC	Word Biblical Commentary

WBCR	Wiley Blackwell Companions to Religion
Wehr	Hans Wehr. *A Dictionary of Modern Written Arabic*. Edited by J. Milton Cowan. Ithaca, NY: Cornell University Press, 1966
WTJ	*Westminster Theological Journal*
WUNT	Wissenschaftliche Untersuchungen zum Neuen Testament
WW	*World and World*
WWSup	Word and World Supplement Series
y.	Talmud Yerushalmi
YOS	*Yale Oriental Series*
ZA	*Zeitschrift für Assyriologie*
ZAW	*Zeitschrift für die alttestamentliche Wissenschaft*
ZBKAT	Zürcher Bibelkommentare Alten Testament
ZNW	*Zeitschrift für die neutestamentliche Wissenschaft*
ZDMG	*Zeitschrift für Deutschen Morgenländischen Gesellschaft*
ZTK	*Zeitschrift für Theologie und Kirche*
ZUR	Zürcher Bibel

1

Introductory Remarks

THE BIBLICAL STORY OF Job[1] is the story of a wealthy "gentleman"[2] who suffers a series of terrible losses, not as punishment for a specific sin or crime,[3] but because two heavenly parties make a "wager" over what might

1. MT איוב; Syr ܐܝܘܒ; Tg איוב (cf. ايوب, Q 38.41, *et passim*); OG Ιωβ; Vg *Iob*; Ιωβαβ (TJob 29.3; cf. Gen 36:33). In line with OG's identification of Job as προϋπῆρχεν δὲ αὐτῷ ὄνομα Ιωβαβ ("formerly called by the name Jobab," OG 42:17b), TJob 1.1 identifies Job as Jobab, the Edomite king who succeeds Bela ben Beor (Gen 36:32, identified in OG Job 42:17d as Balak of Beor), who is then followed by Ḥušam, king of the Temanites (Gen 36:33–34; the homeland of Eliphaz, Job 4:1), who is then identified in Gen 36:11 and OG Job 42:17e as a son of Esau. Talmud ascribes the writing of Job to Moses (*b. B. Bat.* 14b) and reports debates over whether Job is a Gentile or a Jew, and whether he is even an historical individual (*b. B. Bat.* 15a).

2. As Chavalas points out ("Code of Hammurabi," in *HEWS* 1.330–31), ANE society is arranged on three levels: (a) *awīlum* (lit., "man")—"gentleman/aristocrat"; (b) *muškenum*—"workman/palace dependent"; and (c) *wardum*—"slave." Clines (*Parties*, 126–27) recognizes that Job "is not a poor man who once was rich, but a rich man who loses his wealth, regains it, and becomes richer than ever." The name of his homeland (MT עוץ, "Uz") appears in Jer 25:20 and Lam 4:21. TJob reports the name as Αὐσιτίδα ("Ausitis," 28.7), a city Josephus (*A.J.* 1.145) associates with Damascus. Rashi (*Job*, 1.1.1), on the basis of Gen 22:21, also locates it in Syria.

3. Whereas the singular sin of Moses in the wilderness results in his being forbidden to cross the Jordan (Num 20:10–13; cf. Miller, "Moses," 245–55), no such sin is recorded for Job; in fact, the Prologue twice reports that he does *not* sin (1:22; 2:10). Thus Rashi, Maimonides, and Gersonides (cited in Vicchio, *Job*, 8, 14) reckon Job's "flaw" to be simply that he lacks the intellectual tools to make wise decisions. Identifying two types of ברית ("covenant")—one of "salt" (Lev 2:13) and one of "sufferings" (Deut 28:69)—Talmud teaches that as salt flavors meat, "sufferings scour away all of a man's sins" (יסורין ממקרין כל עונותיו של אדם [*b. Ber.* 5a]).

be the rationale behind his piety.[4] The first proudly touts this piety,[5] while the second, unable to deny it, does the next best thing. He challenges its *motivation*,[6] insinuating that should his socioeconomic wealth be removed,[7] Job's "godly fear" would soon deflate into "godly contempt."[8] As Victor Sasson puts it, the second party accuses him of "giving only lip service in return for the great material prosperity God has showered upon him."[9] Unpersuaded by this hypothesis,[10] the first party nevertheless allows the second party to investigate it,[11] allowing him to remove practically everything near and dear to this "gentleman," including his children, his wealth, even his physical

4. Among many others, Bakon ("Enigma," 220) and Leveen ("Job," 833) use the term "wager" to describe what is going on, but since ערב ("wager," 2 Kgs 18:23) does not appear in Job, Day (*Adversary*, 69) prefers to call this a "hypothetical situation," while Good ("Job," 475) avoids the term altogether. Scanning for middle ground, Pope (*Job*, lxxiv–lxxv) insists that "the issue at stake in the testing of Job is not simply the winning of a wager, idle or diabolical, but the vindication of mutual faith of God in man and man in God," and Aimers ("Wager," 362) reports that "more recently, there have been some interpretations which have striven to make the test for piety, especially in terms of Job's integrity, a central unifying theme in the book of Job as a whole. So, in other words, the parameters of Job's test continue in the ensuing Dialogues."

5. A keyword in the Judge's praise is תם ("blameless"; cf. Ps 101:2, 6), a term to which Job and Eliphaz repeatedly return in the Dialogues (Job 8:20; 9:20, 21, 22; 12:4; 22:3). Day (*Adversary*, 81) contends that "Job's sufferings are not initiated by some cruel bet, but rather a profound questioning of the validity of a moral order in which the righteous unfailingly prosper."

6. Crenshaw ("Job," 858) sees in Job "a righteous man whose motives for being righteous are tested through a series of personal tragedies and sufferings." Sasson ("Job," 86) wonders whether the Prosecutor tries "to brand Job a hypocrite, accusing him of having some ulterior motive for his piety." Day (*Adversary*, 80), on the other hand, suggests that the Prosecutor "is not accusing Job, or at least not directly," but "attacking the problem at its source by accusing the creator of perpetrating a perverse world order."

7. In TJob 28.5, Job describes himself as someone accustomed to "great wealth" (πολλῷ πλούτῳ).

8. Cf. Barré ("Fear," 41–43). Wharton's (*Job*, 17) suggestion is cynical: "Maybe Job's deepest motive is no nobler than raw self-interest. Maybe he pretends at faithfulness and integrity only because he believes God's richest blessings are reserved only for those who act out this pious charade." N.B. that "contempt" (Akk *šiṭutum*) is an important motif in ANE texts. Cagni (*L'Epopea*, 248), e.g., argues that the "sin" (*ḫiṭu*) at the end of the *Erra Epic* (*Erra* 5.6) bookends the "contempt" (*šiṭutum*) at the beginning (*Erra* 1.120).

9. Sasson ("Job," 86).

10. Schindler ("Job," 25) speculates that the purpose of the Prosecutor's question is to "goad" the deity.

11. Rashi (*Job*, 1.10.1) suggests that the Prosecutor here tells the Judge, "You have not tested him" (לא ניסית אותו), while Sorge (*Pain*, 1) for some reason sees this as the deity "picking a fight."

health.[12] Not knowing why all these things are happening to him, he bitterly laments the day he was born, cursing not only the *day* of his birth,[13] but the very *fact* of it.[14] Like other "pious sufferers,"[15] he (a) experiences a loss, (b) laments this loss, and (c) tries to determine its meaning through pointed conversations with a few "friends."[16] The result, of course, is a *magnum opus* generally hailed as one of the greatest, if not *the* greatest literary achievement of the ancient world,[17] a sapiential *tour de force* designed to address

12. "Testing" is just as important a motif in Qur'an as it is in the Bible. For example, when Ibrahim receives the divine command to sacrifice his son Isaac, this is perceived to be an البلوا المبين ("obvious test," Q 37.106; cf. the Heb parallel נסה, "to test," Gen 22:1). Clines (*Job*, 28) argues that unlike Abraham's "obedience" test, Job's test "is in reality a test of whether Job's piety stems from his prosperity," but Fyall (*Eyes*, 22) takes issue with any reading inordinately highlighting the wealth motif (*contra* Moore, *Wealth-Wise*, 110–28).

13. Jacobsen and Nielsen ("Day," 187–204; cf. Mowinckel, *Messiah*, 132; Moore, *Babbler*, 45–57). Hartley (*Job*, 106) contends that any sage would be taken aback by Job's curse against the value of his birth, to the point of considering it "a grave act of impiety." N.B. that the "day of death" in Egypt is equivalent to the "day of pain" (*DMS* 10).

14. Job 3:3–26 (cf. Paul, "Imprecations," 401–6). Most read chapter 3 as a "lament," but Pohl (*Job*, 44) calls it a "protest prayer." Responding to Cross's theory (*CMHE* 344, following Jacobsen, *Treasures*, 163) that Job represents a radical critique of prophetic Yahwism eventually clearing the way for the Judaism(s) of the Second Temple period, Janzen (*Job*, 9–12) argues that the primary tension in Job is not between earlier vs. later metaphors for God (Cross), but between Yhwh and the gods of the nations.

15. The "pious sufferer" is more-or-less a stock character in the ancient literary world. In ancient Sumer, e.g., Ur-Nammu complains that "even though I did the gods service and brought great prosperity to the Annunaki . . . no god stood by me" (Kramer, "Ur-Nammu," 112.8–9, 115.155–57). In Babylon, Šubši-mešre-šakkan complains to the god Marduk (*Lud* 1.43—2.120). In *Oedipus Tyrannus* Sophocles laments the gap between human existence and divine reality," particularly humanity's "unfair dependence on divine destiny" (Winnington-Ingram, "Tragedy," 116; cf. Moore, *WealthWarn*, 24–30). Luiselli ("Frommigkeit," 157–82) traces the influence of the "personal piety" motif back through several Egyptian texts.

16. Job 2:11 (רע). "Friend" is a relative term. Job accuses Eliphaz of bargaining over a "friend" (Job 6:27), while one of the participants in *BT* calls his dialogue partner a "friend" (Akk *ibru*, *BWL* 70.12). Neither term necessarily denotes personal intimacy. Pohl (*Job*, 20) finds Job's "friends" to be individuals "appalled and offended by his language," but Knauf ("Elihu," 463) calls them "opponents."

17. Habel (*Job*, 21) calls it a "literary masterpiece." Maimonides (*Guide*, 486) calls it "extraordinary and marvelous." Dell ("Job," 337) calls it a "masterpiece of world literature." Dunham (*Sage*, ix) calls it an "elusive masterpiece." Bakon ("Enigma," 218) calls it "one of perhaps five or six transcendent products of literary excellence in the history of world literature." G. F. Moore (*Literature*, 233) calls it "the greatest work of Hebrew literature that has come down to us, and one of the great poetical works of the world's literature." Seow (*Job*, 2) calls it "one of the most captivating, but unsettling stories ever told," and Larrimore (*Job*, 248) documents how "each part of the book of Job has proven itself a resource and a challenge, a comfort and a provocation to deeper insight into the

the question, "Is God best served from a desire to seek compensation/avoid retribution,[18] or from a condition defined by unconditional trust?"[19]

One of the reasons for the pages below is the fact that so few textbooks on Job read it from the perspective of this *theological* question.[20] Granted, many commentaries do attend to theological concerns, but often only in passing and then quite selectively. The commentaries of Norman Habel, David Clines, and John Hartley, for example, exemplify the best of contemporary English scholarship where Joban theology is dutifully discussed.[21] Marvin Pope's commentary is a *chef-d'oeuvre* of Orientalist erudition, as per the guidelines of the series in which it appears.[22] Samuel Terrien reads Job through what might accurately be dubbed a (post)modern existentialist

---

human and the divine." Reiner ("Literatur," 115–210), Foster ("Literature," 1–47), and Groneberg ("Literature," 59–84) each detail the major attributes of "great literary texts."

18. Talmud presumes that "compensation" is the flip side of "retribution," as Baldwin ("Monochrome," 362) observes: "It is noteworthy that Eliphaz begins his 'retributive-justice' discourse by highlighting the reward of the righteous rather than the destruction of evildoers." Like Job, Qur'an carefully preserves both a "positive" and a "negative" understanding: "O believers, prescribed for you is the 'retribution/compensation' (القصار) for those who have been killed" (Q 2.178). This term, القصار, is derived from the verb قصر ("to shear off, retaliate, settle accounts," Lane 2526–27; Wehr 765–66; cf. the Heb cognate קצר in Job 24:3; Prov 22:8; Ruth 2:9). Kissane (*Job*, xv) believes that "the book of Job is a discussion of the problem of retribution—the apparent contradiction between the doctrine of the justice of God and the facts of human experience." For Jones Nelson ("Job," 519) it "is complex and difficult, but this very complexity is what makes it such an ubiquitous text across religious, philosophical, literary, and artistic traditions."

19. Fox ("Meanings," 7, 10, 17) reports that "the currently dominant readings of the book of Job agree on one essential point: the book refutes the retributory theology assumed to be Jewish orthodoxy, whereby God punishes the wicked and rewards the righteous." But "the book of Job teaches that God does punish and recompense" because "in the book there is divine justice . . . but it is incomplete. It must be so, if human righteousness is to be pure. As the *satan* points out (1:9–11), if Job is invariably and fully rewarded for his virtues, his motivation might be the expectation of a payoff rather than unselfish, uncalculating love and fear of God (cf. Kluger, *Satan*).

20. Raz ("Job," 77) attributes this to the unbridled advance of "enlightenment secularization," designating it the primary factor responsible for leading "modern biblical exegesis . . . to shift the focus away from . . . theological questions . . . towards moral, ethical, and aesthetic concerns." *Caution:* No "theology of Job" disengaged from the speeches of Job in the Dialogues and the speeches of Yhwh in the Theologue can be considered "complete"—thus the subtitle "short theological introduction."

21. Habel (*Job*); Clines (*Job*); Hartley (*Job*). Müller (*Hiob*) surveys most of the predominantly European studies.

22. Pope (*Job*). Ernst (*Muhammad*, 191) reacts negatively to "the Orientalist imagination," accusing it of "collapsing the present into the ancient past, invariably regarding Orientals as trapped in a time warp that prevents them from being part of the present."

lens,[23] while philosopher Margarete Susman rather (in)famously reads the book as a future perfect echo of the European holocaust.[24] Choon Leong Seow examines it from several complementary angles[25] carefully molded into a pluralistic approach Georg Fohrer, among others, finds far preferable to most singular treatments.[26] Gerald Janzen judiciously attends to theological questions, but predominantly from a theodical perspective,[27] as does James Crenshaw in his "literary-theological commentary."[28]

Championing a non-semitic literary approach developed by Mikhail Bakhtin for reading the novels of Fyodor Dostoevsky,[29] Carol Newsom reads Job as a polyphonic text synchronically sensitive to the interchanges recurring between the voices of its main characters.[30] Carol Fontaine reads it as a "poeticized folktale" in which "the narrative and poetic speeches together form a tale of the 'victim-hero.'"[31] Heinz Richter reads it through a legal lens, Tim Johnson through an apocalyptic lens, and William Pohl through a lens contoured by the tenets of contemporary rhetorical theory.[32] Tempering Horace Kallen's reading of Job as a prototypical Greek tragedy, Claus Westermann reads this Oriental text as a "dramatized lament."[33] William Whedbee reads it as a U-shaped comedy,[34] John Burnight as "proto-satire,"[35] and Katharine Dell as a "parody . . . constantly misusing traditional forms from legal, cultic, and wisdom spheres . . . to convey on the level of form what is already conveyed in the content, viz., the book's radical scepticism."[36] Bruce

23. Terrien, *Job*. Cf. Marcel, *Existentialism*.

24. Susman, *Hiob*.

25. Seow, *Job*.

26. Fohrer, *Hiob*, 53.

27. Janzen, *Job*.

28. Crenshaw, *Job*; cf. Gerhards, *Gott*. This list is representative, not exhaustive.

29. Bakhtin, *Poetics*; Dostoevsky, esp. *Crime and Punishment* (1866) and *The Brothers Karamazov* (1880).

30. Newsom, *Job*. Cf. Moore, *Contest*.

31. Fontaine, "Job," 223.

32. Richter, *Hiob*; Johnson, *Job*; cf. Moore, *Apocalyptic*; Pohl, *Job*; cf. Moore, *God-Talk*; Dick, "Legal," 37–50. Gemser ("Controversy-Pattern," 120–37) reads it as a "ריב/court trial."

33. Westermann (*Job*) is influenced by Kallen (*Job*), who in turn credits the reading of Job as a theatrical drama to Theodore of Mopsuestia (cf. Paulus, "Souffrant," 18–66).

34. Whedbee, "Comedy," 1–39; cf. Moore, *Comic*.

35. Burnight (*Job*) "classifies Job as a 'proto-satire' that makes use of both parody and irony to offer a scathing critique of an external target: the traditional Israelite theology represented by his 'friends.'"

36. Dell (*Job*, 110, 148) relies heavily on Fohrer's "Hiobdichtung."

Zuckerman imagines the book as an ideological battleground of sorts upon which the pietistic ideals of the Prologue "provoke the anger of a great literary artist who determines to counterattack its message, using the literary weapon of parody" to produce a composite text in which "Job the Patient" squares off against "Job the Rebel."[37] Ed Greenstein produces a breakthrough translation of the book,[38] while Mark Larrimore traces some of the ways in which it inspires literary texts, theatrical productions, musical scores, films, and other *objets d'art*.[39] Robert Eisen acquaints contemporary readers with the still-insightful medieval commentaries of Maimonides, Rashi, and Gersonides in a history-of-interpretation analysis fleshed out more fully by Steven Vicchio.[40] Lindsay Wilson argues that Job's primary goal is "to correct a fossilized misunderstanding of Proverbs,"[41] while Davis Hankins contends that while Job is sometimes presented as a "trite folktale" about human limitation in the face of confounding and absolute transcendence, it is better described as a drama about the struggle to create a just and viable world in a materialistic environment which is ontologically incomplete and open to radical transformation.[42]

37. Zuckerman, *Job*, 175.

38. Greenstein, *Job*.

39. Larrimore, *Job*. Cf. Moore, *Biography*.

40. Eisen, *Job*; Vicchio (*Job*, xii) lists several of the most common explanations for the problem of evil in Job:

1—*Retributive Justice*—Job suffers because he or someone in his family have done something wrong.

2—*Demonic Forces*—Job's suffering is a product of the *satan* and/or his minions (e.g., the שׁדין; cf. Augustine, Aquinas, and Gregory); Qur'an attributes Job's suffering to *Iblis* and/or *Šaytan* (Q 7.12, 14).

3—*Free Will*—Job's suffering is caused by his own free choices between the יצר הרע ("evil resolve") vs. the יצר הטוב ("good resolve") as illustrated by the "two spirits" discourse at Qumran (1QS 18–19: רוח האמת, "the spirit of truth" vs. רוח העול, "the spirit of evil." Cf. Levison ["Spirits," 169–94] and Nickelsburg ["Seeking," 95–108]).

4—*Original Sin*—The sin of Adam and Eve is inherited by all who come after them.

5—*Contrast View*—Good cannot be understood or appreciated apart from the presence of evil.

6—*Didactic Perspective*—Suffering is permitted to test moral character (Kaufmann, "Job," 66).

7—*Moral Qualities Theory*—Certain moral virtues (courage, fortitude) can only be developed by experiencing evil and suffering.

8—*Divine Plan Theory*—Things may be confusing now, but all eventually "works out for the good" (Rom 8:28).

9—*Deprivation of the Good*—Evil is not ontologically present, only the absence of good (cf. Stoics, Augustine, Aquinas, Gregory).

41. Wilson, *Job*, 3.

42. Hankins, *Job*. My own foray into Job (Moore, "Terror," 662–75) reads it alongside several other ANE texts in the hope of shedding more lexicographical light on one of its more puzzling passages.

Whichever approach is taken, Egyptologist Richard Parkinson rightly insists that "attention to literary form is vital to the understanding of texts (and) should precede (all) other types of analysis,"[43] including many of those just listed. Fully supportive of this approach, the pages below will attempt to examine Job from a literary-historical perspective theologically focused on the Prosecutor's question as well as the various responses to it found in the Dialogues,[44] attending to three basic angles:

(1) *Textual analysis* concentrating on matters of language, translation, and literary structure.[45]

(2) *Intertextual analysis* examining the impact of the compensation/retribution motif in ANE and early Joban tradition.[46]

(3) *Theological analysis* sensitive to the questions and concerns of (post) modern readers.[47]

43. Parkinson, "Form," 163.

44. Janzen (*Job*, 18) recognizes that "all that is narrated or said either moves toward or proceeds from questions of the highest import," distinguishing between four different types: questions seeking information, rhetorical questions, impossible questions, and existential questions. Pelham (*Job*, 30) explains: The fact "that Job actually finds himself living in a world completely different from the world God claims to have created, a world that is consonant with Job's own vision of the world-as-it-ought-to-be, turns the Book of Job from an 'Answer' book, in which the truth about creation is proclaimed, into a 'Question' one."

45. Müller (*Hiobproblem*, 1–140) surveys the major studies of Job published before 1978, and van Oorschot ("Hiobforschung," 351–88) surveys the major studies published up to 2020. Greenstein (*Job*, xvii–xviii) observes that "the book of Job is sometimes touted as the world's greatest poem . . . a remarkable claim, considering that virtually no reader of the original Hebrew has ever felt satisfied at having understood" it.

46. Presuming that "no text is an island," Miscall ("Isaiah," 45; "Texts," 247), very simply defines "intertextuality" as "the reading of two or more texts together and in light of each other," and Tate (*Interpretation*, xv) argues that "the meaning of meaning is meaningless apart from the concept of intertextuality." The pages below are sensitive to the material in Qur'an because it is a pre-medieval Near Eastern text in which Job is claimed to be one of النبيّن ("the prophets" [Q 4.163], and the "compensation/retribution" motif plays a major role [cf. Apt, "Hiobserzählung"]).

47. Cf. Jameson, *Postmodernism*; Butler, *Postmodernism*; and Eagleton, *Postmodernism*. While Mathewson (*Job*) and Wilson (*Job*) are exceptions, one of the constant complaints heard from students is the dearth of textbooks designed to examine Job from an informed theological perspective.

2

The Prosecutor's Question

THE SPEAKERS IN JOB aggressively engage a series of questions generated by the theological notions of "creation,"[1] "redemption,"[2] "retribution,"[3]

1. Perdue (*Revolt*, 20) insists that "order as a unifying center for creation theology in wisdom literature is more comprehensive than either anthropology or theodicy." Fyall (*Job*, 17) finds the creation-chaos polarity central primarily to the Theologue.

2. Ross ("Lament," 42) assigns to Elihu a definition of suffering depicting it "not as the trick of a whimsical, capricious God (so Job) nor the sentence of a hanging judge (so his 'friends'), but a way in which God gets man's attention, so that the angel can interpret its meaning and show the way to repentance. Thus man's ransom is won." Crenshaw (*Defending*, 184) argues that "evil fulfills a vital function in sorting out those individuals who fear God for nothing, gratuitously, in vain. Without the presence of adversity, there would be no way of knowing whether people worship the deity simply because it pays dividends. After all, religion can function quite well as a business, a mercantile transaction of *quid pro quo* in which accurate calculation of costs and benefits governs everything." Cf. Morales, *Exodus*.

3. Alonso Schökel ("Job," 49) observes that Job's "first desire is consolation, but instead they (the 'friends') offer the doctrine of retribution." Richter (*Hiob*, 131) reads the book as a forensic document, chapters 4–14 being an attempt to reach a preliminary settlement between Job and his "friends," chapters 15–31 being a legal social settlement followed by Job's appeal to a higher court, and chapters 32–42 being the final settlement in this higher court. Some rabbis presume that "retributions" have a cosmic dimension: "As the mountains press back the deep lest it ascend and inundate the world, so the righteous press back 'the retributions'" (הפרענות; *Gen. Rab.* 33.1; cf. G. Wilson, *Job*, 82–85).

"theodicy,"[4] and "justification."[5] Each discussion contributes to the book's composite theological profile, but for Walter Moberly only one question identifies "the critical issue around which the whole story revolves; viz., *disinterested piety*."[6] He is not alone. Bruce Waltke calls the Prosecutor's question in 1:9 the book's "ultimate question,"[7] and Choon Leong Seow finds the Prologue "directly and indirectly posing all kinds of theological questions, including the relationship between human conduct and divine reciprocity, the arbitrariness that may be part of divine freedom, the vulnerability of humanity in the face of cosmic malfeasance, and the possibility of disinterested piety," emphasizing that "this last issue . . . is central to the book."[8] Carol Newsom sees in the *character* of Job a veritable "role model for the exercise of disinterested piety"[9] while her student Timothy Sandoval reads

4. Newsom (*Contest*, 17) recognizes "theodicy" not as a major theme in Job, but as a "plot device." Dell (*Evil*, 618), on the other hand, contends that of all the books in the Bible "Job does perhaps give us the most profound airing of theodicy." Based on the Epilogue's treatment of Job's "friends," Gruber ("Job," 59) imagines Job not as a theodicy but as an anthropodicy; i.e., the justification not of deity, but of humanity. Cf. Nicholson ("Theodicy," 71–82); Cohen ("Theodicy," 243–70); Müller ("Theodizee," 249–79); Crenshaw (*Reading*, 7); and Greenstein ("Job," 360–62).

5. Ezekiel refers to Job as a paragon of צדקה ("justice," Ezek 14:14, 20; cf. Gese, "Hiob," 161–79), and Elihu's words to Job are archetypal: אם יש מלין השיבני דבר כי חפצתי צדקך "If you have any words, answer me. Speak, for I desire your justification" (Job 33:32).

6. Moberly (*Bible*, 85). Ticciati (*Job*, 50) insists that the question in 1:9 "is a real and not just 'spurious' obstacle in this opening scene, pointing to depths of Job's integrity that cannot be represented within the terms of its 'naïve' portrayal, and in the absence of which its surface integrity begins to crumble. It functions, therefore, somewhat like a theological irruption into what might otherwise be read flatly (i.e., with little awareness of this deeper plane of meaning), and ultimately brings to the fore what might be seen as the deepest theological assumption of the book, one which will gain the closest of scrutinies in what follows: that God is one who is to be feared for naught."

7. Waltke, *Theology*, 930. Boyd (*Job*, 306) contends that failure to read "disinterested piety" as a predominant motif "inevitably leads to a one-sided view of the book's purpose," citing Kierkegaard (*Wiederholung*, 231) as an example.

8. Seow, *Job*, 262–63. Guffy ("Job," 882) sees Seow "defending the view that the prose and poetry should be conceived as an artistic whole. Historically, Seow points to a number of ANE texts in which poetic content is enclosed in a prose frame. But Seow also sees in the narrator's switch to poetry a literary device signaling the beginning of Job's third trial—the first two are deliberated in heaven, this one on earth. The verdict is still out whether Job (and, by implication, humans) really can 'fear God for naught' (Job 1:9)." Fontaine ("Job," 205) proposes that "no one interpretive scheme seems to account adequately for the symbiotic relationship existing between the prose and poetry in Job."

9. Newsom (*Job*, 181, 50) finds "the focal point" in "Hebrew didactive narratives to be the character of the individual enacted in moments of decision . . . In the moral vision of these stories, for an action to be truly good it must be undertaken without regard to circumstances." Vesely (*Job*, 139–40) believes simply that what Job seeks is "a friend who will demonstrate courageous compassion throughout times of misfortune and loss."

the *book* as an "exploration of the possibility of disinterested piety."[10] Preoccupied with theodical concerns,[11] Peruvian theologian Gustavo Gutiérrez nonetheless insists that the book's main goal is to invite readers to ponder how "human beings can . . . believe in God without looking for rewards (*compensation*) or fearing punishments (*retribution*)."[12] James Crenshaw agrees that Job has fundamentally to do with "the possibility of being good without thought of either reward or punishment,"[13] and Gerald Janzen posits "the universal human question, Why do the righteous suffer?" to presume "a prior and (at least for the narrator) deeper question"; viz., Why are the righteous pious?"[14] In other words, "the question of disinterested piety stands on the shoulders of a much larger one: Is the creator of the world and the divine benefactor of humankind worshipful only by virtue of what he does for humankind?"[15]

Adding another voice to the mix, Jürgen Ebach proposes that the question in 1:9 not only challenges Job's motives, but presumes in the process an organic link between *piety* and *prosperity*,[16] a link David Clines finds noteworthy because it explains why the second heavenly party does not "call into question Job's incomparable piety; nor does he doubt its sincerity, its genuineness." What he *does* question—indeed, "what *must* be questioned (there is nothing 'satanic' about the question)—is the link between Job's godliness and his prosperity." In other words, "Does Job *gratuitously* fear God?"[17]

10. Sandoval, "Wisdom," 497.

11. See Gutiérrez, *Liberation*; *Writings*. Crenshaw ("Theodicy," 644) defines "theodicy" as "the attempt to defend divine justice in the face of aberrant phenomena that appear to indicate the deity's indifference or hostility toward virtuous people" (cf. Tilley, *Theodicy*, 99–102).

12. Gutiérrez, *Job*, 1; cf. Buttenweiser, *Job*, 29–30. Seow (*Job*, 244) suggests that the core of the Muslim tradition shows God permitting (the) "S/satan" (السيطان, Q 38.41) to inflict Job "in order to increase Job's reward." Vicchio (*Islamic*, 115–16) observes that "the question found among ancient rabbis whether Job loved God out of devotion or out of fear is never raised in the Islamic commentaries. Indeed, the interesting question about the possibility of Job's self-interested goodness never occurs to the Islamic commentators." In fact, "if medieval Islamic exegetes are interested in Job's provenance, they seem decidedly disinterested in whether Job worshiped God out of fear or love." Ibn Asakir (d. 1176 CE), for example, "thinks the source of Job's great patience is his foreknowledge that all his goods will be restored, a tradition that may well have its roots in TJob."

13. Crenshaw, "Job," 858.

14. Janzen, *Job*, 2.

15. Janzen, *Job*, 41.

16. Ebach, "Hiob," 321. Hoffman (*Blemished*, 224–53) discusses this question under the rubric of "recompense."

17. Clines, *Job*, 25. Pelham (*Job*, 52) argues that "the point of the scene in 1:6–12 is not to pose, in an abstract way, the question of whether there can be such a thing as

To investigate this question today is to walk a tightrope upon which many have lost their theological balance. Yet one thing is certain. The *piety* </> *prosperity* equation is not unique to Job.[18] In the Egyptian Tale of the Eloquent Peasant, for example, a traveler looking to feed his family is ambushed and robbed, thereby leading him to wonder whether outlaws can do whatever they want without fear of reprisal.[19] In the Babylonian Poem of a Pious Sufferer, Marduk's priests taunt the speaker with the words,

na-piš-ta-šu u-šat-bak-šu	Let's make him hand over his provisions;
ú-šat-bi te-er-tu-šu	Let's deduct his commission;
qip-ta-šú a-tam-ma-aḫ	Let's repossess his loan;
er-ru-ub é-uš-šu	Let's impound his house.[20]

In the Babylonian Theodicy another sufferer chides another "friend" for naïvely presuming that piety *always* leads to prosperity:[21]

il-lu nu-us-su-ku mi-lik-ka d[am-qu]	Dear friend, you do share profitable advice,
il-te-en zik-ra mut-ta-ka lut-t[i-ir]	But let me remind you that sometimes even
il-la-ku ú-ru-uḫ dum-qí la muš-te-'-u .-l[i]	Those who are prosperous neglect the god,
il-tap-ni i-te-en-šú muš-te-mi-qu šá .[l-ti]	And those who petition the goddess become poor.[22]

righteousness unmotivated by the promise of reward and to set up an objective test for the resolution of this question. The point of the scene is to witness to Job's righteousness. Job is at the center, and without Job's presence the discussion would not happen, even though Job is supposedly excluded from the scene. Job looms large for both God and the *satan*, filling their field of vision so that they can talk of nothing else . . . If God had simply answered, 'Yes, I think so,' to the *satan's* query, 'Does Job fear God for nothing?' the *satan* would not have been satisfied, but neither would Job. The *satan*, in fact, prevents God from answering 'Yes, I think so,' by annexing to his question an indictment of God: 'Have you not put a fence around him?'"

18. The symbol </> seeks to depict the difficulties involved in ascertaining whether *piety* leads to *prosperity* or vice versa. Sherwood ("Job," 86) suggests that "the narrative in the Prologue contrasts two opposing views of causality: one is the earthly view, which maintains that piety brings prosperity, the other is the heavenly scenes, which present prosperity as the cause of piety."

19. Cf. Parkinson, "Peasant," 58–75, and below.

20. *Lud* 1.59–62. *Contra* Moore (*WealthWise*, 26), these lines are probably best translated as plural cohortatives.

21. Foster, "Salvation," 1.486. Fee (*Disease*) documents how blind adherence to this presumption *still* misleads.

22. *BWL* 74.71–72; cf. Moore, *WealthWise*, 34–35. Qur'an warns, "Do not be deceived by the 'prosperity' (تقلّب) of unbelievers" (Q 3.196).

In the preamble to the book of Proverbs a Hebrew sage advises:

כבד את יהוה מהונך	Treasure Yhwh more than your wealth
ומראשית כל תבואתך	Or the firstfruits of your produce.
וימלאו אסמיך שׂבע	For then your granaries will be amply stocked
ותירושׁ יקביך יפרצו	And your wineries will produce vintage wine.[23]

Tremper Longman concludes that Job is noteworthy for several reasons, but at the very least it is because "the possibility of reward" can be "a motivation for godly behavior" in other ANE texts, whereas Job presumes an "expectation of godly behavior no matter what."[24]

SEVEN QUESTIONS

However marginalized or dismissed,[25] the disinterested piety motif is critical not only to MT Job, but to the early Joban tradition.[26] It may not *seem* as important as, say, "justification" or "retribution"—the main theological concerns of his "friends"—but careful literary analysis confirms that theodicy cannot be the book's "central theme." More likely it serves merely as a "plot device" designed to "foreground the hero's character."[27] Whether or not this fully defines its role-set, this masterpiece divides into four major sections—Prologue, Dialogues, Theologue, and Epilogue.[28] Relatively overlooked is

23. Prov 3:9–10; cf. Moore, *WealthWise*, 64.

24. Longman, *Job*, 84. Cf. the admonition in 4QInstruction: "Do not sell your soul for money, for it is good to be a spiritually-minded servant serving your supervisors 'without compensation'" (חנם, 4Q16.2.2.17; cf. Moore, *WealthWise*, 137–41).

25. Hamilton (*Theology*, 15–23) discusses how difficult it can be to define what a "theology" is, and Fyall (*Job*, 21–23) examines the presumptions of readers for whom Job is too diverse to have a "theology" (sg.). In Larrimore's (*Job*, 5) opinion, "Job wants his story to be a book" even though "every interpreter tries to be the bookbinder."

26. For Eaton (*Job*, ix), Job addresses "the greatest of all human struggles: to see the world's evil honestly and still believe in good."

27. Newsom, *Job*, 17. Discounting the once dominant redactoral hypotheses of the previous century, Habel (*Job*, 25–26) makes a strong argument for the literary unity of Job. Dell (*Job*, 5–6), however, still believes that "the interpretation of the message of Job is inextricably bound up with literary-critical conclusions regarding which parts of the book are primary and which secondary." Parkinson ("Form," 164) contends that "literary form . . . is integral to . . . meaning . . . although it does not in itself constitute that meaning."

28. Prologue (1:1–2:13); Dialogue (3:1—37:24); Theologue (38:1—42:6); Epilogue (42:7–17). Day (*Adversary*, 71) breaks the book down into "prologue, dialogue cycle,

how much the Dialogues—the book's longest section by far—interface with the Prosecutor's question in the Prologue.[29] Ignored altogether is the fact that the Prosecutor's question stands at the center of a sevenfold coalition of questions framing the "heavenly council" type-scenes:[30]

Question 1—מאין תבא "From where have you come?"[31]

Question 2—השמת לבך אל עבדי איוב "Have you considered my servant Job?"[32]

Question 3—החנם ירא איוב אלהים "Does Job fear God for nothing?"[33]

Question 4—הלא אתה שכת בעדו ובעד ביתו "Have you not erected a fence around him and his family?"[34]

---

wisdom poem, Elihu speeches, whirlwind speeches, and epilogue."

29. Hyun (*Job*, 22) insists that the "voices in the Prologue are complemented by the voices in the Dialogue," and Habel ("Art," 102–4, followed by Day, *Adversary*, 73–75) notes several "signals of continuity" linking the prose portions of the book to the poetic, while Hoffman ("Prologue," 165) points out the number of "elements whose existence in the Prologue is intelligible only if the following speeches are taken into consideration."

30. White (*Council*, 1) reads all "heavenly council" scenes in Tanak (e.g., 1 Kings 22:19–23; Ps 82:1–8; Isa 6:1–13) as "type-scenes," a "literary convention" Alter (*Narrative*, 61) defines as a "reflection of certain social or cultural realities, but bound to offer a highly mediated, stylized image of such realities." N.B. that when Eliphaz affirms the deity's ability to rescue Job, it is deliverance from seven terrors: famine, death, war, the sword, the tongue, destruction, and the beasts of the earth (Job 5:20–23), a sevenfold list recognized by Rashi (*Job*, 5.21.1—24.2).

31. Job 1:7. The rewording of this question in 2:2 (אי מזה תבא) is slightly different, and OG reflects this variation, translating תבא as *πόθεν παραγέγονας* in 1:7 and *πόθεν σὺ ἔρχῃ* in 2:2. Syr simply repeats the question ܡܢ ܐܝܡܟܐ ܐܬܝܬ ("Where have you come from?"). Stump (*Darkness*, 198) suggests that the reason for the Prosecutor's question is to make the heavenly council aware that he is simply and only a "restless outsider."

32. Job 1:8, השמת לבך על עבדי איוב (lit., "have you set your heart on my servant Job?"). Cf. Syr ܥܒܕܝ ("my servant"; so Tg and Vg); OG *παιδός μου* ("my child/son/servant"). Whether עבדי ("my servant") is an honorific title (cf. Gen 26:24; Num 12:7; 2 Sam 7:5; 1 Kgs 11:13, 32) is possible, but indeterminable.

33. Job 1:9 (חנם). OG *δωρεὰν* ("freely"/"as a gift"); Vg *frustra* ("in vain"); Syr ܡܓܢܐܝܬ ("in vain"). Tg reads הפשר די למגן איוב דחל קדם יי ("Is it possible for Job to fear Yhwh freely?"), מגן ("grace") being the Aram translation of Heb חנם (and like Heb חנם, has both economic and non-economic denotations; *DTTM* 729). Interestingly, the Prosecutor says nothing about Job's "integrity" (תם, 1:8), "uprightness" (ישר, 1:8), or determination to "turn away from evil" (סר מרע, 1:8). Qur'an simply posits that الله يحب المتقين, "God loves those who fear him" (Q 3.76).

34. Job 1:10 (lit. "house"). For all intents and purposes, question 4 is a continuation of question 3. N.B. that the rare verb סכך describes both the protective "fencing in" of Job (1:10) as well as the topographical "fencing in" of the sea (ים, "Yam," 38:8).

Question 5—אי מזה תבא, "From where have you come?"[35]

Question 6—השמת לבך אל עבדי איוב, "Have you considered my servant Job?"[36]

Question 7—עדך מחזיק בתמתך, "Why do you still cling to your integrity?[37] ברך אלהים ומת, Curse God and die!"[38]

Four of these questions (1–2 and 5–6) function as parallel pairs of inquiries submitted to the Prosecutor from the Judge[39] through verbatim repetition, a stylistic ploy Western writers are usually taught to avoid.[40] ANE scribes, however, enthusiastically embrace it in what Robert Alter calls "that feature of biblical narrative . . . most 'primitive' to the casual modern eye."[41]

35. Job 2:2. Presuming the deity's love to be all-inclusive, Stump (*Darkness*, 211) proposes that the repetition of the question in 1:7 shows that "there is something new and significant at issue between the Judge and the Prosecutor . . . It is evident now not only that he is wrong about Job, but also that he is unsuccessful in his attempt to introduce into the relations between Job and God that alienation which characterizes his own connection with God . . . Given what happens in response to his attack against Job, given that he is entirely wrong about Job, the circumstances now demand an answer from him that is more, not less yielding than before. But nothing of the sort is forthcoming . . . Instead he simply gives God the same evasive answer as before, only with more intransigence." Schmid ("Job," 889–912), however, is not nearly so inclusive.

36. Job 2:3. Cf. above on 1:8.

37. Job 2:9a. The word תם ("integrity") is the same one used by the heavenly Judge to describe Job's piety (1:8; 2:3). Hartley (*Job*, 36) posits a semi-chiastic posture for the Prologue while Low (*Wife*, 1) remarks: "No other words spoken by a woman in the Hebrew Bible carry more bite and bafflement."

38. Job 2:9b. Heb ברך normally means "to bless," but in 1:11; 2:5; and 2:9 Syr reads ܨܚܐ ("to revile"), thus supporting the likelihood that ברך is intended to be read as a circumlocution (*HAL*; *BDB*; Geiger, *Urschrift*, 267–68; Yaron, "Coptos," 90). Omitting any reference to "cursing" the deity (cf. Vg *benedic Deo*), OG shows Job's wife complaining about (a) her fate as a πλανῆτις ("wanderer") and λάτρις ("slave"), (b) and her role as the wife of a figure defined by the trait of καρτερέω ("endurance"), a portrayal presaging later descriptions of Job as the "athlete of endurance" (ὑπομονή, TJob 1.5; Jas 5:11).

39. Seow's (*Job*, 250) chiastic depiction of the Prologue differs from the structure proposed here; viz., (a) Job's perfect life (1:1–5); (b) an assembly in heaven (1:6–12); (c) a test of Job (1:13–22); (d) an assembly in heaven (2:1–6); (e) a test of Job (2:7–10); (f) an assembly on earth (2:11–13). Granted, it still recognizes the "technique of repetition," but unfortunately it minimizes the significance of the "disinterested piety" motif.

40. In a twentieth-century textbook on speechmaking, e.g., Shurter (*Debate*, 218) admonishes speakers not to engage in "needless repetitions that only weary the hearer."

41. Alter, *Narrative*, 111; cf. Foster, *Muses*, 15–16. The Canaanite Ba`al Epic (*UNP* 87–164), with its constant repetitive choruses, is one of the clearest examples of structural repetition. Whybray (*Pentateuch*, 81) observes that repetition is "a literary device found in literature of many kinds, (but) is particularly common in the literature of the ancient Near East."

This sevenfold coalition has three traits:[42]

(1) Parallel sets of duplicate questions (1–2 // 5–6) framing the overt theological material in questions 3–4 and 7, which suggests that

(2) Questions 3–4 and 7 are intended to be read in parallel, which further suggests that

(3) Question 7, due to its structural symmetry with questions 3–4, is not likely to be an addendum, nor can it be said to signify a "major theme."[43]

This is not the only sevenfold coalition in Tanak.[44] In the story of Ruth, for example, another pious sufferer (Naomi) makes seven declarations designed (a) to release her Moabite daughters-in-law from any responsibility they may feel they still have for her welfare (*anthropological focus*); and (b) pour out her anguish before Yhwh, the deity with whom she is upset for "striking" (ענה) her down in the first place (*theological focus*):[45]

שובנה בנתי	"Turn back, my daughters."
למה תלכנה עמי	"Why would you go with me?"

42. Hoffman (*Job*, 47) observes several examples in Job of the number *seven*, including: (a) the verb ברך ("bless/curse") appears seven times (1:5, 10, 11, 21; 2:5, 9; 42:12); and (b) the number *seven* appears seven times (1:2, 3; 2:13 twice; 42:8 twice, 13). Cf. the Talmudic claim that Job is one of seven prophets authorized to preach to the Gentiles (*b. B. Bat.* 15b), and N.B. that there are seven questions in the conversation between Abališ and Adurfarnbag in the Pahlavi treatise *Gizistag Abališ* (cf. Secunda, *Bavli*, 129–30).

43. Newsom, *Job*, 181. Good (*Tempest*, 390) finds it suspect, if not altogether sexist, that Job's wife does not reappear in the Epilogue, but Wilcox ("Wife," 303–15) finds it just as suspect to read contemporary ideology into this ANE text (so also Keefe, "Hosea," 824). Similarly, Low's (*Wife*, 1–28) attempt (vis-à-vis Schüssler Fiorenza, *Feminist*, 26–28, 48) to turn Job's wife into a major character does not even attempt to identify the Prologue's literary structure, an approach Sasson ("Job," 86) justifiably calls "biased and unfair." More reasonable is Cernucan's ("Sorrow," 137) observation that "her purpose in the narrative is to add one final, crushing blow to Job's suffering before he utters the words that determine whether he has passed or failed the *satan's* test."

44. This is not the first attempt to make structural sense of Job generally or the Prologue specifically. Eissfeldt (*Introduction*, 456) breaks the Prologue down into six scenes, four on earth and two in heaven. Clines (*Job*, 6) breaks it down into five scenes alternating between heaven and earth, each containing the word ברך. Ceresko (*Job*, 125) identifies a chiasm in 1:2–19, Watson (*Techniques*, 17) a chiasm in Elihu's first speech (32:6–10), and Sawyer ("Structure," 55, followed by Habel, *Job*, 54) a chiasm structuring the entire book. Cf. also the proposals of Fokkelman (*Poems*, 211–44); and Dahood ("Chiasmus," 118–30).

45. Gerstenberger, "ענה," 230–52. On the polysemantic character of ענה in Ruth 1:13 cf. Moore, "Anomalies," 234–38. Not to be overlooked is the fact that Ruth is classified in some circles as wisdom literature (e.g., Murphy, *Job*, 83–93).

לכנה שבנה אשה לבית אמה	"Go back, each of you to your mother's house."
זקנתי מהיות לאיש	"I am too old to have a husband."
יצאה בי יד יהוה	"Yhwh's hand has struck me."
כי מר לי מאד מכם	"My bitterness is much deeper than yours."
אל תקראנה לי נעמי קראן לי מרא	"Call me Mara ('bitter'), not Naomi ('sweet')."[46]

Granted, the center of the Ruth coalition only distantly parallels the center of the Joban Prologue, yet two structural parallels beg serious attention: (a) just as the Ruth coalition focuses on the cogency of Naomi's divine protection,[47] so also the Joban coalition focuses on the cogency of Job's divine protection;[48] and (b) just as Naomi's concerns shift from anthropology to theology,[49] so also the Joban Prologue preserves the same sort of shift, only in the opposite direction, reporting first on characters in heaven (Yhwh, sons of Elohim, the *satan*),[50] then characters upon earth (Job, Job's wife, Job's counselors).[51] Should these parallels be taken seriously, it be-

46. Ruth 1:11–20 (cf. Moore, "Ruth," 315–25). Talmud discusses the relationship between Job and Ruth: "Job should be the first book of *Ketuvim* because some believe that Job lived in the days of Moses. But we do not start with 'retributions' (פורענות). But doesn't Ruth also start with 'retributions' (פורענות)? Yes, but the 'retributions' (פורענות) in Ruth hold out a hope for . . . redemption" (*b. Bab. Bat.* 14b). Loader ("Sister," 312–29), however, cautions against any theology predetermined to avoid legitimate critique of the deity, calling it "unnatural."

47. However one defines Boaz's role as גאל (Ruth 4:1), Salisbury ("Naomi," 245) emphasizes that "unless they are married, or otherwise in the care of a man who handles property, women can quickly descend into poverty."

48. Andersen (*Job*, 117) notes that whereas the Prosecutor "sees Job's hedge as a *protection*, the defendant views it as a *restriction*."

49. N.B. that the sequence in Torah's coalition of ten דברים ("words," Exod 20:1–17) also shifts from *theology* to *anthropology*, as Fredriksen ("Commandments," 802) points out in her analysis of *A.J.* 18.116–19: "the first five commandments, the First Table of the Law, concern relations with God, coded here as εὐσέβεια ('piety'); the next five, or Second Table, regulate relations between people, δικαιοσύνη ('justice'/'righteousness')."

50. Job 1:6; 2:1. MT בני האלהים ("sons of God/the gods"); Syr ܒܢܝ ܐܠܗܐ ("sons of God/the gods"); Vg *filii Dei* ("sons of God"); OG οἱ ἄγγελοι τοῦ θεοῦ ("angels of God"); Tg כתי מלאכיא ("bands of angels"). Cf. Ug *p(ḫ)r bn ilm* ("council of the sons of El," *CAT* 1.4.3.14).

51. The most obvious parallel is the use of תם ("integrity") by both the heavenly Judge (1:8) and Job's wife (2:9). OG 2:9 has her saying much more than that reported in MT, lamenting the fact that she is a "wanderer" (πλανῆτις), a "laborer" (λάτρις), "weary" (μόχθος), and "distressed" (ὀδύνη). Similar self-descriptions appear in TJob 21–25. Not to be overlooked is the fact that each of these coalitions ends with a justifiably angry lady challenging the deity.

comes much easier to interpret the spouse's role. The fact that TJob allots to her character so much more attention than MT Job probably reflects the TJob narrator's discomfort with the way her character is depicted in MT.[52]

The argument between Job and his spouse not only plays a significant role in the Prologue, it functionally previews the stroppy interchanges in the Dialogues between Job and his "friends." When they assign to him a piety defined not by unconditional trust, but by the rigid logic of payback perfectionism,[53] this helps explain not only their passivity toward his suffering, but also why their "consolation" intends not so much to comfort him as defend the deity's "honor."[54] Elaborating—and at times camouflaging—this retributional mindset,[55] the Dialogues artfully encase it within some of the Bible's most sophisticated poetry,[56] a situation often producing (a) a struggle among many readers to understand its linguistic/poetic densities,[57] plus (b)

52. TJob 21–25; cf. Mangan, "Women," 100–110. Ignoring structural concerns altogether, some readers imagine Job's wife as (a) an ally of Satan (capital "S"); or (b) a believer tested to her limit; or (c) a vaguely ambiguous figure. Cf. discussions in Schindler ("Job," 25) and Penchansky ("Wife," 223–28). Taking structural concerns seriously, Seow (*Job*, 305) observes that "the second part of Job's wife's speech is reminiscent of the Adversary's prediction that Job will 'bless' God (1:11; 2:5; cf. Mangan, "Blessing," 225–30). She gives voice on earth to (the existence of) doubt in heaven regarding human character, articulating to Job on earth the sentiment of the Adversary in heaven. Hence Augustine (*Psalms* 3.16) calls her *diaboli adiutrix*, 'the devil's helper.'"

53. L. Wilson (*Job*, 115–16) observes that "the concept of retribution is one of several theories of justice that have prevailed in ancient and modern times. It is distinct from other theories such as the *rehabilitation*, *restoration*, and *deterrent* views. These are all theories about how to treat those who have committed wrongs—legal or moral; individual or social; against other people, the environment, or God. The *retribution* view is sometimes called the 'deserts' theory of punishment. According to this theory, punishment should be administered only when it is deserved, and then only to the extent that it is deserved. It has a different goal from one motivated by revenge or retaliation. Punishment is not in order to reach some goal" but to compensate for "some offense. The basic principle is that whatever a person deserves, that should be their punishment, no more and no less. A retributive understanding of punishment sees a penalty imposed on the wrongdoer as a result of, and in proportion to, their offense."

54. Elihu intensely focuses on this issue in his second speech (Job 34:11–12).

55. At one point Job cries out, כלכם מנחמי עמל, "Miserable comforters are you all!" (Job 16:2), an exclamation leading Pohl (*Job*, 248) to suggest that one of Job's rhetorical goals is to defend his protest prayer (Job 3:1–26) against the arguments of his friends (cf. Walton, "Retribution," 648–56).

56. With regard to Hebrew poetry, opinion generally swings from O'Connor's (*Verse*, 3–5) attempt to *refine* Lowth's (*Poesi*) emphasis on poetic parallelism to Kugel's (*Poetry*, 3) attempt to *replace* it. Geller (*Poetry*, 626) sees "poetry" and "prose" as "Hellenistic impositions on the Bible," while Kugel (*Poetry*, 302) finds in Tanak no "precise distinction" between prose and poetry. Hoffman ("Job," 160–70) critiques the pros and cons of viewing Job as a scrapbook of independent texts.

57. Seow (*Job*, 2) observes that the Hebrew book of Job is "widely recognized as an

a speculative inclination (esp. among Continental readers) to "find" within it "hidden clues" to the book's history of composition.[58] Whether such a history is recoverable is impossible to ascertain, however, given the fact that Job is ahistorical wisdom literature.[59] Thus to read it through a *redaktionsgeschichtliche* filter not only tries to force a square peg into a round hole, it too quickly dismisses other approaches more likely to bear legitimate exegetical fruit.[60] For this reason the pages below will seek to show how deeply Job resonates with other "great texts" in its environment,[61] texts like the Egyptian Tale of the Eloquent Peasant,[62] the Dialogue of Ipu-Wer with the Lord of All,[63] the Dialogue of a Man with His Soul,[64] the Babylonian

---

immensely difficult text to understand, and Greenstein (*Job*, xvii) admits that "virtually no reader of the original Hebrew text has ever felt satisfied at having understood the poem at the core of the book."

58. Budde (*Hiob*, 39) and Duhm (*Hiob*, vii) hypothesize the prose narrative to be part of a pre-existing folktale into which the Dialogues are later spliced (so also Penchansky, *Wisdom*, 36), but Kautzsch (*Volksbuch*, 87–88) and Dhorme (*Job*, cxlix–cli) reject this hypothesis. More recent "final form," "new literary," and "deconstructionist" approaches minimize the influence of the Budde/Duhm school (cf. Habel, *Job*; Good, *Job*; Clines, *Job*), and Syring (*Hiob*, 166–67) rehearses how some assign the prose material (Prologue and Epilogue) to an earlier writer and the poetic material (Dialogues and Theologue) to a later one. Day (*Adversary*, 72) suggests that "the folktale told in the Prologue and Epilogue may have had in some form of its telling a life independent of the material now spliced into its middle, (but) there is ample evidence to suggest that it has been retold (and) reshaped in conscious appreciation of the poetic section of the work" (cf. Mathew, "Epilogue"). Beuken (*Job*, vii) summarizes the majority view today: "literary-historical criticism no longer leads to the theory of different origins of the framework in prose and the poetic corpus."

59. Cf. Moore, "Lyric," 9–15. Janzen (*Job*, 15) observes that contemporary "interpretation of Scripture tends prematurely to move to questions of historical fact and literary pre-history . . . It moves too quickly to *what* Scripture means apart from *how* it means." Dell (*Job*, 14–15) adds that "although Job shares certain themes of wisdom such as an interest in just retribution . . . there are other key elements which indicate links with a wider thought-world."

60. Sweeney (*Isaiah*, 13) rightly emphasizes that redaction-historical criticism should be applied only to specific types of texts.

61. Cf. Dever, *Texts*, 629–48; Graf, "Sources," 440–44; Franke, "Nippur," 1119; Hallo, *Belles-Lettres*, 495–633. Reiner ("Akkadische," 151–210), and Groneberg ("Definition," 59–84) outline the definitional features of "great texts," and Waugh ("Preface," xxii) argues that Roman Jakobson's work (esp. his "Poetics," 341–70) "provides . . . a methodology for . . . intertextual analysis."

62. *AEL* 1:169–84; cf. Erman, *Literature*, 116–31. Parkinson ("*Peasant*," 163–78) argues that the "juxtaposition of the two modes of narrative and discourse"—like that found in Job and *TEP*—is a structural "archetype."

63. *AEL* 1:149–63; *ANET* 441–44; Parkinson, "Ipuuer," 166–99.

64. *AEL* 1:163–69; *ANET* 405–7.

Poem of the Pious Sufferer,[65] and the Babylonian Theodicy.[66] These texts show that "there is in fact no lack of ancient works concerned with the testing of a hero or a pious man by all manner of misfortune."[67]

The parallels linking Job to its literary neighbors are remarkable, to be sure, but in no way do they necessarily imply *literary dependence*,[68] either through an academic medium of Canaanite schools attended by newly-settled Hebrews,[69] or by Canaanite scribes working alongside Hebrew colleagues in northwestern urban centers like Alalakh and Ugarit.[70] More likely these parallels demonstrate the simple truth that competent teachers are by definition predominantly interested in training students how to distinguish historical reality from political pretension.[71] Michael Cernucan is thus likely to be correct in his assessment of Job as the product of an author/editor composing/compiling "poetic dialogues in the tradition of Egyptian and Mesopotamian wisdom literature."[72]

65. *BWL* 21–62; Annus and Lenzi, *Ludlul.*

66. *BWL* 63–91; cf. Oshima, *Theodicy*. Stamm ("Theodizee," 104) argues that whereas the Babylonian Theodicy is a straightforward "dialogue of issues," the Dialogues in Job, like the Prologue, follow the juridical format of a "speech in court"; i.e., a "lawsuit" (ריב). Gemser ("Controversy-Pattern," 120–37), shows that this notion is as prevalent in Ketuvim as it is in Nevi'im.

67. Eissfeldt, *Introduction*, 468. Dion ("Job," 187–93) lists several more parallels between Job and the *Erra Epic.*

68. Ball, *Job*, 9.

69. Loretz, "Job," 123–27. Lemaire (*Écoles*, 84) suggests the existence of structured institutional schools in pre-exilic Israel despite the "très pauvre et très fragmentaire" epigraphic evidence ("very poor and very fragmentary," Puech, "*Écoles*," 189–203). Cf. Haran (*Schools*, 81–95) and Grabbe (*Sages*, 173–74).

70. Gray, "Job," 251–69; Dahood, "Word-Pairs," 19–20; Horwitz, "Scribe," 389–94. Berge ("Cities," 77) affirms that Don Benjamin's Claremont dissertation (*City*, 39–90) "convincingly describes Deuteronomic Israel as an urban culture."

71. Fohrer, *Hiob*, 47. Wiseman ("Books," 41) recognizes that "it cannot be doubted that the Egyptian and Mesopotamian epics and historiographies could have been known by the Hebrews. A copy of the Gilgamesh Epic from the 14th century BCE has been found in Megiddo, and other Babylonian texts from roughly the same period have been unearthed in Ugarit and Alalakh."

72. Cernucan, "Sorrow," 111. Most readers date Job to the post-exilic period, but Dunham (*Sage*, 235) suggests a date as early as the 15th century BCE.

HEAVENLY COUNCIL

Heavenly councils[73] mythopoeically[74] mirror the activities of earthly councils because, as Aaron Tugendhaft classically understates it, "cosmological speculation holds political ramifications."[75] The ANE texts examined here do not fall from the sky into desert caves in Arabia or the rolling hills of upstate New York.[76] No, they are in large part definable by their literary-historical contexts, and become more and more definable with every new discovery.[77] In the Babylonian Creation Epic (*Enūma eliš*),[78] for example, an anxious heavenly council recruits a relatively minor deity (Marduk) to stop a formidable sea-dragon (Tiamat) from bullying Babylon.[79] Another Mesopotamian text, the *Atraḫasis Epic*,[80] portrays Babylon's management-labor problem as a primeval conflict between "gentlemen" deities (Annunaki) and "slave" deities (Igigi).[81] In Syria-Palestine the Ba`al Epic begins with a heavenly council compelled to listen to a criminal indictment brought

73. Job 1:6; 2:1. Sasson ("Job," 86) wants to call this an "angelic convention," based on the OG translation οἱ ἄγγελοι τοῦ θεοῦ ("the angels of God"). Alongside Lambert's (*BWL* 7) recognition that ancient scribes "imagine their gods in their own image," Mullen (*Council*, 284) shows that "the parallels among the councils in Canaanite, Mesopotamian, and Hebrew culture suggest that the concept of the council of the gods is a common motif in the ancient Near East," and Lenzi (*Secrecy*, 377) documents how heavenly councils imitate earthly councils in that they "segregate off and control aspects of their more sensitive activities." Mangan (*Job*, 25) notes that the motif of "God consulting the heavenly court" is a "common concept in pseudepigraphal literature" (e.g., 2 En. 22.6).

74. Lewis (*Origin*, 37) carefully distinguishes between "mythopoeic" ("myth-making") and "mythopoetic" ("mythic imagery").

75. Tugendhaft ("Sovereignty," 367). Cf. Jacobsen ("Democracy," 159–72); Moore (*WealthWatch*, 26–29); Jindo ("Courtroom," 76–93); Beckman ("Hittite," 435–42); and Neumann ("Gebühren," 2–4). Komoróczy ("Work," 37) recognizes that the divine world depicted in epic myth is "nothing else than the human world," and Fishbane (*Myth*, 16) observes that "monotheism and myth are neither mutually exclusive nor incompatible."

76. *ODI* 206; Shipp (*Mormonism*, 1).

77. Cf. Rast ("Archaeology," 48–53); Meyers ("Israel," 255–64); Renz and Röllig (*Handbuch*); Cross (*Notebook*, 63–104); and Dever ("Artifacts," 3–36).

78. Lambert, *Creation*, 50–133. Most of the tablets containing *Ee* from Ashur, Kish, Assurbanipal's library at Nineveh, Sultantepe, and other sites date to c. 1200 BCE, but their colophons all indicate that they are copies of a much older version of the myth dating from long before the fall of Sumer (c. 1750 BCE).

79. *Ee* 4.97–104 (cf. Alster, "Tiamat," 867–69; Moore, *WealthWarn*, 17–25). So important is this myth, the Marduk priesthood recites it every year at the annual *akītu* festival (Pallis, *Akītu*; Gabriel, *Weltordnung*, 105–6; Sommerfeld, *Aufstieg*, 185–212). In Egypt the leviathan's name is Apophis (*ANET* 6–7).

80. Lambert and Millard, *Atra-ḫasīs*.

81. *Atr* 1.1–243 (cf. Moore, *WealthWatch*, 73–89).

against the Land-lord (Ba`al) by the Sea-lord (Yam).[82] Each of these mythopoeic texts highlights a different aspect of what goes on in a typical heavenly council.[83]

So what, if anything, is distinctive about the heavenly council in Job, if not its predilection to spotlight a fundamentally *theological* question; viz., Can a mortal creature be disinterestedly blameless, upright, God-fearing, and committed to the renunciation of evil *in the midst of unexplained/innocent suffering?*[84] To introduce *this* question the action starts with a heavenly Prosecutor (השטן)[85] filing charges against a mortal defendant (Job)[86] before a heavenly Judge (Yhwh).[87] Conspicuously absent from this courtroom is the Advocate/defense attorney[88] who, to Job's dismay, never shows up to help plead his case.[89] Deciding to situate the story in a courtroom is likely due to the universal appeal of the law,[90] not to mention the fact that its mythopoeic

82. Cf. *CAT* 1.2.1.18–19, 34–35 (cf. Mullen, *Council*, 113–280; Smith and Pitard, *Ba`al*, 1–3, 185). The conflict between the Sea-lord (Yam) and the Land-lord (Ba`al) is one of the central polarities of Canaanite myth.

83. As Jones Nelson puts it ("Job," 525), "the dialogue between Job and his friends is unique among comparable wisdom literature in the ANE," even though it is not "the only Israelite literature to develop this form."

84. Job 1:6–8. Ellis (*Hermeneutics*, 139–43) documents a debate in Mishnah (*m. Soṭa* 5.5) over whether Abraham or Job is the greater celebrity, the primary variable being whether greatness is based on *love* or *fear* (the former being superior to the latter).

85. Weiss (*Analysis*, 36).

86. Scholnick ("Justice," 521) suggests that Job enacts a role either (a) as plaintiff, charging God formally with specific offenses, or (b) as defendant, addressing the charge of unlawful seizure of his property.

87. Richter, *Hiob*, 131. Seow (*Job*, 548) argues that "Job imagines himself in such a legal setting" in the Prologue, while Stamm ("Theodizee," 104) projects the recurrence of this metaphor deep into the Dialogues.

88. In polytheistic myth this role is usually enacted by the solar deity as Myhrman (*Prayers*, 29–34) points out in his compilation of Babylonian petitions to the sun-god Šamaš (cf. Knudtzon, *Gebete*). Repeatedly utilizing the root جدل ("to argue, debate, advocate"), Qur'an warns believers "not to 'advocate' (يجدل) on behalf of those who deceive themselves" (Q 4.107) because "Who will be their 'Advocate' (كيل; lit., "corn-measurer") on Resurrection Day?" (Q 4.109).

89. At one point Job remarks that he has a heavenly "witness" (עד, 16:19), suggesting to Saadiah Gaon (d. 942 CE) that the "Redeemer" (גאל) in 19:25 is "not a Vindicator to be found in this life or the next" (cited in Vicchio, *Job*, 8). Day (*Adversary*, 89), however, believes that Job "longs for a being who can take both himself and God to task within the context of a trial." Suriano ("Death," 50) idiosyncratically suggests that "the passionate speech in Job 19:23–27 evokes the protagonist's confidence that, after his death, a גאל ('kinsman-redeemer,' v. 25) will perform the proper rituals on his behalf in order to preserve his name and patrimony for posterity."

90. Cf. Gamper, *Richter*, 103–41; Newsom, "Courtroom," 246–59; Roberts, "Metaphor," 159–65; Kensky, *Courtroom*, 13–61. Reading Job in its ANE context, Sheldon

character makes it easier for ANE scribes to post it on something "safe"[91] in order to deal with sensitive social, political, economic, and religious issues.[92] Whether Job is so designed is not impossible to imagine,[93] but given its focus on the journey of one single individual, uncertain.[94]

Not everyone reads Job this way, of course; i.e., as an autonomous religious text operating within an identifiable intertextual literary network.[95] Nor, for that matter, do the majority of contemporary readers appreciate how essential it is to read *all* ancient literature—not just the Bible—in its literary-historical context,[96] in spite of C. S. Lewis' warning that to do otherwise is to risk the likelihood that "what we see when we think we are looking

("Theodicy," 1–2) argues that "questions about divine justice are hosted by the Satan who serves as an ambiguous figure, not unlike Erra in the *Erra Epic*. Unlike the Babylonians who suffer at Erra's hands, however, Job does not remain a helpless victim, but dares to ask Yhwh to meet him in court" (cf. Nielsen, "שׂטן," 73–78).

91. Gardiner (*Grammar*, 1) notes that "the art of writing is always reserved to a conservative and tradition-loving caste of scribes upon whose interests and caprice it depends how far the common speech of the people should be allowed to contaminate *mdw nṯr* ('the god's words')." Yet this in no way diminishes the importance of the socio-political roles enacted by characters in these "great texts."

92. Cf. Lambert, "Ritual," 559; Launderville, *Piety*, 40; Moore, *WealthWatch*, 38. A contemporary example of this literary technique is Arthur Miller's *The Crucible*, a play which, while historically focused on the seventeenth century Salem witch trials, boldly criticizes the contemporary "witch trials" then being conducted by Senator Joseph McCarthy during the Big Red Scare (cf. Fried, *Nightmare*, 3–36). Ricoeur ("Myth," 6372) recognizes that myth alone has the power to project the darkest human conflicts into the Unseen World where they can be "safely handled."

93. Interpreting sapiential literature from a sociological perspective is not new. Weill ("Livre," 137), e.g., suggests that the "arguments" in *DMS* represent two social strata: "La thèse de négation de la religion funérarie . . . en opposition avec la thèse religieuse orthodoxe."

94. Whedbee ("Comedy," 1–39) reads Job as a U-shaped comedy because unlike tragedy, the story ends on a higher note than that with which it begins. The prophet Ezekiel (Ezek 14:14, 20) cites Noah, Daniel and Job as spiritual celebrities whose piety, while legendary, cannot save the land from divine judgment. Pleins (*Visions*, 484–508) argues that Job is a contributor to the "social vision" of the wisdom tradition while Aimers ("Devil," 57) contends that the "broadened scope of the Wager sees a test of Job's and his friends' fear of God in the sense of . . . God's *genuine* will for social justice" (cf. Müller, *Hiobproblem*, 128).

95. On the contours and limitations of intertextuality, cf. Polaski, *Authorizing*, 45–46; Roberts, "Tradition," 110–16; Pope, *Job*, lvi–lxxi; Clines, *Job*, lix–lx; Janzen, *Job*, 5–12; Fuchs, *Hiobdichtung*, 62–63; Andersen, *Job*, 24–33; Dion, "Job," 187–93; Hartley, *Job*, 6–11; and Seow, *Job*, 51–56.

96. Cf. Vicchio, *Job*, 1–45. Of the five approaches presented by Porter and Stovell (*Hermeneutics*)—*historico-grammatical; literary/postmodern; philosophical/theological; redemptive/historical;* and *canonical*—none attends directly to intertextual concerns.

into the depths of Scripture" is but "the reflection of our own silly faces."[97] Applying this caveat to Job, Brian Gault challenges any "simplistic reading of Job" which would encourage the spread of misinformation about one of the world's greatest texts, thereby corrupting the integrity of the whole exegetical process.[98]

In fact, a major misrepresentation occurs right off the bat in the Prologue. Most ETs read השׂטן (lit., "the prosecutor/adversary") as a proper name (i.e., "Satan," capital "S"),[99] even though such a reading is grammatically, structurally, and historically impossible. Here's why:

(1) השׂטן ("the *satan*") is a nominal construction formed by prefixing the definite article ה ("the") to the common noun שׂטן ("prosecutor"),[100] thereby creating a grammatical form never used to designate proper names in Classical Hebrew (or any other language).[101]

(2) Neither the articulated noun השׂטן nor the unarticulated noun שׂטן appear in Job outside of the Prologue.[102]

97. Lewis, *Psalms*, 142.

98. Gault, "Retribution," 165. Jones Nelson ("Job," 519) recognizes that "the format of the book itself seems to kick against any barriers imposed by unified hermeneutical perspectives, holding in tension multiple genres, characters, voices, time periods, perspectives, and perhaps authors." Whereas most read Job as an I-shaped "tragedy," Pope (*Job*, xxxi) contends that "there is no single classification appropriate to the literary form of the book of Job."

99. Job 1:6–7, 8–9, 12; 2:3–4, 6–7. Based on Satan's "title" as "king of the Persians" in TJob 17.1, Pilch (*Bible*, 49) speculates that שׂטן is a Persian loanword (cf. discussions in Magdalene, *Job*, 1–36, and Seow, *Job*, 59). Other suggested titles are "the Adversary," "the Accuser," "the Executioner" (Stokes, *Satan;* Thornton, "Satan," 251–70), "the Challenger," "the divine Policeman"(Lods, "Satan," 660); the "minister of justice" (Kelly, *Satan*) and "Officer Satan" (Handy, "Job," 109). Whether Qur'an refers to "the satan" or "Satan" (capital "S") is not always clear. Cf. وانكر عبدنا ايوب اذ نادي ربه انى مسنى الشيطن بنصب وعذاب, "And remember our servant Job, when he called to his Lord, 'Indeed, (the) S/satan has touched me with hardship and torment.'" (Q 38.41). Rashi (*Job*, 42.7.2) calls him השטן המקטרג את העולם, "the P/prosecutor who brings charges against the world."

100. *HAL* 1227–28, *contra BDB* 966; cf. Seow, *Job*, 272–74. Vicchio (*Job*, 51–53) documents the rise of "Satan" (capital "S") in early Jewish, Christian, and Muslim sources. Gnostic Christians are among the first to deify this character in their transformation of Christianity into a dualistic religion originating not in Tanak, but in a "foreign conceptual world" (Rudolph, "Gnosticism," 1035; cf. Labahn, "Devil," 156–79).

101. Forsyth (*Enemy*, 274) calls השׂטן "the agent *provocateur* in Job." Aimers ("Devil," 66) reckons that "the Joban *satan* deserves the status of a primary character if we allow for the expansion of his role, in connection to the divine wager and 'the satanic agenda,' to extend throughout the Dialogues." In Eliphaz's vision (Job 4:17–21), in fact, Nef Ulloa ("Satán," 39) hears "clear echoes" of the Prologue in "the discussion in the celestial sphere."

102. Gaster ("Satan," 225) and Lemke ("History," 83) suggest that the unarticulated

(3) Prior to the Second Temple period there is no irrefutable evidence for interpreting (ה)שׂטן as an alias of the Devil, the Dragon, the Prince of the Power of the Air, the Evil One, or any other personification of cosmic evil.[103]

Given these facts, Seow suggests that while השׂטן is not a proper name, it may well designate "the appellation of a particular divine being who stands next to the messenger of Yhwh to play an adversarial role," perhaps someone whose "specialized function is to seek out and accuse persons disloyal to God."[104] In fact, השׂטן may well be "an hypostasis, an extension of divine personality, or more specifically, a projection of divine doubt about human integrity."[105] Scrutinizing the term theologically, Crenshaw argues (with Moberly and Waltke)[106] that the Prosecutor's main job is to question "whether Job's religious devotion transcends" the "measure-for-measure calculation" integral to the retributional "demand for punishment."[107] Thus, to translate השׂטן as a proper name is not only grammatically and historically inaccurate; it actually damages the integrity of the reading process.

---

noun שׂטן in 1 Chron 21:1 refers not to Satan, but to an unnamed heavenly prosecutor. Moreover, Clines (*Job*, 20) compares Zech 3:1 (השׂטן עמד על ימינו לשׂטנו, "the prosecutor stood at his right hand to prosecute him") with 1 Chron 21:1, Num 22:22, and 2 Sam 24:1, concluding that השׂטן is "a description of function . . . not a title."

103. Day (*Adversary*, 150) argues that the earliest reference to the proper name "Satan" (capital "S") does not occur until the second century BCE in the pseudepigraphal books of Jubilees and the Assumption of Moses, texts which imagine a Day when לא יעמוד לנגדו שׂטן, "Satan will not survive" (Jub 50.5; As. Mos. 10.1). Pagels (*Satan*, 35–62) traces Satan's history into GNT and beyond. Saadiah Gaon (d. 942 CE) calls השׂטן "the Adversary," but at the same time "refuses to conclude that he is a demonic force responsible for Job's suffering" (cited in Vicchio, *Job*, 7). Rahman (*Themes*, 129) observes that Qur'an is quite ambivalent on "the question whether Satan is the objective *principle* of evil or a *person*."

104. Seow, *Job*, 273. Newsom (*Job*, 74, 76–77) recognizes that "the hostile image of Satan . . . as the opponent of God presumed by the New Testament" is most likely a "later development." N.B. that where Qur'an holds *Satan* responsible for "afflicting Job with distress and suffering" (Q 38.41), Job holds *Šadday* responsible (Job 6:4; 23:16; 27:2).

105. Seow (*Job*, 256), paraphrasing Weiss (*Story*, 42). Another example of hypostasis is the depiction of Sophia (חכמה, "wisdom") as a heavenly "person" (Prov 8:12; Sir 24:1; Wis 10:1). Cf. Emerton (*Goddess*, 127); Cahana-Blum ("Sophia," 469–84); Sinnott (*Personification*); Murphy ("Personification," 222–33); and Moore (*Babbler*, 256–59; *WealthWise*, 65).

106. Moberly, *Bible*, 85; Waltke, *Theology*, 930.

107. Crenshaw, *Evil*, 67, 16.

THE KEYWORD

The keyword in the Prosecutor's question is חנם,[108] a primitive term likely associated with the arithmetical notion of "zero," a concept rooted in old Sumerian, Sanskrit, and Mayan texts.[109] Tanak delimits it to divergent semantic fields: *economic* vs. *non-economic*:[110]

Economic Usage

Often חנם functions as an economic term.[111] In Torah, for example, an Aramean *sheikh* (Laban) bargains with a soon-to-be son-in-law (Jacob) by contrasting one economic term with another:[112]

הכי אחי אתה ועבדתני חנם	If you are my kinsman, should you serve me "without compensation?"[113]
הגידה לי מה משׂכרתיך	Tell me, what are your wages?[114]

Jeremiah reprises this same word-pair in his indictment of King Jehoiakim:

הוי בנה ביתו בלא צדק	Woe to anyone who builds his house by unrighteous means,
ועליותיו בלא משפט	And his upper rooms by injustice,
ברעהו יעבד חנם	Who makes his neighbors work "without compensation"
ופעלו לא יתן לו	Refusing to pay them their wages.[115]

108. Klopfenstein, "Hiobbuch," 117–21.

109. Job 1:9. Kaplan (*Zero*, 6) traces the history of "zero" to such sources.

110. Cf. *HAL* 321. That חנם prompts no dictionary article in *TDOT* or *TLOT* is likely due to the fact that its etymology is more economic than theological. Modern Arabic has a specific term for "nothing" (صفر) but Qur'an indirectly conveys the notion through statements like هل اتى الانسن حين من الدهر لميكن شيا مذكور, "Has there ever been a time when humanity is not worth mentioning?" (Q 76.1).

111. Whereas *BDB* (336) suggests three levels of meaning: (a) "*gratis*, gratuitously"; (b) "for no purpose, in vain"; and (c) "gratuitously, without cause, undeservedly," *HAL* (321) suggests the primary meaning as *ohne Entschädigung* ("without compensation").

112. Gen 29:15. Cf. Gordon, "Nuzi," 25–27; Van Seters, "Marriage," 377–95; and Morrison, "Jacob," 155–64.

113. Gen 29:15 (i.e., "for zero funds"). Arab خلف more often denotes "substitution/exchange" than "reward" (e.g., Q 34.39).

114. Gen 29:15. Cf. Arabic اجر ("to reward, compensate, remunerate" [Q 26.127, 145], and the nominal form اجير ["workman, laborer, employee"]). Lest this line be cited to portray Laban as fair, it is important to note that he "cheats" (תלל) Jacob out of his משׂכרת ("wages") no less than ten times (Gen 31:7).

115. Jer 22:13. Cf. the same term (פעלו) in Job 7:2. Bodner and White ("Recycling,"

Elsewhere Torah warns that any "gentleman" who denies food, clothing, and/or conjugal rights to an indentured Hebrew daughter[116] categorically surrenders *his* "rights" to her:

ואם שלש אלה לא יעשה לה	If he does not take care of these three things,
ויצאה חנם אין כסף	She can walk away "without compensation," owing no money.[117]

Wandering alongside Moses in the wilderness, several Hebrews complain about their daily cuisine:[118]

זכרנו את הדגה אשר נאכל במצרים חנם	We remember the fish we used to eat in Egypt "without compensation";
את הקשאים ואת האבטחים ואת הקציר ואת הבצלים ואת השומים	The pickles, melons, leeks, onions, and garlic.[119]

To Araunah's offer of free land for the Temple, David respectfully declines:

לא כי קנו אקנה מאותך במחיר	No, I will purchase it from you at a fair price,
ולא אעלה ליהוה אלהי עלות חנם	For I will not sacrifice burnt offerings to Yhwh my God "without compensation."[120]

Near the end of the exile an unnamed prophet reminds his comrades:

כי כה אמר יהוה	For thus says Yhwh:
חנם נמכרתם	"You were sold 'without compensation,'[121]
ולא בכסף תגאלו	And will be redeemed without money."[122]

26–31) investigate several later reflections on the Jacob cycle (e.g., 1 Sam 19:9–18).

116. Exod 21:7. MT לאמה, "as a handmaiden"; Syr ܠܐܡܬܐ, "handmaiden"; Tg ברתיה זעירתהא לאמהו, "young(er) daughter as a handmaiden"; OG οἰκέτιν, "housemaid"; Vg *famula*, "handmaid."

117. Exod 21:11 (i.e., "paying zero funds"). Wright (*Law*, 34) cites a parallel statute in *CH* 149.

118. Cf. Wong, "Manna," 56; Maiberger, *Manna*, 9–86.

119. Num 11:5, 11. Q 11.11 promises that "the patient who does good deeds" will receive اجر كبير ("a great reward").

120. 2 Sam 24:24. Josephus (*A.J.* 7.69) describes Araunah as a "wealthy" (πλούσιος) Jebusite who is spared by David, thereby causing him to bear "goodwill" (εὔνοια) toward the Hebrews and "gracious zeal" (χάριν καὶ σπουδὴν) toward David.

121. Isa 52:3. Cf. OG δωρεάν ἐπράθητε ("you were sold 'without cost'"); Syr ܡܓܢ; Tg מגן; Vg *gratis*.

122. Isa 52:3. Goldingay (*Isaiah*, 443) dubs this a "divine wake-up call." Qur'an

Non-Economic Usage

Not all biblical texts, however, treat חנם as an economic term. When Prince Jonathan pleads on behalf of his friend David, for example, he reminds his father (King Saul) that

וישׂם את נפשו בכפו	He took his life in his hand
ויך את הפלשתי	When he struck the Philistine.
ויעשׂ יהוה תשועה גדולה לכל ישׂראל	When Yhwh brought great deliverance to all Israel,
ראית ותשׂמח	You saw it and rejoiced.
ולמה תחטא בדם נקי	Why, then, would you sin against innocent blood
להמית את דוד חנם	And kill David "for no reason?"[123]

Ezekiel uses the term in his *apologia* for the intrinsic power of divine speech:

וידעו כי אני יהוה	And they shall know that I am Yhwh,
לא אל חנם דברתי	That I do not speak "in vain."[124]

After the fall of Jerusalem a bereft Hebrew cries out:

צוד צדוני כצפור איבי חנם	My enemies hunt me down like a bird "for no reason."[125]

In light of this evidence it appears more than a little obvious that חנם straddles two semantic fields,[126] yet in response to what they call a "contemporary consensus" that in 1:9 it means *ends* ("for no reason"), but in 2:3 means *origins* ("without cause"),[127] Tod Linafelt and Andrew Davis propose that the best reading strategy is to translate חנם as "to no effect" in each verse.[128] Should this be the case, they argue, then what the Prosecutor

---

promises a Day when there will be no more بيع ("selling," Q 14.31).

123. 1 Sam 19:5 (cf. 25:31); Vg *absque culpa* ("without fault"). The translation "without compensation" works neither here nor in the following two passages.

124. Ezek 6:10. OG omits; i.e., *καὶ ἐπιγνώσονται διότι ἐγὼ κύριος λελάληκα* ("and they shall know that I the Lord have spoken"); Syr ܘܠܐ ܗܘܐ ܣܪܝܩܐܝܬ ܐܡܪܬ ("that I have not vainly spoken"); Tg לא למגן גזרית בממרי ("that I have not uselessly circumcised my words"); Vg *non frustra locutus sum* ("that I do not speak in vain").

125. Lam 3:52. OG δωρεάν; Syr ܡܓܢ; Tg מגן; Vg *gratis*.

126. So *HAL* 321; *BDB* 336; *DTTM* 484.

127. This "consensus" is highly suspect. Fohrer (*Hiob*) reads חנם as *ohne Entschädigung* ("without compensation") in 1:9 and *ohne Grund* ("without cause") in 2:3. Both Newsom (*Job*, 70) and Hartley (*Job*, 129) read חנם in 2:3 as "for no reason."

128. Linafelt and Davis, "Job," 627–39.

challenges the Judge to consider is not whether Job's piety is gratuitous, but whether the testing process itself is defective, especially when the first round of testing leads Yhwh to say, "You incited me against him to ruin him with 'no effect' (i.e., 'without accomplishing any real purpose')." In other words, not only is the motive for Job's piety inexplicable, the testing process itself is flawed.[129]

Attending more closely to the immediate literary context, Jürgen Ebach suggests that the Prologue is designed to invite readers to ponder whether prosperity is the result of piety or *vice versa*; i.e., *piety </> prosperity*.[130] When Job sacrifices "holocaust offerings" (עלות) on behalf of his children,[131] for example, does he do so to provide them with "insurance" for any sins they might commit?[132] If so, then חנם in 1:9 likely refers to "disinterested piety" as a patriarchal strategy designed to give Job's children the "certainty of security."[133] Climbing aboard this bandwagon, Rainer Kessler suggests that what the Prosecutor *really* wants to find out is whether Job's piety is *fully* חנם; i.e., whether חנם derives from the verb חנה ("to extend grace")[134] or denotes merely a mercantilistic "exchange of equivalents."[135]

129. Linafelt and Davis, "Job," 627–39.

130. Ebach, "Hiob," 321. Davies (*Narrative*, 15) argues that "the effect of the narrative's ambiguity is to draw readers into the fictive world of the story, setting in motion their own decision-making processes, and forcing them to come to their own moral judgment" after engaging in "a readerly interaction with the characters that a more explicitly detailed account would not have made possible."

131. MT Job 1:5 reads העלה עולות (lit., "he lifted up the lifted-up things"; cf. Lev 1:3–17); OG προσέφερεν περὶ αὐτῶν θυσίας ("he offered sacrifices for them; cf. Moore, "Sacrifice," 533). Coogan ("Children," 138) concurs that Job's intention is to "make exculpatory offerings for any hypothetical sins they may have committed."

132. The keyword in MT Job 1:5 is אולי ("perhaps"). The verse ends with a note explaining that Job repeats his routine כל הימים ("every day").

133. "Logik der Versicherung"; Ebach, "Hiob," 321. It's important to remember that Job is not a Hebrew individual (though he eventually "joins the family" via his marriage to Dinah, according to TJob 1.5–6), so his theology of sacrifice doubtless looks more like that of, say, Balaam than, say, Aaron; cf. Moore, *Balaam*, 87–96.

134. Brockelmann (*VG* 1.474) suggests the final *mem* is likely due to mimation, while Bauer-Leander (*BL* 529y) read it as a "fossilized suffix." Regardless of morphology, the חנם > חנה relationship parallels the same adverbialization process as ריק ("to empty, pour out") < ריקם ("vainly, wantonly," Ps 25:3).

135. "Austausch von Äquivalenten," Kessler ("Erlöser," 147). This is Kessler's interpretation of עור בעד עור, "skin for skin" (2:4). For Clines (*Job*, 43) "the most natural view is that this saying comes from the world of bartering, where 'one skin for another skin' could well be a phrase for a fair exchange." Following Calmet (*Job*, 9), Duhm (*Hiob*, 11) argues that "skin for skin" probably refers to the trading of animal skins, a view congruent with the interpretations of Ewald (*Job*, 91) and Dhorme (*Job*, 14).

Other possibilities may be discussed, of course, but suffice it to state here that serious exegetical interpretation takes three perspectives into account: (a) the content and function of the biblical text; (b) the nuances of meaning derived from an examination of its literary structure; and (c) the nuances of meaning derived from an investigation into its intertextual network. Trumping all discussion about "etymology," "tradition," and/or "scholarly consensus," holistic interpretation of the Prosecutor's question is impossible without explaining why every major lexicon defines חנם within economic/non-economic parameters.[136] In short, חנם *may* be, but does not *have* to be an economic term.

THEOLOGICAL REFLECTION

Holistic interpretation of the Joban Prologue attends to (a) how much its *Sitz im Leben* compares to that underlying other ANE "heavenly council" texts;[137] (b) how much its metaphorical imagery reflects a courtroom populated by a defendant, a Prosecutor, a Judge, and a (conspicuously absent) Advocate;[138] (c) how much the Prosecutor in this courtroom theorizes the defendant's piety to be determinable in some way by the scope of his wealth; (d) how much the Judge in this courtroom is willing to permit the testing of this hypothesis; and (e) how much the quarrelsome behavior of this mortal couple contributes to the tone of the forthcoming Dialogues.[139] Of particular significance is the keyword חנם and how it (c)overtly elucidates the *prosperity* </> *piety* equation in the Prologue (Job's wife vs. Job), the Dialogues (the "friends" vs. Job), and the Theologue (Yhwh vs. Job).

At any rate, the Prologue raises five theological questions:

(1) Why does the Judge ask the Prosecutor about his whereabouts?

(2) Why does the Judge depict the defendant's piety as blameless, upright, God-fearing, and evil-avoidant?

(3) Why does the Prosecutor challenge the defendant's motives?

136. Cf. *HAL* 321; *BDB* 336; *DTTM* 484. Cf. Delekat ("Wörterbuch," 7–66).

137. Cf. Pss 82:1; 89:7; Jer 23:18, 22 (cf. Breitkopf, "Gunkel," 54).

138. Eissfeldt (*Introduction*, 456) calls the goings-on in the Prologue a "trial."

139. Hoping to find in TJob 21–25 a "visionary precedent to feminism," Garrett ("Sex," 63–70) regretfully concludes that "those searching for such a precedent will have to look elsewhere" because the "wifely and maternal passions" of Job's wife "bind her to the corruptible earthly realm," thereby "providing an easy avenue of access for Satan."

(4) Why does the Judge permit the Prosecutor to test the *prosperity* </> *piety* equation?

(5) Why does the defendant's spouse advise him to "curse God and die?"

Prosecutor's Whereabouts

When the heavenly Judge asks the Prosecutor to report his whereabouts and hears (not learns) that he has been "roaming the land,"[140] Pope Gregory I (d. 604 CE) interprets this to mean that "the Devil has been stamping the footprints of his wickedness into the hearts of the Gentiles."[141] Norman Whybray, however, argues that the Judge's question is an "ignorant enquiry" betraying his "seduction" via the "Devil's cynicism."[142] Presuming "omniscience" to be an innately divine trait, Eleonore Stump posits that the Judge's inquiry cannot be designed to solicit previously unknown information, but may well signal the deity's intention to pull an errant "son" back from the edge of the Abyss.[143] More pragmatically, John Hartley suggests that the *satan* in the Prologue is less a prosecutor than an "emperor's spy"[144] endowed with "powers to coerce and torture"[145] like those *still* deployed by "secret police."[146] Each of these readings has merit, but none of them seriously attends to the significance of the disinterested piety motif.[147]

140. Job 1:7. MT משוט בארץ; OG περιελθὼν τὴν γῆν ("encircling the earth"; so Vg *circuivi terram*); Syr ܡܚܕܪܐ ܒܐܪܥܐ ("to go around/beg on the land"—cf. Satan's beggar disguise in TJob 6–8). Tg מן שוט בארעא ("from roaming the land").

141. Gregory I, *Moralia*, 96.

142. Whybray, *Job*, 24.

143. Stump (*Darkness*, 198) speculates that the deity is as concerned about השטן as he is for any other בן האלהים ("son of God," 1:6; 2:1). Contrast this with Whybray's ("Oppression," 1–19) portrayal of the deity as an "oppressor" and Lasine's (*Knowing*, 263) depiction of a "jealous and demanding father."

144. Hartley, *Job*, 73.

145. Bartlett, *Signs*, 52.

146. Clines, *Job*, 23. Andrew ("Spies," 13–26) charts the history of "secret police" throughout the ancient world.

147. Jindo ("Courtroom," 76) depicts the courtroom not as "an independent theological category," but as a "complex category of biblical religion through which biblical authors grasp the operation and meaning of the world and the self."

Defendant's Piety

Plastered to the facade of the library of Celsus in Ephesus stand four statues depicting qualities "attributable," in Garrett Ryan's judgment, "to any cultivated man in public service"—Σοφία ("wisdom"), Ἐπιστήμη ("knowledge"), Ἔννοια ("intelligence"), and Ἀρετή ("virtue").[148] The virtues of the "ideal gentleman" in Job, however, look very different: תם ("integrity/blamelessness"),[149] ישר ("uprightness"),[150] ירא אלהים ("godly fear"), and סר מרע ("avoidance of evil").[151] Discounting all attempts to hyper-segregate East from West,[152] it nonetheless remains difficult to describe the virtues billboarded in Ephesus as in any way comparable to those found in Job.[153] Yet, as Patricia Vesely points out, the mere fact that "godly fear" parallels "resistance to evil" in this virtue-list clearly indicates a close connection "between piety and ethics."[154]

Defendant's Motives

Question: Does the Prosecutor question Job's motives because he finds this to be a feasible legal strategy, or does he do so simply because it's his job? *Answer:* "Yes." The former is possible, of course, but the latter cannot be impossible. Prosecutors prosecute, plaintiffs complain, counselors counsel, defendants defend, and judges judge. These roles are as old as the law itself,

148. Ryan, *Cities*, 166. Virtue-lists are commonly found in several ancient texts (cf. Plato, *Resp*. 4.427–45; Wis 8:7; 14:22–27; 4 Macc 1:2–4; 5:23–24; Gal 5:22–23).

149. Vesely (*Job*, 168) contends that where "blamelessness in the prose narrative demonstrates a willing acceptance of the superiority of God's plan, no matter what the outcome may be, in the poetic dialogues it manifests itself as commitment to honesty and justice."

150. Clines (*Job*, 12) views ישר ("uprightness") as a relational term, as opposed to the more abstract term צדקה ("justice/righteousness").

151. Job 1:1, 8; 2:3 (always in this order).

152. Avrahami (*Bible*, 23) acknowledges that "alongside the essentialist dichotomy between Hebrew and Greek modes of thinking found in some scholarly works, other scholars (mainly from the social scientific approach) attribute both Hebrew and Greek cultures to a larger pan-Mediterranean culture" (cf. Hagedorn, *Moses*, 14–37).

153. A possible exception is the fourth virtue, ἀρετή. Xenophon (*Mem* 2.1.21), e.g., depicts youth as a time "when the young, now becoming their own masters, show whether they will approach life by the path of 'virtue' (ἀρετή) or by the path of 'vice' (κακία)" (author's translation).

154. Vesely, *Job*, 167. Cf. 2 Pet 1:5–7; Gal 5:22–23. Without dismissing the reality of legitimate East-West polarities it nevertheless remains prudent to be "concerned," with Pohl ("*Friendship*," 310–11), about Vesely's "use of Greek philosophy as a lens through which to read Job."

a cultural institution predating Job by centuries, if not millenia.[155] For Raymond Westbrook, in fact, it's important to realize that "the ancient Near East is home to the world's oldest known law, predating by far the earliest legal records of other ancient civilizations, such as India or China."[156]

Exactly how a prosecutor might build a case against a defendant based on "evidence" hidden within the *mind* of said defendant, however, is an entirely different matter. None of the ANE law codes (including Torah) make provision for such a procedure, so one can only wonder why the heavenly Judge entertains it here.[157] Indeed, this is one of the book's great mysteries, one which Janzen explains as part and parcel of the "human question" vs. the "divine question." That is, "from the human side the question arises as to the meaning of innocent suffering for one's understanding of one's own life and of human existence in general, and for one's understanding of the divine character and purposes. However, this human question is correlative to—and in Job presented as arising within the context of—the divine question as to the motivation and character, and therefore the meaning, of human piety and rectitude."[158] Doubtless this tension explains why Job so strongly emphasizes his compassion for widows and orphans—because he wants to quell any attempt to prosecute him on the basis of "hidden evidence."[159]

Judge's Permission

Why does the Judge permit the Prosecutor to test Job? Realizing that the goal of every prosecutor is to gather enough evidence to secure a conviction,[160]

155. Cf. Wilcke, *Law*, 9–27; Couturier, "Loi," 177–92; and Blenkinsopp, *Law*, 74.

156. Westbrook, "Law," 1. Richter (*Hiob*) bases his forensic analysis on Alt's ("Weisheit," 139–48) hypothesis that 1 Kgs 5:26 references two kinds of wisdom: *Naturweisheit* ("nature wisdom"—carpentry, architecture, engineering, etc.) and *Lebensweisheit* ("life wisdom"—ethics, scribal midrash, law, etc.). Audet ("Origines," 352–57) documents the close relationship between *wisdom* and *law*.

157. A possible exception is the first law in the Code of Hammurabi: *šumma awīlum awīlam ubbirma nērtam elišu iddima la uktīnšu mubiršu iddâk*, "If a gentleman accuses another gentleman of homicide, but cannot prove it, he is to be killed" (*CH* 5.26–31). The Joban Prosecutor makes a similar unsubstantiated accusation. Simonetti ("Trial," 285) observes that *CH* "employs no less than five paragraphs (*CH* 6.70—8.24) to explain how the evaluation of evidence should be made in a trial." So "we should conclude that, evidently, the problem of judicial malfunction is keenly perceived."

158. Janzen, *Job*, 20.

159. Job 29:12–13 (cf. 24:3–4). Evidently Job takes seriously the responsibility of "gentlemen" to "judge the cause of the widow and adjudicate the case of the orphan" (*ydn dn almnt yṯpṭ ṯpṭ ytm*, *CAT* 1.17.5.7–8).

160. Birzer ("Crime," 36) is blunt: "The ability to identify and properly collect

LaSor points out (a) that the legal activity in the heavenly council stands in dramatic contrast to the peaceful activity in Uz and (b) that the text subtly highlights this contrast by "alternating between the land of Uz, where Job lives with integrity and piety (in prosperity or in disaster), and the court of Yhwh, where the *satan* challenges Yhwh to test Job."[161] In other words, the Prologue introduces the dynamics of Job's suffering simply by the way it is structured.

Spousal Advice

Why does Job's spouse advise him to "curse God and die?"[162] Having lost everything with her husband except her health, she says:

עדך מחזיק בתמתך	Are you still clinging to your integrity?
ברך אלהים ומת	Curse God and die.[163]

Job's response highlights the significance of the disinterested piety motif:

כדבר אחת הנבלות תדברי	You speak like one of the foolish women.
גם את הטוב נקבל מאת האלהים	Shall we accept that which is good from God
ואת הרע לא נקבל	And not the bad?[164]

Most ETs read this proclamation as "Curse God and die!"[165] but Edwin Good suggests several ways to interpret it: (1) *Farewell*—"Say goodbye to

physical evidence is . . . critical to prosecuting . . . crimes."

161. LaSor et al. (*Survey*, 475) dub the events in the Prologue a "drama on a double stage."

162. TJob explains the giving of this advice to her husband as the final stage of a three-stage meltdown, the first two being (a) she is driven into slavery to support him (21.1—22.2), after which (b) she sells her hair to Satan (capital "S") for three loaves of bread (22.3—23.11). After this TJob goes so far as to insert a poem commemorating *her* suffering (TJob 25.1–8).

163. Job 2:9.

164. Job 2:10. MT repeats קבל twice ("to receive, take"), but OG translates the first with δέχομαι ("to take, accept, welcome") and the second with ὑποφέρω ("to endure"); Vg twice repeats the verb *suscipio* ("to honor, respect, suspect"), but conjugates it differently, reading *si suscepimus* ("if we have honored"), followed by *non suscipiamus* ("shall we not honor"); Syr reads ܩܒܠ (cognate of קבל) twice, conjugating it first as a participle ܡܩܒܠ ("having received the good"), then as a 1 fut c pl ܠܐ ܢܩܒܠ ("shall we not receive the bad?"). Regardless of the wording, it's difficult to imagine a more concentrated testimonial to the power of disinterested piety.

165. Job 2:9. MT ברך normally means "to bless" (Vg *benedic* "to bless"), and Tg reads בריך מימרא דיי ומית ("bless the word of Yhwh and die"), but Syr ܓܕܦ ("to revile") influences most ETs to read ברך as a circumlocution (cf. Anderson, *Blessing*, 273–97).

Elohim and die"; (2) *Rebellion*—"Throw the whole thing in Elohim's face and take the consequences of death"; (3) *Encouragement*—"Go on holding fast to your integrity, even if it leads to your death"; and (4) *Pity*—"Bless Elohim and be released from your suffering."[166] Other possibilities include (5) *Pain*—"I can no longer watch you suffer, so please put an end to it"; (6) *Resignation*—"I do not trust your deity, why should you?"; and (7) *Inconvenience*—"To get herself out of her commitment and thus betray her husband in his terrible adversity." Sasson suggests that "she does not ask for a divorce," but "finds a better, convenient alternative at hand: she simply tells her husband to commit suicide!"[167] OG aligns with #1 and #3 and perhaps #5,[168] but early Christian leaders tend to lean toward #2 and/or #6.[169] Frank Andersen suggests that "by tempting her husband to self-damnation, Sitis[170] urges him to do exactly what the *satan* predicts he would do," thereby becoming a pawn of the Prosecutor whose accusation, though it "does not reach Job openly," touches him "more subtly through the solicitude of a loving wife."[171] Whichever reading is preferred, what can most surely be affirmed is that the antagonistic mood generated by this marital dispute effectively sets the tone for the Dialogues.[172]

SUMMARY

Backboned by a coalition of seven questions, the Prologue introduces the book of Job by forthrightly stating its central polarity—*retribution* vs. *reality*. Is God to be served only to receive a reward or avoid punishment? Or is he to be served without preconditions because he is God, the Sovereign Lord? The first half of this polarity presumes a willingness, however difficult,

166. Good, *Job*, 200.

167. Sasson, "Job," 88. *DMS* is interpreted by some as a tract on suicide (see below).

168. OG 2:9–10 portrays this marital conflict as follows: "After time passed his wife said, 'How long will you patiently say, "Let me wait a bit longer as I look for the hope of my salvation" while your memory is expunged from the earth along with our children, the labor and travail of my womb, whom I apparently raised for no reason? Meanwhile you sit in wormy decay passing the nights outside while I tread and drudge from place to place and house to house, waiting for the sun to go down so that I may rest from the toils and griefs which now grip me. So *say a word to the Lord and be done with it*'" (εἰπόν τι ῥῆμα εἰς κύριον καὶ τελεύτα).

169. Cf. sources cited in Vicchio, *Job*, 58–59.

170. Job's wife's name in TJob 25.1 is Σίτιδος ("Sitidos").

171. Andersen, *Job*, 97–98.

172. Balla ("Relationship," 107–26) traces some of the difficult realities of male-female relationship into Sir 25:26, 36.

to process wisely the reality of suffering while the second half presumes a prerequisite "as long as"; i.e., "I will serve only *as long as* I get paid, or I will serve only *as long as* I am not punished." The Dialogues take up this polarity and debate it vigorously.

3

The Counselors' Questions

GIVEN THE PROLOGUE'S DECISION to spotlight the disinterested piety motif, the Dialogues next turn to Job's "friends" in order to see what theological ideas are most important to them. Before examining the speeches of these characters, however, it's important to recognize from a structural standpoint that the initial response of each counselor, beginning with Eliphaz the Temanite, is a barbed methodological query:[1]

הנסה דבר אליך תלאה	If you are exhausted by a single trial,[2]
ועצר במלין מי יוכל	Who will endure *your* words?[3]

This initiatory response does not determine everything which follows, of course, but it does lay the groundwork for a cumulative demand that Job recant his "inappropriate" remarks,[4] whether through "rhetorical questions

1. Teman is another name for Edom (Jer 49:7, 20) and OG Job 2:11 calls Eliphaz ὁ Θαιμανων βασιλεύς ("king of the Temanites").

2. Job 4:2a (lit., "testing of a word"; cf. Gen 22:1). OG μὴ πολλάκις σοι λελάληται ἐν κόπῳ ἰσχὺν, "Do you often speak of exhausting matters?"; Syr ܠܐ ܠܡܡܠܠܘ ܥܡܟ ܠܐܝܐ, "Is not conversing with you exhausting?"; Tg נסיון פתגמא דמטה לותך העל, "Is dialogue (lit., "testing of a word") going to be possible with you?" Qur'an emphasizes the importance of "testing the unjust" (فتنة للظالمين, Q 37.63), and Rashi (*Job*, 4.2.1) imagines Eliphaz to be "dumbfounded" (לשון תימה, lit., "tongue of astonishment") by Job's "exhaustion."

3. Job 4:2b. OG ῥημάτων σου τίς ὑποίσει, "Who can endure your words?"; Syr ܘܠܡܠܠܐ ܗܟܢܐ ܣܓܝܐܐ ܡܢܘ ܡܨܐ ܢܣܝܒܪ, "Who can consume so many words?"; Tg תשתלהי ולמעכבא במליא מן יכול, "Who can prevent the planting of words?" Hartley (*Job*, 105) thinks that what Eliphaz "politely asks" for here is "Job's indulgence before offering a word."

4. N.B. that some synonym for "word" (דבר, אמר, and/or מלה) occurs in the opening speech of each counselor. Citing Morrow (*Protest*, 139–45), Pohl (*Job*, 129) identifies chapter 3 as a bitter lament saturated with "complaints against God" bordering on the "theologically problematic."

he is not expected to answer,"[5] or by "convincing him that his words are dangerous and destructive."[6] Thus Bildad the Shuhite asks:[7]

עד אן תמלל אלה	How long will you say such things[8]
ורוח כביר אמרי פיך	Through the windy words gusting out of your mouth?[9]

Zophar the Naamathite asks:[10]

הרב דברים לא יענה	Should a swarm of words go unanswered,[11]
ואם איש שפים יצדק	Or an impudent mortal justified?[12]

Elihu asks:

5. Clines, *Job*, 121. Seow (*Job*, 381) observes that "many perceive Eliphaz to be a sly rhetor who resorts to diplomatic doublespeak, constantly saying one thing, but meaning another." Scher ("Macho," 84) catalogues similarly abusive professors' perceptions of students via "academic machismo," esp. when berating their intellectual capacities before their peers (cf. Mewburn, *Academic*).

6. Pohl, *Job*, 132. Cf. Westermann, "Job," 81; Koch, *Formgeschichte*; and Moore, *Babbler*, 222. Brown (*Vision*, 173–81) contends that an entire book can be written about the ways in which Job's "friends" twist his words out of context. Among other sources, Qur'an views the "twisting of words out of context" (يحرفون الكلم من مواضعه, lit., "cutting the words from their places") as something which "cannot stand" (اقوم, Q 4.46).

7. OG Job 2:11 calls Bildad a ὁ Σαυχαίων τύραννος ("ruler of the Shuhites"). Knauf ("Shuah," 1026) identifies Shuah as *Sūḫu*, an Assyrian province on the middle Euphrates.

8. Job 8:2a. OG μέχρι τίνος λαλήσεις ταῦτα, "How long will you say these things?"; Syr ܥܕܡܐ ܠܐܡܬܝ ܬܡܠܠ ܗܠܝܢ, "How long will you chant words?"; Tg עד אימתי תמלל כאלין, "How long will you speak such words?" Pope (*Job*, 132) reads "How long will you set word snares?"

9. Job 8:2b. OG πνεῦμα πολυρῆμον τοῦ στόματός σου, "the windy words of your mouth"; Syr ܘܪܘܚܐ ܪܒܬܐ ܡܠܐ ܦܘܡܟ, "and the word from your mouth be a great wind"; Tg וזעפא רבא מימרי פומך, "and the great hurricane of words from your mouth."

10. Knauf ("Naamathite," 968) thinks that "the homelands of Job's friends encircle the whole Arabian peninsula: Bildad is from Shuah, i.e., the middle Euphrates, NE Arabia; Eliphaz the Temanite comes from either Edom or Tayma, NW Arabia in either case; and Zophar comes from South Arabia." Yet OG Job 2:11 calls Zophar ὁ Μιναίων βασιλεύς ("king of the Minoans").

11. Job 11:2a. OG ὁ τὰ πολλὰ λέγων καὶ ἀντακούσεται, "Should the one saying so many things be answered?"; Syr ܣܘܓܐܐ ܕܡܠܐ ܠܐ ܚܝܐ, "Should a multitude of words go unanswered?"; Tg אפשר דמסגי מליא לא יתותב, "Is it possible to respond to so many words?"

12. Job 11:2b (lit., "man of lips"; i.e., "smart aleck"). OG καὶ ὁ εὔλαλος οἴεται εἶναι δίκαιος εὐλογημένος γεννητὸς γυναικὸς ὀλιγόβιος, "should such a sweet talker be expected to be righteous, having been 'cursed' (?) to have been born of a mortal woman"; Syr ܘܐܦܠܐ ܓܒܪܐ ܡܡܠܠ ܒܒܨܝܪܘܬܐ ܙܕܝܩܘܬܗܘܢ; "nor a great man speaking disparagingly of their vindication"; Tg ואין בר נש מרי שפון יזכי, "and is a son of man not vindicated by humble words?" To prepare humanity for the يوم الفصل ("Day of Judgment," Q 77.13), Qur'an commands *muslims* to preach a message consisting of عذرا اونذرا ("justification and/or warning," 77.6; note the alliteration), depending on what is most needed by the audience at hand.

והוחלתי כי לא ידברו	Should I wait until they (Job's "friends") stop arguing?[13]
כי עמדו לא ענו עוד	Or until they come to a conclusion bereft of evidence?[14]

Even Yhwh begins with a question:

מי זה מחשיך עצי במלין בלי דעת	Who is this darkening my counsel with such nonsense?[15]

Reckoning Job's lament to be a natural response to "the severity of the pains burdening and overwhelming him," Rashi (d. 1105 CE) condemns Job's "friends" for failing "to console him as Elihu does,"[16] and the fact that they express what *appears* to be "consolation" only masks their belief that Job's real problem is a profound "disregard (for) the infallible justice of God in punishing wrongdoers."[17] Postmodern readers may expect from the word "counselor" a reference to professional healthcare workers committed to administering a type of psychotherapy like, say, Transactional Analysis ("I'm OK—You're OK").[18] But such expectations, however well-intended, are

13. Job 32:16a. The difference here, of course, is that Elihu begins not by responding to Job, but to the "lack of progress" he sees in Job's three "friends." Cf. OG ὑπέμεινα οὐ γὰρ ἐλάλησαν, "Shall I wait until they stop speaking?"; Syr ܡܛܠ ܕܠܐ ܡܡܠܠܝܢ, "Wherefore do they not speak?"; Tg ואוריכית ארם לא ימללון, "Waiting out their debate, will they ever shut up?"

14. Job 32:16b. OG ὅτι ἔστησαν οὐκ ἀπεκρίθησαν, "Because they do not give an answer on where they stand"; Syr ܘܩܡܘ ܘܠܐ ܐܗܦܟܘ ܠܝ, "Though taking a stand they give me no answer"; Tg שתקו ולא אתיבו תוב, "They are silent and do not answer." Elihu seems to refer here to the type of *waiting* later reflected upon in Qur'an: "Say to the unbelievers, 'Keep on doing what you are doing (عمل; cf. עמל in Job 3:10, 20; 4:8, *et passim*), and so will we. Keep on waiting (نظر), and so will we.'" (Q 11.121–22; 44.59; 52.31; cf. Ps 37:34).

15. Job 38:2 (reading עצי based on OG με βουλήν).

16. לנחמו כאשר עשה אליהוא (Rashi, *Job*, 42.7.2). Rashi's definition of "consolation" is different from that of Job's "friends." For Rashi, Yhwh singles Eliphaz out for judgment because אתם פשתם על אשר הרשעתם אותו ("When you disobeyed you did evil to him," Job 42:7). Buttenweiser (*Job*, 41) thinks that Rashi views Job's counselors as "exponents of the religious views of their age, upholders of tradition, and as such, all three, without appreciable difference, tenaciously defending the doctrine of retributive justice."

17. Diewert, "Elihu," 1. Longman ("Disputation," 285) is more inclined to see "sarcastic dismissal" than "disregard."

18. Harris (*OK*) and Berne (*Games*) are two of TA's best-known advocates. Opinion is divided, of course, over the definitional parameters of "therapy." Gabriel ("Damage," 25), e.g., reminds postmodern readers that

> "in the early years of this country's history, suffering—both physical and psychological—was widespread and generally considered a normal part of everyday life . . . As a result there was no sense that emotional or mental distress might harm the individual

driven by dynamics utterly foreign to the literary-historical environment responsible for producing this "great text." What is unquestionably clear, however, is that Job's opening lament triggers a deeply rooted reflex in these sages to defend at all costs the deity's "integrity" (תם).[19] Everything else, including Job's pain, is secondary to what they perceive to be his *primary* problem; viz., his arrogant refusal to confess and submit. Because Job refuses to submit to "wise counsel," they therefore conclude that his real intention is to challenge God's integrity, thereby forcing them to defend it (a) by attacking Job directly, or (b) by camouflaging their counsel behind ivy-covered walls of "sage advice."[20] Whatever their methods, William Henry Green follows the deity in holding *them* responsible for making Job feel "wounded by their harshness, stung by their censures, and exasperated by their reproaches."[21]

ELIPHAZ

With the character of Eliphaz, however, there is much more beneath the surface than first meets the eye.[22] It goes without saying that his language hardens considerably over the course of his three speeches,[23] but for Da-

in a lasting way . . . People simply did not think of those who suffered as damaged in the way that we do today." Since the Civil War, however, "psychological suffering has been reconceptualized as anomalous and potentially threatening to the normal functioning of the self" so that today "a central assumption in the popularization of therapeutic culture" is that this damage "can be ameliorated through therapeutic intervention." Of course, there is no need to reject "the importance of therapeutic culture in making the world a better place . . . (but) not its tendency to foreclose other possible responses to the troubles of the world."

19. In Ps 82 the psalmist sharply criticizes the "gods" for failing to take care of the marginalized, a critique which leads him to insist, to quote Crenshaw (*Defending*, 45, 54), that they have "forfeited their claim on terrestrial devotees," thereby leaving only a "single deity" in whose "integrity and commitment to justice the psalmist rests all hope for rectitude among humans." Further, "the move away from many gods to a single God comes at a high price" in that "the presence of evil in the world is sacrificed for ethical monotheism." Frymer-Kensky (*Goddesses*, 213) similarly believes that "the transformative insights of biblical monotheism are insufficient."

20. OG, TJob and other early readers moderate this portrayal through what Dunham (*Sage*, 32) calls an "interpretive polarity." That is, sometimes Eliphaz is "eloquent and respectable," and sometimes he is "hasty and violent."

21. Green (*Job*, 113), referencing Job 42:7.

22. Dunham, *Sage*, 232–33. Clines ("Arguments," 275) reckons that "only genuinely distinctive argumentation would fully justify the introduction of three interlocutors." Further, Habel (*Job*, 121) underlines the importance of "distinguishing between the role Eliphaz plays as a character and the poet's way of playing with Eliphaz and his speeches in the overall plan of the book."

23. On the slowly-revealed differences between Job and Eliphaz over the

vid Clines his first words intend only to comfort a "friend" in a "most conciliatory manner."[24] Similarly, Samuel Terrien sees "gentleness and courtesy" in his opening remarks,[25] while Marvin Pope sees an "apology for presuming to lecture his friend in such a state of misery."[26] Maimonides (d. 1204) commends Eliphaz's "exhortations to patience, words of consolation, and appeals to amicability,"[27] while Andrew Davidson wonders whether he is "the most dignified . . . most considerate, and perhaps oldest of Job's friends."[28]

Kemper Fullerton, however, takes sides against Job by arguing that Eliphaz's "affirmations, doctrinally so sound and steadying, bring a welcome relief" from Job's "vehement, almost ungovernable outbursts."[29] Tremper Longman similarly thinks that Eliphaz's opening words "intend to challenge Job's complaint,"[30] while Choon Leong Seow finds in them a note of "caution."[31] Norman Habel sees in Eliphaz a "compassion matched by a compulsion to speak,"[32] while John Hartley sees a diffident professor caught in the throes of "reflecting on his own dilemma" because (a) he does not want to alienate Job, and (b) he does not want Job's "bitter words" to "alienate God."[33] Similarly, Marvin Pope sees in Eliphaz a nervous professor unwilling to "get involved in a contradiction," and so for this reason "withdraws himself from consideration of Job's particular case" choosing instead to share only a few "generalizations."[34] Clines agrees, suggesting that there is no reason to doubt the sincerity of Job's respect for Eliphaz,[35] but that the

benevolent-vs.-malevolent character of Šadday, cf. Moore (*Babbler*, 217–19).

24. Clines, *Job*, 121.

25. Terrien, "Job," 932.

26. Pope, *Job*, 35.

27. Maimonides, *Guide*, 491.

28. Davidson, *Job*, xxiv. Fohrer (*Hiob*, 134) sees him as "*ruhig und freundlich*" ("calm and friendly"). Peake (*Job*, 77) labels him "considerate and tender."

29. Fullerton ("Eliphaz," 326) is hardly the first to notice Job's flaws. Talmud preserves a comment that because Job says כלה ענן וילך כין יורד שאול לא יעלה ("as a cloud fades and vanishes, so the one who descends into Sheol does not ascend," Job 7:9), then he must surely "deny the resurrection of the dead" (בתחית המתים, *b. B. Bat.* 16a). Polzin ("Framework," 184) characterizes Job's speeches as "some of the most anti-Yhwh sentiments of which we have any record," and Dunham (*Sage*, 25) suggests that OG's depiction of Eliphaz as an "urbane interlocutor" is doubtless responsible for "later sympathetic readings in Jewish and Christian interpretation."

30. Longman, *Job*, 115.

31. Seow, *Job*, 382.

32. Habel, *Job*, 124.

33. Hartley, *Job*, 105.

34. Pope, *Job*, 36.

35. Responding to Eliphaz's first speech, Job tries to meet him halfway: הורוני ואני

latter's "reproofs" amount to little more than rambling "generalities" about "the inevitability of human sin."[36] In light of these variegated responses it thus seems clear that Eliphaz is not a flat, one-dimensional character, even though the jury is still out on whether he is, as Kyle Dunham wants to claim, a "sophisticated counselor who has at his disposal the best of human wisdom and insight."[37]

Intrigued by the aforesaid "generalities," Carol Newsom suggests that what Eliphaz sees in Job's "moment of crisis" is "something which can be integrated and endowed with meaning," as opposed to Job's treatment of it as "simply and irreducibly 'turmoil.'"[38] More to the theological point, Habel finds Eliphaz paralyzed by the possibility of being accused of empathizing with Job, fearing that his colleagues might brand *him* as an "enemy of God."[39] Other opinions may be cited, of course, but so wide a spectrum of opinion from so small a sample is sufficient to show that this character, like most major characters in most "great texts," is not easily cartooned.[40]

First Dialogue

John Burnight suggests that Eliphaz's opening remarks (4:2–6) are an intratextual response to what looks to be a "tacit indictment" of the deity in Job's opening speech (3:20–26). If so, "what at first glance may appear to be concern and encouragement . . . is in fact a sharp rebuke to Job for complaining about his 'fear' and inability to find 'rest.'"[41] This proposal is intriguing, but whatever its plausibility, Eliphaz's ambivalence plainly surfaces when he applauds Job for his ministry to the poor (4:3–4)[42] then immediately derides

---

אחריש, "Teach me and I will be silent" (6:24).

36. Clines, *Job*, 181.

37. Dunham, *Sage*, 232.

38. Newsom, *Job*, 102. Cf. Job 3:26.

39. Like Jung (*Job*, 51) and Lasine (*Kings*, 239, 61), Habel (*Wisdom*, 50) has no qualms imagining the deity as just another flawed character.

40. Cf. Alter, *Narrative*, 143–62. Eliphaz's character resembles that which Mikhail Bakhtin (*Poetics*) sees in the characters animating Dostoevsky's 1880 novel *The Brothers Karamazov* (cf. Newsom, *Contest*, 21–24). Cf. the character of Solomon son of David who, after receiving a positive assessment (1 Kgs 3:3), soon receives a negative one (11:6; cf. Frisch, "Solomon," 51–52).

41. Burnight, "Eliphaz," 348.

42. Nef Ulloa ("Job," 99–102) highlights the parallels between a *theology* of retribution and an *economy* of retribution.

him for (misleadingly?) portraying his abandonment of "godly fear" as a "tragic loss":[43]

הלא יראתך כסלתך	Is not your fear your confidence?[44]
תקותך ותם דרכיך	Your hope your integrity?[45]

The *corpus callosum*[46] here linking the Prologue to the Dialogues thickens considerably because while the Prosecutor challenges the *motivation* behind Job's piety, Eliphaz bemoans its *dissolution*.[47] If Job's "godly fear" is authentic, he wonders, then what happened to his "confidence?"[48] Several of the Dialogues covertly allude to this puzzle,[49] but the irony here is twofold: (a) that the traits listed by Eliphaz are elsewhere attributed to Job by the heavenly Judge,[50] while (b) their poetic replay in the Dialogues comes

43. Gibson, *Job*, 37. Pope (*Job*, 36) finds in Eliphaz a character who, like the Prosecutor, is forced "to concede that Job's piety and conduct have been exemplary."

44. Job 4:6a (cf. 15:4; 22:4). OG ἀφροσύνη ("folly"); Syr ܣܒܪ ("complaint"); Tg סבוי ("outlook, hope"); Vg *patientia* ("patience"). For MT כסל "confidence" seems preferable to "foolishness" because the term תם ("integrity") parallels it in the next line. Rashi (*Job*, 4.6.2) translates "foolishness" (כסילות) even though כסל elsewhere in Job means "confidence" (Job 8:14; 31:24; cf. *b. Sanh.* 89b; Schüpphaus, "כסל," 266).

45. Job 4:6b. Rashi (*Job*, 4.6.2) argues that Job's "foolishness" comes from a lack of דעת שלמה ("complete understanding"), and Seow (*Job*, 384–85) suggests that Eliphaz here "implies that Job's approach . . . is too self-centered and individualistic, (and that) Job seems to judge God solely on the basis of his personal experience." Bildad later underlines this "fault" in Job's thinking (8:8–10).

46. The *corpus callosum* is the large bundle of c. 200 million myelinated nerve fibers connecting the left hemisphere of the brain to the right one (Hellige, "Brain," 248–57).

47. Cut-and-paste diachronic theories designed to segregate the Prologue from the Dialogues, though not as elaborate as they used to be, are today giving way to newer approaches more sensitive to the text's synchronic literary structure (cf. Habel, *Job*, 25–31; Day, *Adversary*, 72–74; and R. Moore, "Integrity," 17–31).

48. Bildad mocks the wicked man's loss of "confidence" (כסל, 8:14), but like the psalmist, Eliphaz wonders whether Job can say, טרם אענה אני שגג ועתה אמרתך שמרתי, "Before I was afflicted I went astray, but now I keep your word" (Ps 119:67). Qur'an asks, "Are you 'confident' (امين; cf. אמן, 'amen') that the Heavenly One will not make the earth collapse . . . . Are you 'confident' (same term, امين) that the Heavenly One will not unleash a violent storm?" (Q 67.16–17).

49. Dunham (*Sage*, 2, 33–35) rightly observes that Eliphaz's "speeches," while genuine and authentic, "touch upon each of the various theodicies put forth by the human speakers in Job." N.B. how the apostle Paul tries to unite a divided Corinthian congregation with a line from Eliphaz's first speech (OG Job 5:13, cited in 1 Cor 3:19), a citation Dunham takes to be an example of irony (39–41).

50. Job 1:8; 2:3. Unless Eliphaz is somehow aware of this identification it is difficult to explain how these traits just "happen" to appear. So, it makes more sense to attribute this replication to the narrator, who, after all, is the only party aware of *all* the text's voices (cf. Newsom, *Job*, 17–18).

embossed not by the words of a delighted deity, but by the legalistic counsel of a payback perfectionist.[51] His next question underscores this:

מי הוא נקי אבד	Who among the innocent perishes?[52]
איפה ישרים נכחדו	Where are the upright cut off?[53]

Regardless of rationale,[54] Eliphaz's attraction to such questions indicates either clueless misconstrual or stubborn denial of a very simple truth: *suffering is endemic to the human condition.*[55] No one is immune to it. The innocent suffer just as much as the guilty, whether they be "crack babies,"[56] abused toddlers,[57] massacred schoolchildren,[58] cyber-bullied adolescents,[59] cartel-terrorized refugees,[60] "honor-killing" victims,[61] or some other situation.[62] To hide behind a socioreligious veil and ignore the reality of innocent

51. Longman (*Job*, 159–60) defines "retribution theology" as a worldview "based on the idea that sin leads to suffering and thus that suffering is a sign of sin." Even Dunham (*Sage*, 232), a reader supportive of Eliphaz, describes him as a figure shaped by an "archetypal paradigm" exemplifying a "system of retribution."

52. Job 4:7a. MT אבד ("perish, destroy"); ἀπώλετο ("perish, destroy"); Syr ܐܒܕ ("perish, destroy"). Qur'an tells the story of a dinner hosted by Potiphar's wife to counter her husband's support of Joseph's innocence, where though her guests "witness the signs" (راوا الآيت) of his innocence, they still condemn him (Q 12.35; cf. Gen 39:1–20).

53. Job 4:7b. Holbert ("Eliphaz," 471) observes that "Eliphaz's traditional theology forces him to claim that 'the upright' are never cut off," even while "the case that gives the lie to that claim sits before his very eyes." In this way "the reader is immediately made aware that the book of Job launches an attack on a theology that would offer simple solutions to a person in the condition of Job, namely, an 'upright' person who has lost everything." Granting Eliphaz the benefit of the doubt, Hartley (*Job*, 107) notes that the sage "does not say that the upright will not suffer hardship," only that one must be "careful not to put the emphasis on the final outcome of one's life."

54. Bergant ("Motifs," 164), e.g., argues that the purpose of these questions is to promote a "poetic statement of the inability of human beings to be clean/righteous before God."

55. Cf. Job 21:7–26; Hab 1:4; Pss 10:1–3; 73:2–14 (Pope, *Killings*; Moore, "Lamentations"). Doubtless the death of Job's children exemplifies the phenomenon of "innocent" suffering, *contra* Bildad's view that the most likely explanation for their fate is unconfessed "sin" (חטאת, Job 8:4).

56. Barone, "Myths," 67–68; Black, "Children," 23–25.

57. Nurse, *Abuse*, 77–105.

58. Shah, ("Guns," 1); Cook ("Columbine," 107–17); Viano ("Kindergarten," 253–79).

59. Bingöl ("Bullying," 138–43); Mishna (*Bullying*, 73–86); Litwiller and Brausch ("Suicide," 675–84).

60. Slack (*Deported*, 1–39).

61. Shoro (*Honour*). Husseini ("Honor," 264) argues that "the origin of honor-based violence against women . . . is not exclusive to any ethnicity, religion, or geography," but in point of fact it is most common in Muslim families in the Middle East.

62. Bales (*Disposable*, 1–5). Like Eliphaz, Qur'an presumes that there is no such

suffering is pathetically myopic, if not altogether blind. In fact, an argument can be made that such a response makes the innocent suffer more than they otherwise would because it practically *invites* religio-political demagogues to read texts like Ruth and Job through distorted lenses shaped not by the texts themselves, but by their own twisted prejudices.[63] Granted, it is sad to watch Eliphaz pick and choose only those attributes of the deity with which he is comfortable,[64] but theological myopia is not new, especially among "enlightened" professors more prone to ideological extremism than biblical theology.[65]

Struck by its complexities, Kyle Dunham suggests for the character of Eliphaz three possibilities. Either he is (a) a pernicious counselor with no theological contribution; or (b) a sophisticated counselor making a substantive theological contribution; or (c) a normative ANE counselor making a substantive (though flawed) theological contribution.[66] Seow more pragmatically suggests that what Eliphaz wants from Job is that he learn how to embrace the "common-sense principle of cause and effect."[67] Psy-

---

thing as "innocent" suffering. For example, "Imagine if God's punishment were to overwhelm you with or without warning. Who would be destroyed other than 'the wrongdoers' (الظالمون)?" (Q 6.47). To those who, like Eliphaz, minimize the reality of innocent suffering, Niebuhr (*Nature*, 2:45–46) suggests that the suffering of Christ is a reminder that "the contradictions of history are not resolvable in history," but "only on the level of the eternal and the divine."

63. Examples: (a) the politicized paternalism predetermining the way some Muslims define شريعه (*shari'ah*, Q 45.18); (b) the paternalistic way some Christians define ὑποτάσσω ("to submit," Eph 5:21); and (c) the understandable, but parochial way some Jews define ציון ("Zion," 2 Kgs 19:31). Note also the debate among classicists on whether the "hidden thoughts" of Homeric heroes can be identified by "reading between the lines": *YES*—(de Jong, "Hidden," 27–50); *NO*—(Redfield, *Iliad*, 21).

64. Cross (*CMHE* 344) singles out especially the "covenant God of Deuteronomy," but Dunham (*Sage*, 93–94) is quick to reject any depiction in which Eliphaz "espouses dogmatically the Deuteronomic principle of retribution." In Islam, as Farook (*Reformation*, 3–4) observes, "many Muslim-majority countries are leaning toward traditional Islam by way of implementation of the *shari'ah*." Yet, "the more a country leans this way, the more not just the West, but conscientious Muslims around the world become anxious" (e.g., Jasser, *Battle*) because "the *shari'ah* is being distorted through the association with its partial and discriminatory implementation via dictatorial, authoritarian, or hereditary rule, often applied to the general, largely poor populace, while those in power or the wealthy are immune to the harsh punishments." The same applies to the thinking of Job's "friends."

65. "Biblical theology" has taken an academic beating the last few decades (see Childs, *Crisis*), but to paraphrase Mark Twain, "the rumors of its death have been greatly exaggerated."

66. Dunham (*Sage*, 4–7) naturally leans toward the third of these options as a "golden mean" between the first two (Aristotle, *Eth. nic.* 2.1).

67. Seow (*Job*, 385). Jastrow (*Job*, 210) sees Eliphaz warning Job that he "ought to be

chologically this may imply that he wants Job to become more sensitive to the discipline of "left-brain" thinking,[68] but anthropologically it may mean that he wants him to learn how to champion the "trade language" of the marketplace over the "heart language" of the home/village.[69] Whatever else it may be, however, the book of Job does not promote one language at the expense of another,[70] not least because to do so would make it that much easier for sages like Eliphaz to fall prey to "defective speech."[71]

Of course, this does not mean that the theological motif upon which Eliphaz *does* focus is unimportant or insignificant. Far from it. *Justification* is no minor motif, seeing as it shapes and contours texts as diverse as the Prophecy of Habakkuk,[72] the Proverbs of Solomon, the Gospel of John, and Paul's Letter to the Romans (just to name a few).[73] To his credit, though, Eliphaz apparently thinks that the Presence of the *mysterium tremendum* stands at the center of a just cosmos,[74] even when a mysterious "night-spirit"[75] shows up to ask:

---

willing to take some of the medicine that he has so frequently poured down the throat of others."

68. McGilchrist (*Master*, 16–31); Williams (*Mind*, 1–12).

69. Influenced by cultural anthropologists like Eller (*Anthropology*, 109), Inouye (*Foundations*, 19–21) promotes the "trade-language-vs.-heart-language" polarity as a helpful descriptor, but Selmier and Oh ("Trade," 486–514) prefer to think in terms of a variety of factors signalling the measurement of what they call "linguistic closeness," including *same language, direct communication,* and *language distance.*

70. Von Rad (*Wisdom*, 79) believes that the sages of the ancient world do not intend to "do theology," and that "to speak of a 'doctrine of retribution' is highly misleading because this is not a question of ideological postulates, but of experiences which hold true over a long series of generations." Attracted to this argument, Perdue (*Wisdom*, 20) adds that the "creation order" championed by many sages can sometimes lead to "a hardened doctrine of retribution" which in turn degenerates into "an inflexible, mechanistic system of reward and punishment disallowing or restricting divine freedom." Yhwh censures Job's "friends" (Job 42:7) for professing this "twisted perversion of sapiential thought."

71. Job 42:7.

72. Cf. Koning ("Habakkuk," 120–24).

73. See Hab 2:4; 1QpHab 7.1–17; John 5:30; Rom 1:16–17, *et passim*. Not everyone is convinced that the מורה הצדק ("Teacher of Righteousness") at Qumran (1QpHab 7.5) is Sadducean/Zadokite, but Schiffman's (*Qumran*, 127) arguments are compelling (cf. Murphy-O'Connor, "Teacher," 400–20). In Qur'an "righteousness" is not about "turning one's face toward the east or toward the west. Rather, the 'righteous' (البر) believe in God, the Last Day, the angels, the Books, and the prophets. They give from their means to relatives, orphans, the poor, needy travelers, and beggars. They free captives, establish prayer, pay alms-tax, keep their pledges, and patiently endure 'suffering' (البسغ)" (Q 2.177).

74. Cf. Otto (*Holy*, 80); Moore ("Presence," 166–70).

75. Illustrating the depths to which anti-Eliphaz animus can sink, R. Shimon bar

האנוש מאלוה יצדק Can a mortal be more righteous than God?[76]
אם מעשׂהו יטהר גבר Can a gentleman[77] be purer than his Maker?[78]

Eliphaz may or may not be interested in helping Job find an Advocate, but evidently he doubts whether *any* mediator—earthly or heavenly—has the power to cross the "great gulf" separating the Seen from the Unseen World, not only because Šadday does "profoundly great things,"[79] but because mortals generally tend to behave like "troublemakers."[80] Raising his eyes aloft, he thus asks:

קרא נא היש עונך Call now! Who will answer you?
ואל מי מקדשׁים תפנה To which of the holy ones will you turn?[81]

Abba suggests that what Eliphaz hears in his "night-visions" (חזונות לילה, 4:13) is the voice of Satan (שטן, *b. Sanh.* 89b). Disagreeing with this notion entirely, Rashi (*Job*, 4.12.1; 14.1) contends that what this "night-spirit" relays is a דבר נבואה ("word of prophecy"; cf. 5.1.1) from a מלאך ("angel"). Pointing out that the "pious sufferer" in *Lud* 3.8–45 receives a "special revelation," Dunham (*Sage*, 172) concludes that the character of Eliphaz stands "smugly within the Mesopotamian wisdom tradition."

76. Job 4:17a. *Contra* NRSV, NIV reads the *mem* in each couplet as comparative (Joüon 141g). Janzen (*Job*, 73) emphasizes that "in imputing to humankind the qualities of inevitable untrustworthiness and inevitable error, he (or his 'revelation') is speaking on one side of the issue already joined in the heavenly meeting between Yhwh and the Satan." Seow (*Job*, 389) interprets this to be "divine doubt reminiscent of the Adversary's perspective in the Prologue." Whatever the substance of Eliphaz's views, the doctrine of justification cannot reasonably be described as biblically peripheral (cf. essays published in Beilby and Eddy, *Justification*).

77. Doubtless גבר not only provides a poetic parallel to אנוש, but signifies the upper echelon of ANE society. Cf. the description of Boaz as a גבור חיל ("wealthy gentleman," Ruth 2:1).

78. Job 4:17b. Pelham (*Job*, 108–9) sees an inherent contradiction within Eliphaz's worldview, noting that his "inclusion of the spirit's message (4:12–17) that humans have no righteousness because of their mortality plainly contradicts the views expressed in the rest of his first speech . . . As Eliphaz sees it, humans can be righteous" but "according to the spirit, humans cannot be righteous . . . Strangely, although the spirit's words contradict Eliphaz's own, Eliphaz does not argue with them, but instead *pretends* that they support his position." Brown (*Job*, 12–50) observes that contemporary interpreters read Eliphaz's vision from several angles: (a) as central to Eliphaz's argument; (b) as ambiguous or subversive; (c) as a late addition; and/or (d) as Job's vision.

79. Job 5:9 (עשׂה גדלות ואין חקר).

80. Job 5:7 (לעמל יולד; lit., "born to/for trouble"). Cf. Otzen ("עמל," 196–202) and N.B. that Eliphaz's use of עמל ("trouble") resonates with Job's use of the term in his opening lament (3:10). Prioritizing ecology over theology, Habel (*Nature*, 45–46) suggests that Eliphaz's problem is not the challenge of dealing with Job as a sage-counselor, but that he "views humans as corrupt and impure because they originate in . . . their mother, Earth."

81. Job 5:1 (OG reads ὄψῃ, "see"). MT קדשׁים ("holy ones") can refer to beings earthly (cf. קדשׁים אשׁר בארץ, "holy ones on the earth," Ps 16:3) or heavenly (cf. יהוה אלהי כל קדשׁים, "Yhwh my God and all the holy ones," Zech 14:5). Most see

In short, Eliphaz's emphasis on the justification motif is not what makes his theology problematic. It's his insistence that it replace all others, including "disinterested piety."[82]

Second Dialogue

Having listened to Job's rejoinders—to himself in chapters 6–7, to Bildad in chapters 9–10, and to Zophar in chapters 12–14—Eliphaz begins his second speech (chapter 15) with a shrill denunciation of "blowhards."[83]

החכם יענה דעת רוח	Should the wise respond to "blowhards"[84]
וימלא קדים בטנו	Who inflate their bellies with the east wind?[85]
הוכח בדבר לא יסכון	Should they argue over things unproven,[86]
ומלים לא יועיל בם	Or words bereft of profit?[87]

Dwelling on what he believes to be the most likely explanation for Job's newfound timidity,[88] Eliphaz plies him with "creation" questions much like

---

here the latter of these two options (e.g., *HAL* 998), yet Seow (*Job*, 389) suggests that Eliphaz doubts whether "even divine intermediaries are perfect in the eyes of God."

82. Dunham (*Sage*, 173) rehearses the outdated notion that Job's wisdom is "Hebrew" and Eliphaz's "Gentile," but this proposal reopens an interreligious can of worms, not least because Job is not Hebrew. Dating the book to c. 500 BCE, Gese ("Lebenssinn," 161–79) sees rather in Job a "new piety" in which human welfare is processed and promoted through a type of חכמה ("wisdom") rooted in personal relationships with the deity.

83. Job 15:1–35 (cf. Signer, *Demagogue*, 32–37). Given Job's decision to characterize his counselors as "worthless physicians" in the first speech cycle (13:4), Yu ("Speeches," 287) characterizes the second speech cycle (chapters 15–21) as dependent upon a "change in the friends' rhetorical situation." Qur'an similarly censures "indulging in reckless talk with the careless" (نخوض مع الخايضين, Q 74.45; from خوض, "to plunge, dive, rush," Wehr 265).

84. Job 15:2a (lit., "the knower of wind"). Vg *ventum loquens* ("windy talker"); Syr ܪܘܚܐ ܢܣܒ ("busybody"); OG *συνέσεως πνεύματος* ("spiritual insight"); Tg האפשר דחקימא דדמי יתיב דעתא ("Can the wise man compensate for suspect knowledge?").

85. Job 15:2b. The קדים ("sirocco/east wind") blows through the Middle East at regular intervals (cf. Drinkard, "East," 248).

86. Job 15:3a. In 8:8, Bildad contends that unproven terms are inferior to those articulated by ראשון דור ("former generations"), and Qur'an proverbially says "a kind word of forgiveness is preferable to a charitable deed dripped in hate" (Q 2.263).

87. Job 15:3b. "Profit" (יעל) is an important term in the sapiential lexicon (cf. Job 30:13; Prov 11:4; Moore, *WealthWise*, 32). Hartley (*Job*, 244) recognizes that חכם ("wise man") here refers either to Eliphaz or Job, but suggests the latter to be the more likely option because Eliphaz here responds to Job's insistence that his wisdom is much deeper than that of his counselors (12:3; 13:2). In other words, what Eliphaz wants is فذكر ان نفعت الذكر, "to admonish where admonishment is profitable" (Q 87.9).

88. Job 15:4. Unlike the Prosecutor in 1:9, Eliphaz does not go so far as to insinuate

those rehearsed in the Theologue.[89] For Leo Perdue this signals a determination on his part to "counter Job's destabilizing curses through sapiential instruction and pious praise" for the "creator and sustainer of a just world order."[90] Balentine similarly sees a "broad consensus that Job extensively appropriates creation imagery, especially in the Prologue-Epilogue, which effectively frames the book as a sequel to the primordial creation accounts in Genesis."[91] For Dunham, however, Eliphaz's speeches disclose the thinking of a "theological legalist . . . embodying the highest achievement and most profound perspectives of human wisdom in the ancient Near East," even though "his outlook remains, in the end, merely human":[92]

הראישון אדם תולד	Are you the first man?[93]
ולפני גבעות חוללת	Were you spawned before the mountains?[94]
הבסוד אלוה תשמע	Do you attend the divine council,[95]
ותגרע אליך חכמה	Or do you restrict wisdom to yourself alone?[96]

---

that Job fears God only when "compensated" (חנם; cf. above); he simply wonders why his "godly fear" is "crumbling" (פרר).

89. "Creation" motifs pop up repeatedly in the speeches of Zophar and Elihu before reaching full bloom in the Theologue. As Schifferdecker (*Whirlwind*, iv) points out, the whirlwind speeches in chapters 38–42 connect more closely to the Dialogues in chapters 4–37 than most people realize because each section presumes "creation" to be "radically non-anthropocentric." Unlike most readers, Crenshaw (*Introduction*, 100) imagines Job as a "triptych (Prologue, Dialogue, and Theologue) with Job's two monologues in chapters 29–31 as the hinge connecting the three panels."

90. Perdue (*Creation*, 137).

91. Balentine ("Animals," 3).

92. Dunham (*Sage*, 13–14).

93. Job 15:7a. Syr ܩܕܡ ܐܢܫܐ ("first man"); OG πρῶτος ἀνθρώπων ("first of the humans"); Vg *primus homo* ("first man"); Tg reads בלא אבא ואמא אתילדת ("were you born without father or mother?"). Given the versions and the fact that בכור ("firstborn") appears in 18:13, ראישון is probably best translated here as "first." Talmud preserves a tradition where God "gives the 'first man' (אדם הראשון) a knowledge similar to that found above" (*b. Pes.* 54a), and Paul says something similar in his "first Adam—second Adam" argument (Rom 5:12–21; cf. Wallace, "Adam," 64). Chrysostom (cited in Hagedorn, *Hiob*) imagines Job as "a second Adam, the first falling to the Prosecutor in Eden, but the second sitting on a dunghill victorious" (cf. Sorlin and Neyrand, *Chrysostom*).

94. Job 15:7b (cf. the repetition of חול in the *polel* form in 39:1). Perdue (*Wisdom*, 20) believes that "order as a unifying center for creation theology . . . is an inevitable mystery," not least because it imposes "limits on human perception," thereby "making epistemological certainty an illusion."

95. Job 15:8a (lit., "listen to, hear"). MT סוד ("council"); OG σύνταγμα κυρίου ("the Lord's contingent"); Syr ܐܪܙܗ ܕܡܪܝܐ ("the Lord's council"); Tg אפשר דברז אלהא ("the midst of God's council"). Evidently בני האלים ("sons of God") in 1:6 is equivalent to סוד אלוה ("God's council") in 15:8.

96. Job 15:8b.

Acknowledging the presence of Bildad and Zophar, he asks:[97]

מה ידעת ולא נדע	What do *you* know that *we* do not know?[98]
תבין ולא עמנו הוא	What do *you* understand that *we* do not understand?[99]

Annoyed by Job's resistance to "sage counsel,"[100] Eliphaz takes another pass at the "consolation" motif, this time from the deity's perspective:

המעט ממך תנחמות אל	Do the "consolations" of El seem trivial to you,[101]
ודבר לאט עמך	Or the word which treats you gently?[102]
מה יקחך לבך	What are you thinking?[103]

97. Bildad makes a similar cohortative shift in 18:2. ANE scribes are well aware of the impact generated by changes in perspective (cf. Q 67.17; Endo, *Hebrew*, 236; Moore, *Babbler*, 239–42).

98. Job 15:9. In an earlier response to Eliphaz Job insists that he "knows nothing" (8:9), but this is not how tenured professors usually think. On the surface this question may *look* rhetorical, but underneath lurks the deepest of all academic prejudices; viz., that students are definable by what they know, not by who they are. For Botterweck ("ידע," 448–81) this prejudice betrays a skewed understanding of "knowledge" because, as Barnett and Bengsten (*Knowledge*, 111) observe, "knowledge is not merely a power we draw upon when we wish to solve a specific problem or seek an answer to a difficult question. Rather, it brings the whole world close to us and in ways for which we do not necessarily even wish." Whether or not Eliphaz adheres to *this* definition of "knowledge" is a slippery question because, as Dunham (*Sage*, 212) points out, people like Job "threaten Eliphaz's very epistemology."

99. Job 15:9 (lit., "is not with us"). OG οὐχὶ καὶ ἡμεῖς ("we do not"); Vg *nesciamus* ("we are aware"); ܕܠܐ ܗܘܐ ܠܢ ("which it is not for us"); Tg ולא גבנא הוא ("and it is not appropriate").

100. For example, Job earlier remarks: גם לי לבב כמוכם לא נפל אנכי מכם, "I have as much wisdom as any of you. I am not inferior to any of you" (Job 12:3).

101. Job 15:11a. Cf. OG ὀλίγα ὧν ἡμάρτηκας μεμαστίγωσαι μεγάλως, "If you seldom sin should you be constantly flogged?"; Syr ܐܪܐ ܡܢܟ ܟܠܝܢ ܟܘܢܫܐ ܕܐܠܗܐ, "Should the rebukes of God be withheld from you?" MT תנחמות ("consolations," note the play on נחמה in 6:10, ignored by all vss except Vg) derives from the polysemantic term נחם ("to console, repent"), translated in Vg 42:6 as *ago paenitentia*, "I do penance." Breitkopf (*Job*, 13) sides with Vg, but Martin ("Job," 299–318) classifies the major interpretations of 42:2–6 as "penitentialist," "consolationist," and "existentialist" (see below).

102. Job 15:11b. OG ὑπερβαλλόντως λελάληκας ("Should you speak endlessly?"); Syr ܘܡܡܠܠ ܫܝܢ ܠܗ ܢܦܫܟ ("and speak peacefully to your soul?"); Vg *numquid grande est ut consoletur te Deus sed verba tua prava hoc prohibent* ("Is it a great thing that God might console you, but your crooked words prohibit it?"). In 2 Sam 18:5, David commands Joab to "deal 'gently' (לאט) with the young man Absalom."

103. Job 15:12a (lit., "what is your mind thinking?"), reading יקח as "thinking" (cf. Job 11:4; Deut 32:2) and taking לקח לב as a parallel to נשא לב (cf. *libba(ša)-ka na-ši-ka*, OB *GE* 3.191). Seow (*Job*, 713) thinks that Eliphaz here demands to know why Job is so "arrogant."

ומה ירזמון עיניך	Why do your eyes roll[104]
כי תשיב אל אל רוחך	When you vaunt your spirit against El[105]
והצאת מפיך מלין	And spew such words from your mouth?[106]

Then he robotically defaults to his favorite motif—*justification*:

מה אנוש כי יזכה	How can human beings be made innocent?[107]
וכי יצדק ילוד אשה	Or the offspring of women be made righteous?[108]

Third Dialogue

In his final speech Eliphaz responds to Job's complaint—"Now I realize that you find me defective"[109]—and in so doing gives in to the temptation to castigate Job for even *imagining* he has the power, not to mention the *right*, to "advise" God:[110]

הלאל ליסכן גבר	Can a gentleman advise El?[111]
כי יסכן עלימו משׂכיל	Or a professor counsel the Most High?[112]

104. Job 15:12b. *HAL* 1129 defines MT רזם as *zwinkern* ("to wink, give a secret sign"), but OG apparently reads ירמון, translating ἐπήνεγκαν ("to afflict, be haughty"; cf. discussion in Seow, *Job*, 714). The English idiom "rolling the eyes" translates this well.

105. Job 15:13a. Syr ܘܡܪܝܡ ܐܢܬ ܠܘܬ ܐܠܗܐ ܪܘܚܟ ("for you raise your spirit against God"); cf. Vg *contra Deum* ("against God"); Tg לאלהא ("against Eloah").

106. Job 15:13b. OG ἐξήγαγες δὲ ἐκ στόματος ῥήματα τοιαῦτα, "cause these words to exit the mouth"; Vg *ut proferas de ore huiuscemodi sermones*, "as you pour out such sermons from your mouth"; Syr ܘܡܦܩ ܐܢܬ ܡܢ ܦܘܡܟ ܡܠܐ, "you let the word exit your mouth."

107. Job 15:14a. (lit., "What is a man, that he is innocent?"); Tg בר נש ("son of man"). OG βροτὸς ("mortal") frequently reflects the human side of the "immortality"-"mortality" polarity (cf. Homer's use of βροτοί in *Il.* 5.304).

108. Job 15:14b. Job earlier alludes to the justification motif (9:2) first enunciated by Eliphaz (4:17), then echoed by Bildad (8:6), now restated by Eliphaz (15:14). Yu ("Eliphaz," 85) contends that how these interlocutors respond to one other is secondary to the fact that this is the primary way the book schedules the appearances of its literary motifs.

109. הן ידעתי מחשבותיכם ומזמות עלי תחמסו. These are Job's words in 21:27.

110. Q 2.165 reads "there are some who take others as Allah's 'equal' (اندادا)—they love them as they should love Allah—but the true believers love Allah even more. If only the wrongdoers could see the horrifying punishment awaiting them, then they would realize that all power belongs to Allah."

111. Job 22:2a. Heb סכן repeats twice in this verse, and although elsewhere in Job it means "to be useful" (15:3; 35:3), the vss here imply something else. Cf. Syr, "Why do you say to Eloah, 'a gentleman (ܓܒܪܐ) among you is equal to him in wisdom?'"

112. Job 22:2b. Pope (*Job*, 164; cf. 7:20; 35:7) suggests that "the point . . . seems to be that God can have no ulterior motive in dealing with Job, since there is nothing Job can do to benefit him." Dunham (*Sage*, 211) thinks that "Eliphaz wants to prove to Job

Determined to champion Šadday's "rights" against Joban "opposition," Eliphaz keeps clanging on the "justification" bell regardless of whether or not it helps Job weather his crisis:

החפץ שדי כי תצדק	Does Šadday care whether you are "righteous?"[113]
ואם בצע כי תתם דרכיך	Is it profitable to him if your way is "blameless?"[114]

Weary of Job's "iniquities,"[115] he confronts him head-on:

המיראתך יכיחך	Does your "piety" make it more likely that he will meet you in court,[116]
יבא עמך במשפט	Or otherwise respond to your litigation?[117]
הלא רעתך רבא	Is your wickedness not great?
ואין קץ לעונתיך	Is there no end to your iniquities?[118]

This last of Eliphaz's speeches signs off with trumped-up accusations of cheating the poor, robbing widows, abusing orphans, and other "crimes."[119]

BILDAD

Grabbing the "justification" baton, Bildad runs the next leg of this "sage relay" insisting that the only way to explain Job's suffering is the payback

(and his colleagues) that God is 'wholly other,' sufficiently removed and disinterested in the created order as in no way beholden to it." Habel (*Job*, 338), however, believes that "Eliphaz seeks to protect God from any hint of weakness or any flaw that might endanger the doctrine of divine justice."

113. Job 22:3a. OG *τί γὰρ μέλει τῷ κυρίῳ ἐὰν σὺ ἦσθα τοῖς ἔργοις ἄμεμπτος* ("Is it any care to the Lord if your works are blameless?"); Syr ܡܢܘ ܝܘܬܪܢ ܕܡܫܠܡܘܬܟ ("What is the advantage of being blameless?").

114. Job 22:3b. OG *ἢ ὠφέλεια ὅτι ἁπλώσῃς τὴν ὁδόν σου* ("Is it an advantage for you to make your path plain?"); Syr ܐܠܐ ܐܘܪܚܬܟ ܡܢ ܕܚܠܬܟ ("on your path away from fear"). Eliphaz is likely unaware of the Judge's appreciation of Job's תם ("integrity," 1:8; 2:3), but as Vesely (*Job*, 153) points out, Eliphaz feels that "even if Job were blameless, the disparity between humanity and God is so great that God's justice would not be called into question by Job's misfortunes."

115. עונות (Job 22:5).

116. Job 22:4a. N.B. the similar use of יכח ("mediate") in 9:33 (cf. Mayer, "יכח," 66–67). Gordis (*Job*, 245) reads יכח and בוא משפט as courtroom terminology delineating the litigation process.

117. Job 22:4b (cf. Scholnick, "משפט," 524). Jeremiah gravitates to the stronger legal term ריב ("to sue," Jer 12:1).

118. Job 22:5.

119. Job responds to these charges in his farewell speech (chaps. 29–31), while in 23:10 he admits that even though Eliphaz's judgment is flawed, El's is not: כי ידע דרך עמדי בחנני כזהב אצא, "For he knows the path before me (and) after he tests me I shall come out like gold" (23:10).

principle. As Hartley puts it, he thinks that "whoever experiences calamity must have sinned."[120] Dismayed but not surprised, Elaine Phillips holds Bildad responsible for a particularly "harsh and personalized statement of the doctrine of retribution."[121]

First Dialogue

To Job's inquiry as to whether or not it is possible to be righteous before El (9:2) Bildad simplistically advises that he "look to El and petition Šadday,"[122] blithely recommending the pursuit of "purity and decency" so that he too may someday enjoy "protection and peace."[123] The irony here, of course, is that Bildad, like Eliphaz and Job himself, is evidently unaware that the heavenly Judge has already attributed these traits to Job.[124] Yet still he asks:

האל יעות משפט	Does El cheat justice?[125]
ואם שדי יעות צדק	Does Šadday pervert what is right?[126]

Rhetorical questions usually presume "obvious" answers,[127] but to Bildad there is nothing "obvious" about why anyone would want to drag Šadday into the mess and muck of creaturely defilement. So when Job accuses the deity of seizing him by the back of the neck, shattering him into pieces and positioning him as his "target" (מטרה), puncturing his "kidneys" (כליות)

120. Hartley, *Job*, 156. Bildad is the "friend" who argues (in 8:4) that Job's children die because they deserve it. Carson (*Sovereignty*, 217) finds the focus of the book to be about "biblical writers grappling with the . . . tension of divine sovereignty and human responsibility."

121. Phillips, "Job," 34.

122. Job 8:5 (אם אתה תשחר אל אל ושדי תתחנן).

123. Job 8:6. MT יעיר עליך ושלם נות צדקך doubtless parallels the Canaanite blessing *ilm tġrk tšlmk*, "May the gods protect you and give you peace" (*CAT* 2.13.7–8).

124. Cf. Yhwh's praise of Job in 1:8; 2:3 and Eliphaz's advice to Job in 4:6. Like Eliphaz, Bildad is doubtless unaware of the heavenly conversation in the Prologue, but this hardly deflates the reader's sense of irony.

125. Job 8:3a (so Elihu in 34:12). OG *μὴ ὁ κύριος ἀδικήσει κρίνων* ("Does the Lord do wrong to the one who judges?"); Syr ܕܠܡܐ ܐܠܗܐ ܡܥܘܠ ܕܝܢܐ ("Does Eloah pervert justice?"); Tg אפשר דאלוהא יעקם דינא ("Is it possible for Eloah to circumvent justice?"). Amos 8:5 uses the term עות ("to cheat") to describe the behavior of corrupt merchants (cf. Moore, *WealthWarn*, 103–7).

126. Job 8:3b. OG *ὁ τὰ πάντα ποιήσας ταράξει τὸ δίκαιον* ("Does the one who makes all things throw justice into jeopardy?"). As in the Ugaritic texts (e.g., *CAT* 1.2.12; 1.10.27–28; 1.15.17–18; cf. Michel, *Job*), MT twice repeats the same verb (עות), doubtless for emphasis (cf. discussion in Seow, *Job*, 527–28). The versions, however, champion synonymity over repetition, as does Elihu in 34:12 (רשע // עות).

127. Adams (*Questions*, 1–20); Black (*Questions*, 135–46).

with "arrows" (רבים), and releasing the "gall" (מררה),[128] this pushes Bildad beyond the boundaries of his comfort zone. In fact, for the Bildads of the world such talk comes perilously close to what writers elsewhere call the "unpardonable sin,"[129] a malady Shimon Bakon defines as the human "propensity to project its standards of conduct and knowledge onto the Almighty."[130] What Bildad begins to realize, in other words, is that his "problem is not with the insignificant prattle of a 'desperate' man, as Job styles himself (6:26)," but with "a 'mighty wind' (8:2) . . . too dangerous to go unattended."[131] John Goldingay insists that Job never "pretends to be totally without sin,[132] but such a claim fails to satisfy Bildad because he believes that (a) it is his duty to teach that "the moral universe . . . is founded upon the principle of retribution," which in turn means (b) that Job's "complaint against God's arbitrary and disproportionate treatment of him implicitly charges God with injustice."[133] In other words, Job's suffering "proves" to Bildad not only Job's "impenitence," but his refusal to confess his sin is itself a passive-aggressive indictment of the deity. Why? Because he thinks that "Job does not acknowledge that to deny the universal applicability of retribution is to deny the righteousness of God."[134]

Contra Eliphaz's openness to mystical revelation,[135] Bildad encourages Job to rely on the tried-and-true testimony of "former generations":[136]

128. Job 16:12–13.

129. ἡ δὲ τοῦ πνεύματος βλασφημία οὐκ ἀφεθήσεται, "Blasphemy against the Spirit will not be forgiven" (Matt 12:31; cf. *TDNT* 6:406). Trying to explain this verse, Litfin ("Sin," 713) argues that since Christ's opponents are the "beneficiaries of an extraordinary measure of both verbal and apodictic light," the fact that some "respond with maximum rejection . . . prompts the adamant verdict of Jesus."

130. Bakon ("Enigma," 226).

131. Seow (*Job*, 515).

132. Goldingay (*Job*, 76) underscores the narrator's remark in 1:22: MT לא חטא איוב ולא נתן תפלא לאלהים ("Job does not sin or ascribe unseemliness to God"); Syr ܠܐ ܣܟܠ ܐܝܘܒ ܘܐܦܠܐ ܫܘܐ ܥܠ ܐܠܗܐ ("Job does not sin or pile scorn upon God"); Tg לא חב איוב ולא מסדר מלי מחטי קדם יי ("Job does not sin or assign sinful words to Yhwh").

133. Clines (*Job*, 202). Talmud (*b. Ber.* 57b) posits that "there are three great texts one might see in a dream: he who sees the book of Psalms should anticipate 'piety' (חסדות); he who sees the book of Proverbs should anticipate 'wisdom' (חכמה); and he who sees the book of Job should anticipate 'retribution' (פורענות, lit., 'paybacks,' from the verb פרע, "to pay back").

134. Clines (*Job*, 203).

135. Job 4:12–17. Rashi (*Job*, 4.12.1) refers to Eliphaz's "night-vision" as דבר נבואה ("a word of prophecy"). Elihu's mention of "night vision" (33:15) may be an indirect allusion to Eliphaz's vision.

136. Job 8:8 (דור ראשון). Cf. Eliphaz's question in 15:7, "Are you the 'first' (ראשון) human being?" Brown (*Vision*, 265) wonders whether Bildad's appeal to tradition is meant "to deny implicitly that Job has seen what even the ancestors have not."

הלא הם יורוך יאמרו לך	Do the sages not teach you[137]
ומלבם יוצאו מלים	When they express their insights?[138]

To illustrate the value of this strategy he cites a proverb:

היגאה גמהבלא בצה	Does papyrus grow outside a marsh?
ישׂגה אחו בלי מים	Do reeds survive without water?[139]

Crenshaw's explanation is straightforward: "Devoid of moisture, plants like these swiftly die; so, in like manner, do those who forget El lose hope."[140]

Second Dialogue

So negative are the invectives in Bildad's second speech, many wonder whether his denunciation of "wickedness" refers to Job's wickedness or to wickedness in general.[141] For Clines it cannot refer to Job's wickedness alone because Bildad perceives "Job's claim for his innocence" to be "an affront to

137. Job 8:10a. Cf. Ps 119:95, לי קוו רשעים לעבדני עדתיך אתבונן ("The wicked lie in wait to destroy me as I ponder your testimonies"). Job's response to Bildad is that God is the source of wisdom, not the "traditions of the elders" (Job 12:13–25; cf. Matt 15:6). Indeed, it is God who possesses "wisdom" (חכמה), "strength" (גבורה), "counsel" (עצה), and "understanding" (תבונה). God's impartiality is what renders him greater than counselors, judges, kings, priests, elders, and/or princes. He is consistently reliable while the so-called "wise men" show partiality and speak falsely (Job 13:1–12).

138. Job 8:10 (מלים, "words"). Cf. OG ῥήματα; Vg *eloquia* ("sayings/speeches"); Tg מילין ("words"); Syr ܡܠܐ ("word"). Bildad is not the only sage to revere tradition (cf. Ps 143:5), nor is he the only professor to deemphasize the power of personal experience/revelation. Gese ("Lebenssinn," 172) contends that "it is in the humble acceptance of suffering that suffering becomes meaningful and salvation from suffering becomes possible."

139. Job 8:11. Whether this proverb is original to Bildad seems doubtful, given his preference for tradition. Irwin ("Bildad," 206) suggests that the images here have to do with "the prosperity yet sudden ruin of the wicked" metaphorically expressed by "the life history of the swamp reeds and rushes. They have every advantage; they grow in rich mire with abundance of water, yet presently disaster comes: the water fails and then they wilt and dry up at the very height of the growing season." Pinker ("Bildad," 432), however, asks, "If Job and his children are wicked, then why are they not disciplined by society's normal restraining agencies?" *Answer:* Their wickedness makes "heavenly intervention necessary." In other words, "the wicked benefit from a natural support system," but "the retribution doctrine predicates their sure demise."

140. Crenshaw (*Defending*, 123), to which Bildad might well add, "because they lose touch with their traditions." Qur'an insists that ignorance of "the Book" (الكتب) is no excuse for denying the reality of divine revelation, and further, that all deniers will someday be "*compensated* with an evil punishment" (Q 6.157).

141. Cf. Driver and Gray (*Job*, xxv–l); Murphy (*Literature*, 32); and Habel (*Job*, 282–83).

the stable moral order in which he has always found his own security."[142] With this assessment Clines follows the lead of Robert Gordis, who sees in Bildad a conventional representative of the traditional belief that "the laws of the universe remain unshaken, and that retribution ultimately overtakes the evildoer."[143] To underscore this the sage launches (like Eliphaz earlier) an abrupt shift in perspective:[144]

מדוע נחשבנו כבהמה	Why do you treat us like beasts?[145]
נטמינו בעיניכם	Why are we perceived to be defiled in your eyes?[146]
הלמענך תעזב ארץ טרף נפשו באפו	Should the land be abandoned because unsavory characters, bent on destruction,[147]
ויעתק צור ממקמו	Regularly remove the boundary-stonesfromtheirrightfulplaces?[148]

142. Clines, *Job*, 409. Hartley (*Job*, 272) thinks that "Bildad emphasizes the possibility that Job might have a bright future" in his first speech, whereas in his second speech "he details the horrid fate that befalls the ungodly."

143. Gordis (*Job*, 187). Ghantous ("Job," 25) thinks that the compensation/retribution motif anchoring "the traditional concept of wisdom is adopted in the book of Job neither by Job nor by God, but rather by Job's 'friends' and the young Elihu, who insist on interpreting Job's sufferings as a divine punishment for a certain sin Job must have committed." In 34:33, Elihu criticizes Job for demanding that the deity "compensate" him (שלם; OG ἀποτίνω, "to pay back"; Syr ܣܓܐ, "to increase"; cf. Gerleman, "שלם," 1–14).

144. Job 18:3a (cf. 15:9). Hyun (*Job*, 147–48) points out that Eliphaz's critique is distinguishable from Bildad's in that Eliphaz responds to Job, but Bildad responds to both Eliphaz *and* Job. Salakpi ("Job") emphasizes that grammatical shifts in person and/or number often signal significant nuances of meaning (cf. Moore, "Lamentations," 534–55).

145. Cf. בהמות in the Theologue (Job 40:15). One wonders what sort of zoology Bildad has in mind when "the Joban theophany encourages humanity to treat the most stigmatized and marginalized animals, ecosystems, and people with compassion and reverence. It embraces those on the peripheries as central to God and those designated detestable as delightful to God. It revels in and provides for those labeled unclean or an abomination. Rather than separating humans as superior, it weaves them into the sublime tapestry of life" (Huff, "Animals," 258).

146. Job 18:3b. 11QtgJob 1.6 reads דמינא ("to resemble," if deriving from דמה); OG σεσιωπήκαμεν ἐναντίον σου ("silent before you"); Syr ܘܐܬܛܦܫܢ ܩܕܡܝܟ ("stupid in your eyes," if deriving from ܛܦܫ); "defiled in your eyes," if deriving from ܛܡܐ). While "fornication" (הזנות), "avarice" (ההון), and "defilement" (טמא) make up the "three nets of Belial" (CD 4.17–18; cf. Eshel, "Belial," 244), the fact that the versions so obviously differ on how to read MT Job 18:3 suggests that דמה is polysemantic (cf. Grabbe, *Job*, 73–74; Seow, *Job*, 780–81).

147. Job 18:4a (lit., "tear up his soul; cf. 14:18). Bildad here responds to Job's use of אף ("anger") and טרף ("to tear up," 16:9), redirecting it to quasi-heavenly figures like the בכור מות ("Firstborn of Death," 18:13) and the מלך בלחות ("King of Terrors," 18:14; cf. Moore, *Babbler*, 212–25).

148. Job 18:4b. Removing boundary stones is a crime condemned in Torah (Deut

Third Dialogue

Bildad now returns to the "justification" motif, projecting it through lenses tinted by the exegetical principle of *qal waḥomer*:[149]

ומה יצדק אנוש עם אל	How is a man made righteous before El,[150]
ומה יזכה ילוד אשה	Or a woman's offspring made innocent?[151]
הן עד ירח ולא יאהיל	If the moon is not radiant enough,
וכוכבים לא זכו בעיניו	Nor the stars bright enough in God's eyes,[152]
אף כי אנוש רמה	How much less a maggoty mortal,[153]
ובן אדם תולעה	Or the wormy spawn of a hominid?[154]

In short Bildad's angst, as Adriane Leveen recognizes, is a predictable response to Job's questioning of his "reliance on traditions influenced particularly by Deuteronomic ideas"—a response made all the more distinctive by contrasting it with Job's "reliance on his experience of present suffering."[155]

19:14; 27:17), Nevi'im (Hos 5:10), and Ketuvim (Prov 22:28). Here it serves as a figure of speech; i.e., those who "remove boundary stones" are the type of people who cut moral corners to get what they want. N.B. that Bildad's apprehensions about chaos and turmoil echo those of the Egyptian sage Ipu-Wer (see below).

149. קל וחמר ("light and heavy"). The first of seven hermeneutical מדות ("methods") attributed to R. Hillel (*t. Sanh.* 7.11), *qal waḥomer* defines "analogy" as that which applies to the "light" applies to the "heavy" case as well. Cf. Lat. *a minore ad maius* (Longenecker, *Exegesis*, 20–21; Sloan and Newman, "Hermeneutics," 68).

150. Job 25:4a. OG's use of βροτὸς ("mortal") echoes its use in Eliphaz's second speech (15:14a).

151. Job 25:4b. Eliphaz uses similar language in 14:1 (אדם ילוד אשה, "man born of a woman") and 15:14 (אנוש . . . ילוד אשה, "man . . . born of a woman"), and Job shows no desire to disagree with him (9:2; 14:4).

152. Job 25:5 (the *protasis*). Mention of the moon and stars indirectly reflects Torah's stern warnings against worshiping them (Deut 4:19; 17:3; cf. 2 Kgs 23:5), not to mention the lunar-solar preferences lurking at the center of what Brooke (*Calendars*, 108) calls the "war of the calendars."

153. Job 25:6a. Another instance of *qal waḥomer* occurs in the GNT Letter to the Hebrews: "If the blood of bulls and goats can sanctify, how much more so the blood of Christ" (Heb 9:13–14).

154. Job 25:6b (cf. Isa 41:14; Ps 22:7). Denigrating an enemy via "worm-language" is not uncommon in ANE texts (cf., e.g., *KAI* 222A.27). *Example:* Esarhaddon (cited in Parpola and Watanabe, *Treaties*, 53.570–72) threatens potential treaty-breakers: "Just as a worm (*tūltu*) eats fresh cheese, may worms eat your flesh, the flesh of your wife, and the flesh of your children while they are still alive."

155. Leveen ("Job," 835).

ZOPHAR

Several adjectives tend to cluster around this last of Job's three "friends." Some see in him the youngest of the three because he is the last to speak.[156] Others see him as a "miserable comforter who disposes of the mystery of human suffering quite easily" because "for him there is no mystery—suffering is a product of sin."[157] Still others see him as "impetuous,"[158] even "cruel."[159] Maimonides thinks his goal is to make Job submit to the simplistic equation that "suffering is a wage of sin."[160]

First Dialogue

Having voiced with his colleagues the now-obligatory warning about Job's "inappropriate language,"[161] Zophar reviews Bildad's concern for "appropriate" boundaries before reframing it within a conceptual discussion about "creation" systemically resonating with the thinking of his colleagues while echoing the words of the deity in the Theologue.[162] Along the way he gravitates to words and phrases sprinkled throughout the book (esp. the wisdom poem in chapter 28) to goad Job into admitting that there is something "out there" he needs to "find":[163]

החקר אלוה תמצא	Can you find God's pathway?
אם עד תכלית שדי תמצא	Can you determine the extent of Šadday's endeavors?[164]

156. Gordis (*Job*, 83).

157. Goldsmith ("Scourge," 7–8).

158. Delitzsch (*Hiob*, 92).

159. Reichert (*Job*, 66).

160. Maimonides, *Guide*, 100. Contrast the Pauline view that death, not suffering, is the "wages of sin" (Rom 6:23).

161. Job 11:2–3 (see above).

162. In 11:10, Zophar uses the expression מי ישיבנו ("Who will restrain him?") to refer, in Perdue's opinion (*Job*, 136), "to God's uncontested might and the power . . . to judge and imprison."

163. Job 11:1–4 (cf. 17:10; 23:3). As Wolde ("Job," 25) sees it, Job 28 focuses on what can and cannot be "found," while Greenstein ("Poem," 253) argues that the question, "Where is wisdom?" is "remarkable more by virtue of the subtle way it is conveyed by the poet than on account of its constituting a new idea in ancient thinking" (cf. Jones, *Rumors*, 174–78; Lo, *Rhetoric*, 198–201; Geller, "Wisdom," 155–88).

164. Job 11:7. Like MT מצא (Heb "to find), Tg twice repeats the same verb (שכח, Aram "to find"), but OG, rather than repeat the same verb, reads ἦ ἴχνος κυρίου εὑρήσεις ἢ εἰς τὰ ἔσχατα ἀφίκου ἃ ἐποίησεν ὁ παντοκράτωρ ("Can you find the Lord's pathway or discover the extent of the Almighty's accomplishments?").

גבהי שמים מה תפעל	What do you know about the heavenly expanse?[165]
עמוקה משאול מה תדע	What do you know about the depths of Sheol?
כי הוא ידע מתי שוא	Does he (Šadday) not know what is worthless?
וירא און ולא יתבונן	Can he not detect wickedness without fixating on it?[166]

Recognizing that the Theologue repeats many of these same details, Gersonides concludes that what Zophar wants to emphasize is the inability/unwillingness of mortal creatures to "find" an accessible path to the Creator.[167]

Second Dialogue

Unlike Bildad (and to a lesser extent Eliphaz) Zophar resists the temptation to blame Job for the world's problems. Instead he invites him to ponder the fragility of his mortality:

הזות ידעת מני עד	Do you understand this old notion,
שים אדם עלי ארץ	That ever since mortals appeared on the earth
כי רננת רשעים מקרוב	The rejoicing of the wicked has been fleeting,
ושמחה חנף עדי רגע	And the A/accuser's delight short-lived?[168]

In his critique of the wicked, however, Zophar singles out the wealthy, warning them that the extermination of Job's children is a warning to *their* children that eventually they must learn how to practice the principles of wise stewardship; i.e., that it is truly "more blessed to give than receive."[169] They may decide to go on guzzling their wealth like greedy little children, but if so they should not be surprised that such behavior is more likely to trigger regurgitation than prosperity:[170]

משיב יגע ולא יבלע	They will return the fruit of their labor, not guzzle it;

165. Job 11:8a, reading with Syr ܪܘܡܐ ܕܫܡܝܐ ܡܢ ܐܫܟܚܗ.

166. Job 11:11. Maimonides (*Guide*, 3.17, 23) suggests that Zophar's commitment to absolute divine sovereignty parallels that of the Muslim Asharite sect following the teachings of Al-Aša`ri (d. 936 CE).

167. Gersonides, מלחמות, 4.2.153–55.

168. Job 20:4–5.

169. Acts 20:35.

170. Job 20:10, 15. Ward (*Abundance*, 1) is bemused by the fact that so many believers in "a God of abundance" often display a "scarcity-mindset."

כחיל תמורתו ולא יעלס	From the profit of their trade they will take no enjoyment.[171]

Pushing the metaphor to extremes, he adds:

יהי למלא בטנו ישלח בו חרון אפו	To fill their bellies to the full he will send his fierce anger into them
וימטר עלימו בלחומו	And rain it upon them as their bread.[172]

Summary

Carol Newsom concludes that Job's counselors want to "defend traditional understandings of divine justice against the skeptical onslaught of the sufferer. Though the 'friends' are often understood simply to be 'blaming the victim,' their arguments are more nuanced than this. Like many in the ancient world, they believe that the deity can be unintentionally or unknowingly offended.[173] Thus the natural response to inexplicable suffering is, in their minds, to acknowledge any possible wrongdoing and appeal humbly to God for deliverance."[174] Tosefta censures Job's counselors for insensitivity in their approach, but not for the legality of their indictment. Some find Job's words circumstantially excusable, but theologically inexcusable.[175] In other words, both Job and his counselors have flaws, an oft-overlooked fact which leads Gersonides to be very careful in his understanding of Job's "friends":

- (a) Eliphaz finds suffering to be something not always undeserved and often the result of one's own folly;
- (b) Bildad believes that both good and bad events are the result of divine compensation/retribution, but that suffering is eventually rewarded by its final outcome, even though most mortals cannot see it;
- (c) Zophar believes that when sin occurs, it is not because the sinner fails to evaluate human behavior correctly, but because no mortal is consistently able to distinguish right from wrong.[176]

171. Job 20:18. Tg reads MT תמורה ("trade") as פרוגה ("compensation").

172. Job 20:23 (doubtless an allusion to the "raining down" of manna in the wilderness, Num 11:9). Tg reads ויחת עלוי מטרין בשלדיה ("he will send upon them rains of recompense into their dead carcasses").

173. Cf. 2 Sam 21:1; Hanson ("When the King," 11–25).

174. Newsom ("Job," 4932).

175. *t. Bab. Meṣ* 3.25 (cf. Kraemer, *Suffering*, 69).

176. Gersonides, מלחמות, 4.2.153–55 (cited in Eisen, *Job*, 150–51). Debating the pros and cons of each position, Gersonides eventually throws the weight of his support behind Zophar, and Breitkopf (*Job*, 145) argues that the polysemantic verb נחם in 42:6

Susanna Baldwin more concisely concludes that Eliphaz focuses on God's moral justice, Bildad on God's immutable decrees, and Zophar on God's unsearchable wisdom.[177] Presuming Job's "friends" to be inhabitants of a "flat, deistic universe," Elaine Phillips concludes that it is impossible for them "to perceive and/or acknowledge the vast complexity and powers in the heavenly court."[178] Thoughtful opinions all, but the point here is not so much what Job's counselors say as what they do *not* say; viz., that these professors make no effort whatsoever to recognize, much less champion the pivotal significance of "disinterested piety" in their dealings with Job, either because they find it irrelevant, or because they do not find it nearly as important as compensation/retribution.

ELIHU

At first glance Elihu's speeches look similar to those delivered by Job's "friends,"[179] but due in part to the persistent influence of nineteenth- and twentieth-century *redaktionsgeschichtliche* approaches to the book,[180] many still consider them to be far less authentic than the foregoing speeches because (a) Elihu does not appear in the Prologue, Epilogue, or Theologue;[181] (b) the prose preamble of the Elihu cycle (32:1–9) differs significantly from the preambles of the first three cycles, especially with regard to genealogical

conveys "penitence" only "in the sense that the character Job retracts his comments regarding existence" (see below).

177. Baldwin ("Comforters," 359–75).

178. Phillips ("Job," 35).

179. Opinion is divided. Habel ("Elihu," 83) understands the Elihu speeches to be forensic in character, the first being Elihu's *apologia* for being Job's "arbiter." Jones Nelson ("Job," 535–37) publishes a good thumbnail survey of rabbinic, medieval Christian, and contemporary analyses of these speeches.

180. "Redaction-history." Citing Duhm (*Job*, 10–11) as an example, Day (*Adversary*, 71) observes that a generation of nineteenth- and twentieth-century scholars (esp. in Continental universities and Protestant divinity schools) "view Job as something of a cut-and-paste job none too carefully executed." Polzin ("Job," 182) overreacts to the *redaktionsgeschichtliche* approach by denigrating it as a "dehusking procedure," while Carr (*Bible*, 36) finds in it little more than "hypothetical reconstruction." The presumption of this study is not that redaction criticism is altogether invalid, but that apart from hard evidence interpreted within clear methodological parameters it too easily drifts off into feathery speculation (cf. Perrin, *Redaction*, 1–13; Vermeylen, *Job*; and Moore, "Revolution," 151–53).

181. Cf. the discussion in Newsom (*Job*, 282). Cernucan's ("Sorrow," 2) method of distinguishing prose from poetry draws more from Russian formalism than German *Redaktionskritik*.

detail;[182] (c) Elihu mentions Job by name no less than nine times, often in conjunction with citations from previous counselors' speeches; and most importantly (d) these speeches "interrupt the connection between Job's final challenge and God's appearance."[183]

Individually any one of these observations is vulnerable to critique, but taken altogether they carry significant weight, enough to make anyone take pause. Carol Newsom, for example, believes that a single writer is responsible for both the prose and the poetry, but that the Elihu speeches most likely come from a different hand, if not a different source.[184] Harald Wahl sees Elihu as one of the Bible's "most differently judged personalities,"[185] while Donald Johns suggests that his character "draws heavily from the traditions (of) his namesake, Elijah."[186] Larry Waters finds the Elihu speeches to be (a) "a genuine and original part of the book playing a significant interpretive, explanatory, and theological role . . . integral to a full understanding of the enigma of suffering," as well as (b) "a preparatory component to understanding the Yhwh speeches."[187] Pope finds these speeches to be "diffuse and pretentious,"[188] but Seow finds in them "a necessary transition from the passionate and self-righteous asseveration of Job to the overwhelming response of the theophany."[189] Habel agrees, reading the Elihu *speeches* as "a bridge between the discourses of the friends and the majestic answer of God,"[190] even though the Elihu *character* is, in his opinion, a "windbag" whose sophomoric theology derives from an "image of El . . . manipulating the forces of creation to enforce the principle of justice."[191]

182. This oft-heard remark, however, fails to recognize how similarly each speech-cycle (including Elihu's) begins with a critique of Job's "inappropriate language" (see above).

183. Bewer (*Literature*, 329). Eissfeldt (*Introduction*, 457) sees the Elihu speeches "violently disturbing the artistic structure of the original book," while Cornill (*Einleitung*, 249) diametrically dubs them the "crowning point of the book." Newsom (*Job*, 200) speculates that many dislike Elihu because he appears to them to be "someone who has defaced a cultural monument with his graffiti."

184. Newsom (*Job*, 201–2) gives no reason for this opinion, but perhaps it is because Elihu speaks λόγους θρασεῖς ("insulting words") to Job as somebody ἐμπνευσθεὶς ἐν τῷ Σατανᾷ ("inspired by Satan," TJob 41.6).

185. Wahl (*Elihurede*, 1).

186. Johns ("Elihu," 1). TJob, however, depicts Elihu's speeches as coming not from Elijah or any other "human" (ἄνθροπος), but from the mind of a "beast" (θηρίον, TJob 42.2).

187. Waters ("Elihu," 1).

188. Pope (*Job*, xxvii; cf. Driver and Gray, *Job*, xl–xlvii).

189. Seow, *Job*, 37.

190. Habel, *Job*, 8.

191. Habel, *Nature*, 95. Cf. Eliphaz's passive-aggressive description of Job as a

One of the more complex theories about the Elihu speeches comes from David Noel Freedman, who suggests that they most likely originate as contrapuntal responses to the speech cycles of the three "friends," the first after the first cycle (i.e., after chapter 14), the second after the third cycle (i.e., after chapter 27), the third after the second cycle (i.e., after chapter 21), and the fourth after Job's farewell speech (i.e., after chapter 31). That they now appear altogether in one place is likely due, in his opinion, to the original editor's abandonment of the project until a later editor, unwilling to discard them, relocates them after Job's farewell speech as a conclusion to the Dialogues.[192] Unpersuaded by this theory, Clines nonetheless rejects all attempts to treat the Elihu speeches as secondary, yet posits for them a secondary *location* before Job's farewell speech.[193] Whatever the possibilities, Cooper Smith level-headedly proposes that even though the "judgments of Elihu and his arguments widely differ," their ultimate value "depends on the vantage point and inclinations of the interpreter." In other words, "their beauty lies in the eye of the beholder."[194]

First Speech

Elihu's first speech addresses two audiences: (a) Job's counselors and (b) Job himself. Vexed by Job's unwillingness to submit to Eliphaz, Bildad and Zophar, Elihu censures them for failing to put him in his "theological place," asking,

מדוע אליו ריבות	Why do you go on arguing with him, (saying)
כי כל דבריו לא יענה	"He does not respond to anything I say?"[195]

"blowhard" (15:2).

192. Freedman ("Elihu," 58) believes that "the author composes the four speeches as part of a general plan to reorganize the book of Job, and that he intends to place each of the speeches at a turning point in the Dialogues, namely, at the end of each cycle of speeches, and in direct correspondence with Job's closing speech in that cycle. The fourth and last speech is to serve the same function in relation to Job's final address." Yet "the project is never carried through to completion, and seems to be abandoned entirely, since no effort is made to link Elihu to the story in the Prologue or Epilogue, or with any of the characters except Job." Gray (*Introduction*, 122–23) posits more connections between the Elihu speeches and the Theologue than with the preceding Dialogues.

193. That is, *before* chapters 29–31 (Clines, "Elihu," 243–53). Pohl (*Job*, 229–30) believes that the Elihu speeches are genuine and belong right where they are.

194. Smith ("Elihu," 2) identifies no less than twenty-three allusions in these speeches to the rest of the book.

195. Job 33:13. On ריב ("to sue"), cf. sources as diverse as *Inanna's Descent* (Sum DI MU-UN-DA-KU5-RU-NE, lit. "cut a lawsuit," *ID* 167), the Former Prophets (Judg

Insisting that "Eloah is greater than any human being,"[196] he then turns his attention to Job. Like Job's "friends," Elihu finds "pointless suffering" to be an oxymoronic phrase, yet what he proposes in its place is a worldview more nuanced than the retributional ruminations of Job's three "friends"; viz., (a) that someone can commit sin and, if penitent, not always be required to "pay compensation,"[197] and (b) that suffering may serve as a first step toward "redemption" (פדה)[198] in response to divine "grace" (חנן)[199] imputed through (sacramental?) "atonement" (כפר).[200] This "redemption-grace-atonement" sequence continues to develop over time, of course,[201] but its appearance here is revolutionary. Seeking to understand its *raison d'être*, Newsom concurs with Elihu that the road to redemption sometimes begins with suffering.[202] Citing the *Sefat Emet*,[203] Judith Kates thinks that "to become aware of the pain of one's existence, to resist assimilation into one's condition of need, pain, or suffering is to begin a process of change. The

---

6:32), and the Latter Prophets (Jer 25:31; Hos 2:4). On the PN Jerubba`al (ירובעל, "Let Ba`al sue") cf. Moore (*WealthWarn*, 60).

196. Job 33:12, כי ירבה אלוה מאנוש.

197. Job 33:27. MT שוה (lit., "make equal"); OG ἐτάζω ("to afflict"); Vg *recepi* ("to be taken back"); Syr ܫܘܐ ("to profit").

198. Job 33:24. MT פדעהו is problematic. Weiser (*Hiob*, 218) and Terrien (*Job*, 223) read פדהו ("redeem him"), while Budde (*Hiob*, 211) and Fohrer (*Hiob*, 28) read פרעהו ("liberate him"). In OG Elihu trusts in a deity who "repays men (for their) righteousness" (ἀποδώσει δὲ ἀνθρώποις δικαιοσύνην, OG 33:26); Syr ܘܢܦܪܘܥ ܠܒܪܢܫܐ ܙܕܝܩܘܬܗ ("and justice be repaid by the son of man"). Cf. 33:28 and Eliphaz's remarks in 5:17–27 (Moore, *WealthWatch*, 148–58).

199. Job 33:24. See above for Kessler's ("Erlöser," 147) suggestion that the Prosecutor's keyword חנם (1:9) derives from חנה ("to show favor"). Linebaugh (*Wisdom*, 175) suggests that the theology of grace championed in Paul's letters is "a daring, and from Wisdom's perspective, dangerous deduction." Yancey and Brand (*Pain*, 5–6), on the other hand, recognize that "such conditions as leprosy, diabetes, alcoholism, multiple sclerosis, nerve disorders, and spinal cord injury . . . can bring about the strangely hazardous state of insensitivity to pain," and that "while most of us seek out pharmacists and doctors in search of relief from pain, these people live in constant peril due to pain's *absence*."

200. Job 33:24 (פדעהו מרדת שחת מצאתי כפר, "Free him from going down into the Pit; I have found an atoning ransom").

201. Cf. ἀπολύτρωσις ("redemption," Rom 3:24; 8:23), χάρις ("grace," Eph 2:5, 8), and ἱλαστήριος ("atonement," Rom 3:25; Heb 2:17). Gilkey ("Redemption," 169) believes that "God does not so much judge, repudiate, condemn, or destroy evil as he transforms it, embraces it, participates in it, and overcomes it."

202. Newsom (*Job*, 215–16).

203. *Sefat Emet* ("Words of Truth") is the *fin de siècle* commentary on Torah written by R. Yehuda Leib Alter (d. 1905). The passage referenced here is *Shemot* (Exodus) 1.2.18 (cf. Green, *Truth*, 81–82).

Sefat Emet calls this opening of awareness כאצת גאלה ('a little bit of redemption'), which is all the deity needs to redeem the truly penitent."[204] Whereas Nebuchadnezzar's "awareness" begins with a descent into madness,[205] Job's "awareness" begins when the burden of his losses pushes him over the edge into an abyss of "inappropriateness."[206] The Prologue reports that Job "does not sin with his lips," but this "glass-half-empty" assessment comes from the mind of an appreciative narrator.[207] Maintaining his piety in the face of emotional, economic, spiritual, social, and physical chaos—much of it intensified by his "friends"—is "glass-half-full" behavior reflecting Yhwh's sanguine assessment of him to the Prosecutor.

Second Speech

Reacting to Job's seventh lament, where he says, "I know I am right, even though El has taken away my rights,"[208] Elihu joins his colleagues in exposing Job to a strong dose of *ad hominem* radiation:

מי גבר כאיוב	Is there anyone like Job,
ישתה לעג כמים	Who drinks mockery like water,[209]
וארח לחברה עם פעלי און	Who accompanies scoundrels into taverns,[210]
וללכת עם אנשי רשע	And promenades with the wicked?[211]

Having made a politically-correct decision to mimic his colleagues' negative assessment of Job, Elihu then lays out three concerns. The *first* is the deity's "honor":[212]

204. Kates ("Redemption," 49).

205. Dan 4:1–33.

206. Mende (*Elihureden*, 419–20) sees an intentional orthographical variation: (a) Elihu uses דע to designate *his* divinely-inspired "knowledge" (Job 32:6, 10, 17), but (b) דעת when referring to the "knowledge" of Job's three "friends" (33:3; 34:35; 36:12).

207. Job 2:10. R. Joseph bar Ḥama hastily concludes that Job does not sin with his lips, but he *does* sin "in his heart" (בלבו, *b. B. Bat.* 16a). TgJob 1.22 simply states that he utters no מלי מחטי ("guilt-incurring words").

208. צדקתי ואל הסיר משפטי (Job 34:5).

209. Job 34:7. Syr "who drinks up ܡܘܝܩܐ ('scorn, derision') like ܡܝܐ ('water')"; OG μυκτηρισμὸν ("sneering"), from μυκτηριάζω ("to turn up the μυκτήρ"—i.e., "the nostril"). N.B. Jeremiah's complaint that "everyone 'mocks' me" (לעג; OG μυκτηριζόμενος, Jer 20:7). Cf. Moore (*Babbler*, 90).

210. Job 34:8. 11QTgJob 24.1–2 reads ומתחבר לעבדי שקרא ("and mingles with servants of deceit"); cf. Syr ܥܒ̈ܕܝ ܥܘܠܐ, ("servants of evil"); OG ποιούντων τὰ ἄνομα ("those doing lawless things").

211. Job 34:8.

212. Recognizing that "*honor* is a major concern," Crenshaw (*Defending*, 66, 19)

כי פעל אדם ישלם לו	He compensates[213] a man for his work,
וכארח איש ימצאנו	And according to his behavior lets him "find" it.[214]
אף אמנם אל לא ירשיע	El never acts wickedly,
ושדי לא יעות משפט	Nor does Šadday pervert justice.[215]

His *second* concern is the eagerness with which Job maligns, undermines, and/or misrepresents the "righteous." Oblivious to the negative ink for which Elihu is well-known,[216] John Eaton reckons that most "right thinking" readers will agree with his "indignance" toward Job for his "harangues against God."[217]

האף שׂונא משפט יחבש	Should those who hate justice govern?[218]
ואם צדיק כביר תרשיע	Would you condemn the strong with the righteous?[219]
האמר למלך בליעל	Would you say to a king, "O Belial?"[220]
רשע אל נדיבים	Or to a nobleman, "O Wicked One?"[221]
אשר לא נשׂא פני שׂרים	Would you extend impartiality to princes,
ולא נכר שׂוע לפני דל	But show no appreciation to the rich *or* the poor?[222]

His *third* concern is that should Job be in any way correct in his critique of Creation, such a situation would open up a door to a reality too horrifying

points out that "salvaging divine honor may come at the expense of men and women" who, granted the blessing of free will, immediately find themselves forced "to bear ultimate responsibility for their own suffering." Sessions ("Honor," 206–24) discusses the notion of "honor" from a contemporary philosophical perspective.

213. Job 34:11a. MT שלם ("to make whole, compensate"); OG ἀποδίδωμι ("to pay, reward, compensate"); Syr ܦܪܥ ("to make compensation"); Vg *restituet* ("to provide restitution"); Tg ישלם ("to compensate"; so also 11QtgJob 24.5).

214. Job 34:11b. Cf. 11:1–4; 17:10; 23:3. Elihu's point is that God always keeps his promise to compensate the righteous for their "labor" (פעל).

215. Job 34:12. Not to compensate the righteous for their labor is to do "evil" and pervert "justice"—behavior in which an honorable deity does not indulge.

216. Apparently the negative press starts with TJob 43.5 where Elihu is called ὁ μόνος πονηρὸς ("the only evil one").

217. Eaton (*Job*, 24).

218. Job 34:17a. Cf. *TEP* 134: "Those who are supposed to punish injustice now practice it" (see below).

219. Job 34:17b.

220. Job 34:18a. OG ἀσεβής ("ungodly"); Vg *apostata* ("apostate"); Syr ܒܝܫܐ ("evil"); Tg רשיעה ("wicked").

221. Job 34:18b. Cf. *DILA* 12:11–12: "Utterance, Perception, and Justice accompany you, yet you bring chaos and the noise of tumult into the land" (see below).

222. Job 34:19.

to contemplate, a world so brutally damaged that even the most courageous, impartial Judge cannot restore it:

והוא ישקיט ומי ירשע	If he is silent, who will pass sentence?
ויסתר פנים ומי ישורנו	If he hides his face, who will see him?[223]
כי אל אל האמר	Has anyone ever said to El,
נשׂאתי לא אחבל	"I forgive, but I do not pledge?[224]
בלעדי אחזה אתה הרני	Will you reveal to me what I do not see,
אם עול פעלתי לא אסיף	So that if I do evil I will not continue in it?[225]
המעמך ישלמנה כי מאסת	Should he compensate you for something you have rejected?"[226]

The speech closes with Elihu criticizing Job for jumping to conclusions, ignoring the advice of his "friends," and generally behaving like "Job the Rebel."[227]

Third Speech

In his third speech Elihu (a) recalibrates the justification motif to mount a challenge against Job's claim of being a צדיק ("righteous man"),[228] then (b) asks how it might be possible, even should this claim be true, for *any* mortal to demand the deity's attention:

הזאת חשבת למשפט	Does it sound appropriate
אמרת צדקי מאל	For you to claim, "I am more righteous than El?"[229]

223. Job 34:29.

224. Job 34:31. MT חבל ("to take as a pledge of repayment, to borrow"; *HAL* 274; cf. Deut 24:12). OG ἐνεχυράζω ("to pledge"); Syr ܐܢܐ ܠܐ ܣܟܠܬ ("I will not sin"); Vg *non prohibeo* ("I will not offend"). Cf. Akk *ḫabālu* ("to borrow"); e.g., *abua ma'da ḫabulli ša PN*, "my father borrowed much belonging to PN" (cited from *CAD* Ḫ.7). Ezekiel describes a צדיק ("righteous person") as someone who חבלתו חוב ישיב ("returns to the debtor his pledge") and חבל לא חבל ("never demands a pledge," Ezek 18:7, 16). In pre-Islamic Arabic اخبال signifies the "act of lending" (Lane 1.699).

225. Job 34:32. Cf. ἐπιμένωμεν τῇ ἁμαρτίᾳ, ἵνα ἡ χάρις πλεονάσῃ, "Shall we continue in sin that grace may abound" (Rom 6:1)?

226. Job 34:33. MT שלם ("to compensate, make whole"); OG ἀποτίνω ("to pay back"); Syr ܠܘܬܟ ܠܐ ܢܦܢܐ ܝܬܝܪܬܐ ܥܡܟ ("Will he not return something greater to you?"); Tg אפשר די מעמך ישלמנה ("Should he perhaps compensate you?").

227. Job 34:33–37 (חטאת, "sin"; פשע, "transgression, rebellion"); cf. Parmentier ("Rebel," 227–42).

228. In Job 10:15, Job says אם רשעתי . . . וצדקתי ("If I am wicked" . . . "then I am righteous"), but it is unclear whether the conditional particle אם applies to the apodosis. OG, Syr, and Vg think it does; Tg does not (cf. *GKC* 159*l*).

229. Job 35:2. Unlike OG, Vg (*iustior Deo*, "I am more just than God") reads the

כי תאמר מה יסכן לך	For you say, "What advantage do I have over you?
מה אעיל מחטאתי	How am I better off than when I am sinning?"[230]
אם חטאת מה תפעל בו	Well, if you sin what do you accomplish with him?[231]
ורבו פשעיך מה תעשׂה לו	If your transgressions multiply, how does that affect him?
אם צדקת מה תתן לו	And if you are righteous, how does that profit him?[232]

Fourth Speech

Elihu's fourth speech raises epistemological, soteriological, and cosmological questions about Job's new reality:[233]

כי חמה פן יסיתך בספק	Beware of wrath lest it provoke you to ridicule,
ורב כפר אל יטך	And let not the size of the ransom corrupt you.[234]
היערך שועך לא בצר	Will your cry for aid hold your anxiety at bay?
וכל מאמצי כח	Will every ounce of your strength?[235]
מי פקד עליו דרכו	Who manages God's path for him?
מי אמר פעלת עולה	Who can say, "You have done evil?"[236]

Echoing the words of Zophar, he then defers to the created order of things:

---

mem in מאל as comparative.

230. Job 35:3. In a roundabout way Elihu here acknowledges the disinterested piety motif.

231. Job 35:6. Like MT (בו), Syr (ܒܗ) reads "with him"; Vg (*contra eum*) reads "against him," but OG omits (εἰ ἥμαρτες τί πράξεις, "if you sin in what you do"). Smith ("Allusion," 176) reads this question as an echo of Job's earlier question in 7:20, "If I sin, what is that to you?").

232. Job 35:7. Syr ܡܘܬܪ (from ܝܬܪ, "to profit").

233. Poser (*Ezechielbuch*, 261) reads Ezekiel as an attempt to help returning exiles "appreciate and participate (fully) in the (hi)story of their trauma" in order to "soften up their traumatic stiffness." Cf. Schöplin (*"Herz"*).

234. Job 36:18 (lit., "turn you aside"); cf. OG δώρων ὧν ἐδέχοντο ἐπ' ἀδικίαις, "gifts which are received through injustice" (i.e., a bribe). Cf. Ps 49:8: "No one can ransom themselves before God." The מבין issues a similar warning: ובמחיר אל תמכור כבודכה, "Do not barter your birthright for a fee" (4Q416.2.2.17; Moore, *WealthWise*, 140).

235. Job 36:19.

236. Job 36:23.

אף אם יבין מפרשי עב	Can anyone understand how the clouds disperse,
תשאות סכתו	Or the thunderclaps over his domain?[237]
התדע בשום אלוה עליהם	Do you know how God exercises his will,
והופיע אור עננו	Or how he makes lightning electrify the clouds?[238]
התדע על מפלשי עב	Do you understand how clouds hover,
מפלאות תמים דעים	Or how miracles occur through perfect knowledge?[239]

SUMMARY

David Penchansky thinks that even though "many try to discern a progression in the arguments between Job and his friends," all he sees are "distinctions and subtleties between the friends' various monologues," each attending to the same point; viz., that "God would not afflict Job in such a manner if he were innocent."[240] Robert McCabe, on the other hand, argues not for a "progression" but a "recapitulation"; i.e., that Elihu's arguments recapitulate those already proffered by Job's three "friends." Elihu's "understanding of the 'fruits of suffering' (33:15–27, 36:8–10) . . . echoes that of Eliphaz (5:17–27) and his defense of God's justice in chapter 34 echoes that of Bildad in chapter 8." Moreover, "Job's suffering is the direct result of unconfessed sin (33:17, 27; 34:10–12, 36–37; 36:8–10),"[241] and Elihu's citations of Job in 33:9–11, 34:5–6, and 35:2 preserve the book's "key tension": Job's 'integrity' (תם) vs. God's 'justice' (צדקה)."[242]

The goal here is not to pit one polarity against another, but to accentuate the fact that the counselors' arguments in the Dialogues are just

237. Job 36:29.

238. Job 37:15.

239. Crenshaw ("*Revolt*," 232) recognizes that Job contains "competing viewpoints" because "on the one hand, Job's friends emphasize the myth of divine rule by strict justice, and on the other hand, Job insists on integrity characterized by rebellion. A mediating position, represented by the poem about wisdom's inaccessibility in chapter 28 and the Elihu speeches in 32–37, strives for a return to naiveté," but in the process "produces a sterile faith."

240. Penchansky (*Wisdom*, 36).

241. McCabe ("Elihu," iii). Following Bakon ("Enigma," 228), Dunham (*Sage*, 239) extrapolates from this that Elihu may well be the author/compiler/editor of the book.

242. Cf. 33:9–11 (responding to 9:21); 34:5–6 (responding to 27:2a); and 35:2 (responding to 27:6).

that—the *counselors'* arguments.[243] They do not reflect Job's thinking, nor do they reflect the thinking of the deity, who eventually tells Eliphaz:

חרה אפי בך	My anger boils against you
ובשני רעיך	And against your two friends;[244]
כי לא דברתם אלי נכונה	For you have not spoken correctly about me,[245]
כעבדי איוב	Like my servant Job.[246]

So if the counselors' theology is not נכונה ("correct"), then what is?[247] At this point many throw up their hands in exegetical despair, some responding to this question by slicing up the book into hypothetical fragments, others by portraying it as an unfinished cacophony of conflicting voices, still others by imagining the Epilogue to hold the "key" to the "message of the book."[248]

The question here, however, is twofold: (a) whether the keyword in the Prosecutor's question (חנם) articulates the book's key tension (*pace* McCabe) as *compensation/retribution* vs. *disinterested piety* (i.e., *retribution* vs. *reality*); and (b) whether the book's intertextual context buttresses or challenges this conclusion. The fact is that Job moves from a *disinterested piety* focus

243. Cho ("Job," 230) admits that "the theological questions, indeed the perspective from which they are asked, changes" between the Prologue and the Dialogues.

244. Job 42:7. Whether Yhwh's censure applies to the fourth counselor (Elihu) is a classic *argumentum ab silentio*, but what can be said with certainty is that no one ever calls Elihu a רע ("friend"). In fact, the anti-Elihu passage in TJob 43.5 goes so far as to call him "the *only* evil one" (ὁ μόνος πονηρὸς).

245. Job 42:7. MT נכונה (derived from כון); Tg כונתא ("correctly," same root); Syr ܟܝܢܬܐ ("correct," derived from the cognate root ܟܢ); OG ἀληθὲς ("truthfully"); Vg *rectum* ("correct, in order"). Dunham (*Sage*, 232–33) interprets this divine indictment to mean that "Eliphaz fails as a counselor because in his *hubris* he does not acknowledge the true source of wisdom—which lies not in shadowy dreams, the traditions of the ancients, nor the customary cleansing rituals of the ANE religious milieu—but in Yhwh." N.B. that the "friend" in *BT* similarly wonders whether the gods Enlil, Enki, and Mami may on occasion be responsible for allowing mortals to fall prey to "twisted speech" (*itguru dabābu*), particularly when this makes it easier to "flatter the fortunes of the wealthy" (*ša šarî idabbubū dumqišu*, *BWL* 88.279–83).

246. Job 42:7. OG reads simply "you have 'sinned' (ἥμαρτες), you and your two friends, for you have not spoken before me what is correct." Nam (*Job*, 13) suggests that Yhwh does not commend Job for speaking "correctly," only "constructively."

247. Perdue (*Revolt*, 20) thinks that "order as a unifying center for creation theology in wisdom literature is more comprehensive than either anthropology or theodicy" even though "this approach may distort wisdom thought in a number of ways. First, order as 'justice' may take on a too legalistic definition and lead inevitably to a hardened doctrine of retribution" in which "the outcome often is an inflexible, mechanistic system of reward and punishment." Welz (*Theodicy*, 172) explains Kierkegaard's (*Wiederholung*, 231) reaction to Job as "looking not at the given and the lost, but at the *giver*," so that "he could even take loss as a gift."

248. Cf. Guillaume and Schunck ("Job," 457–72).

in the Prologue to a *compensation/retribution* focus in the Dialogues, then back to a *disinterested piety* focus in the Epilogue. So it seems abundantly clear (a) that the Prosecutor challenges the existence of Job's disinterested piety, and (b) that Job's "friends" patently sidestep this discussion.

The bottom line for Varunaj Churnai is that the book of Job is a genuine "re-evaluation and ultimate rejection of the theology of retribution."[249] For Jason Kalman the sages' goal is to "defend God at Job's expense."[250] For Clement Grene the book's major polarity consists of the counselors' "endlessly complacent clichés on divine justice" vs. "Job's far more honest, heartfelt questions."[251] For Gustavo Gutiérrez, Job's counselors "think that the world has been made in order to be made immediately useful for human beings and to be of service in temporal retribution: a reward for the just, a punishment for sinners." For Yhwh, however, "the doctrine of retribution is not the key to understanding the universe" because to maintain such a focus is to "give rise to a commonplace relationship of self-interest with God and others."[252]

249. Churnai (*Justice*, xi).

250. Kalman ("*Iyov*," 77).

251. Grene ("*Pain*," 310).

252. Gutiérrez (*Job*, 70). For Goldingay (*Theology*, 2:607), Yhwh "can be urged to rise up to pay back the important people who exult in their wrongdoing, act destructively in relation to the community and conspire to bring about the death of the innocent," even as "this "redress can (also) be described in terms of Yhwh's bringing peoples' wickedness back on them, which suggests something like diverting the force of the wrongdoing, like a tennis player utilizing the force in a powerful serve to return it—indeed, God puts an end to them *through* their wrongdoing."

4

The Compensation/Retribution Motif in Ancient Near Eastern Wisdom

THE DISINTERESTED PIETY MOTIF is conspicuously absent in ANE wisdom literature contemporary with Job, but not so for the compensation/retribution motif dominating the thinking of Job's "friends."

EGYPTIAN TEXTS

Whether or not "wisdom" is definable as a full-fledged "genre,"[1] Donald Redford finds Egypt's participation in the "literary heritage of the ancient world" to be significant, and that "its principal contributions are the short story and the wisdom text."[2] For Samuel Adams the primary purpose of *sebayit* ("instruction/discipline")[3] is to teach students "how to conduct

1. Kynes (*Obituary*, 2) thinks of "wisdom" as "an unwieldy scholarly category developed in mid-nineteenth century Germany to meet the ideological demands of that time and place." Sympathetic to Kynes' arguments, Fox ("Theses," 75), nevertheless rejects them, insisting that they hardly justify abandoning (a) the concept of wisdom literature, or (b) the recognition of wisdom literature as a "genre." Sneed ("Grasping," 39) believes that "genres exist, but that the important question is, 'Where do they exist?' The reality is that genres do not exist in texts themselves, but only in the minds of authors and readers." So, following Frow (*Genre*, 63–67), Sneed ("Methods," 30) prefers the word "mode" to the word "genre." Weeks (*Introduction*, 1) pronounces this taxonomical debate "an untidy business."

2. Redford ("Literature," 2238). Otto (*Vorwurf*) examines the bulk of the Egyptian dialogical literature.

3. Shupak ("Literature," 267) sees the closest Heb equivalent in the term מוסר ("discipline, instruction," Prov 5:12, 23).

themselves in the public sphere and with family members," and that it is often "through colorful scenarios" that they "present ethical requirements and vivid motifs in the pursuit of character formation."[4]

The Tale of the Eloquent Peasant

One of these "colorful scenarios" is the Tale of the Eloquent Peasant, a spirited text Nili Shupak calls "a good example of the genre of Egyptian wisdom literature."[5] Comprised of multiple speeches within a narrative framework, it is one of the best attested examples of a "great text" from the Middle Kingdom period (c. 2040–1780 BCE).[6] While it may be examined from several angles, no reputable Egyptologist ever proposes that the narrative framework in *TEP* must come from a different time and/or place than the speeches.[7] In fact, noting how in some ways it "approaches the level of a hybrid genre,"[8] Richard Parkinson joins several of his colleagues in classifying its colloidal mixture of material as a "literary archetype" similar to the one housing the Tale of the Sporting King (and, of course, Job).[9] The main difference between *TEP* and Job is that instead of multiple dialogues spoken by multiple speakers, *TEP* consists of nine "increasingly despairing speeches" spoken by one speaker.[10]

4. Adams ("Egypt," 310–27). Brown (*Character*, 1) suggests that one of the reasons why wisdom literature "is troubling to Jews, and more so to Christians," is because it "appears to lack a readily identifiable theological center."

5. Shupak ("Judiciary," 1). Erman (*Literature*, 116) calls it "The Complaints of the Peasant."

6. Parkinson ("Literature," 310). ETs appear in *AEL* 1.169–84; Allen ("Peasant," 229–326); Wilson ("Peasant," 407–10); Shupak ("Peasant," 98–104); and Parkinson (*Peasant*). All references below are cited according to Parkinson's line-numbering schema ("Peasant," 58–75).

7. *Alttestamentler* Siegfried Herrmann (*Untersuchungen*, 92) attempts to apply *redaktionsgeschichtliche* methods to *TEP*, but with negligible results. Parkinson ("Literature," 310) recognizes that some identify *TEP* as a "hybrid genre," and Shupak ("Peasant," 2–3) theorizes that *TEP* "consists of two parts—prosaic and rhetorical, the former consisting of the plot, the latter of the peasant's complaints against the legal establishment."

8. Parkinson ("Literature," 310).

9. *ANET* 243–45; Parkinson ("Peasant," 164; "Literature," 310). Cf. Goedicke (*Report*, 62) and Brunner (*Literatur*, 24). Allen ("Peasant," 229) prefers to call *TEP* "an unusual blend of two genres: stories and wisdom texts."

10. Lichtheim (*AEL* 1.169); cf. *TEP* 120–21; The Babylonian Dialogue of Pessimism (*BWL* 144–48); Bottéro ("Pessimiste," 4–24); Baines and Yoffee ("Order," 199–260); Richards ("Wealth," 36–45); and Denning Bolle (*Dialogue*).

This speaker, a straight-talking salt miner named Ḥueninpu,[11] is a *sẖty* ("rustic, peasant")[12] whose story (like the Tanak story of Jacob's sons)[13] features a sojourn into the Nile delta to buy food.[14] But like the diviner/exorcist Balaam ben Be`or, he runs into trouble along the way.[15] Whereas Balaam encounters a heavenly messenger blocking the road, Ḥueninpu encounters an all-too-earthly messenger, a corrupt government official named Nemtinaẖt.[16] Determined to take Ḥueninpu's goods, Nemtinaẖt exemplifies the culture of corruption so vigorously condemned by the Egyptian sage Ipu-Wer, who complains to Pharaoh that mid-level officials like Nemtinaẖt *habitually* "set ambushes against peasants."[17] Tricking one of Ḥueninpu's donkeys into munching a "wisp of barley" on a patch of road next to his land, he uses this "theft" as a pretext to seize *all* the peasant's donkeys as "just compensation."[18] Appalled by the brazenness of this thievery,[19] Ḥueninpu pleads for justice, first to the perpetrator of the crime (Nemtinaẖt), then to the perpetrator's boss (Rensi), then by proxy to *his* boss, Pharaoh Nebkaure Kheti III,[20] asking not just for the return of his donkeys, but the return of law and order. As Parkinson explains, "his complaint about a theft becomes a larger questioning of why society ignores justice."[21]

11. "Protected by Anubis."

12. *TEP* 1–3, 5, 7, *et passim*. The classic example of Egyptianized dialogue is *DMS* (*AEL* 1.163–69; *ANET* 405–7; Allen, "Dispute," 327–60). Parkinson ("Peasant," 54) characterizes Ḥueninpu's role as that of a "noble savage." Whereas the protagonist of Job is a "gentleman," the protagonist of *TEP* is a "peasant."

13. Gen 42:3. Staubli ("Levant," 64) calls Joseph the "Israelite Sinuhe."

14. Ḥueninpu is from the Wadi Natrun, a region several miles NW of the Nile delta known for the mining of *nṯrj* (Lat. *natrium*—Na on the periodic table), an element found in compounds like sodium chloride and sodium bicarbonate.

15. Num 22:22–27.

16. Num 22:23; *TEP* 6.6–7. Nemtinaẖt is the employee of a *wr* ("great man") named Rensi.

17. *DILA* 13.4. Whereas *DILA* addresses the problems created by widespread social chaos, *TEP* concentrates its attention on a specific situation.

18. While an Egyptian "law code" has yet to be found, several ANE law codes condemn property theft in no uncertain terms (e.g. *CH* 6.31–69; cf. Moore, *Wealth-Wise*, 14–15). In Ps 140:5 the poet complains of the "trap" (פח) hidden for him by the "arrogant."

19. Another brazen example is King Ahab's decision to seize Naboth's land, then execute him for complaining about it (1 Kings 21.1–29; cf. Moore, *Pressure*, 37–44).

20. Cf. Beckerath (*Königsnamen*, 74); Grimal (*Egypt*, 140).

21. Parkinson ("Peasant," 55). Like *DILA* (*AEL* 1.149–63; *ANET* 441–44), *TEP* has both prophetic and sapiential properties. If nothing else, it shows that the attraction of Job's "friends" to the compensation/retribution motif is hardly unique.

Meanwhile the Pharaoh, though initially sceptical of his motives,[22] provisions Ḥueninpu and his family with bread and beer while he reviews his speeches. Then he makes an executive decision: Nemtinaḫt must hand over to Ḥueninpu not only his donkeys, but *all* his property as "just compensation." In this way another "pious sufferer" winds up with more possessions at the end of his story than the beginning. More to the point, in both *TEP* and Job the compensation/retribution motif shines brighter in the speeches than it does in the framework.[23] Drawing from everyday life (grain harvesting, shipping, construction), these speeches address several concerns:

Leaders Should Be Incorruptible

Ḥueninpu insists that the exemplary *sšmw* ("leader") should be "free of greed," a "father to the orphan," a "husband to the widow," a "destroyer of lies," an "architect for M3`t,"[24] a "cop who refuses to steal," a "captain who refuses to take bribes," a "trader who refuses to skim off the top," a "heavenly rudder," an "earthly pillar," and an "impartial judge."[25] Citizens forced to endure such "leaders" are like a "town without a mayor," a "troop without a leader," a ship without a captain," and/or a "business without a boss."[26] "Great ones" (*wr*) are by definition "free of arrogance" because they recognize (a) that all bosses report to bosses of their own; and (b) that those who ignore this truth are "blind to what they see and deaf to what they hear."[27] Denial of their leadership responsibilities is proof positive that M3`t is no longer guiding them.[28]

22. Pharaoh initially suggests that Ḥueninpu might be a disgruntled employee with an ax to grind (*TEP* 75–77).

23. In addition to *TEP* and perhaps also the Tale of the Sporting King (Parkinson, "Literature," 310) another variation of this "archetype" occurs in the GNT Acts of the Apostles, a rambling *Geschichte* comprised of thirty-six speeches embedded into a prose narrative (cf. Soards, *Speeches*, 1–17; Kucicki, *Speeches*, 1–10).

24. M3`t is the Egyptian goddess of truth/justice/wisdom (cf. Smelik, "Ma`at," 534–35). For Lopes ("Peasant," 922) *TEP* is a veritable "treatise on M3`t." Even as Lady Sophia personifies "wisdom/truth" in Israel (Prov 1–9), so M3`t personifies "wisdom/truth" in Egypt (Carenga, *Ma`at*, 5–11).

25. *TEP* 97, 93, 94, 98, 122, 223, 136. N.B. the similar honorifics used to describe Marduk (*Ee* 6.124; 7.1, 7–8, 20–22, 57–59, 65) and Hammurabi (*CH* 2.16—3.46). Cf. D'Andrade ("Bribery," 239–48).

26. *TEP* 221–23.

27. *TEP* 144 (*pr m3w šp jrwt sḏmw sḫw*). Cf. Isa 6:10.

28. *TEP* 128, 219. Cf. Yhwh's dramatic abandonment of the Jerusalem temple (Ezek 1–11; Kutsko, *Ezekiel*, 94).

The Justice System Should Function Properly

Not content to indict a single *individual*, Ḥueninpu extends his critique to the entire justice *system*, denouncing it in a lament Parkinson calls "particularly descriptive."[29]

mk mꜣ`t wtḫ=s ẖr=k	Look! Mꜣ`t has abandoned you,
nš.tḏ m st=s	Having been exiled from her abode.
srw ḥr ḏrt ḏyt	Officials do evil
tp-ḥsb n mdt ḥr rḏjt ḥr gs	When "normal" speech becomes so biased
sḏmyw ḥr ḫnp jṯt=f	That judges carry off whatever they can seize.[30]
sḏꜣṯḏ pw n mdt ,`qꜣ=s	Are those who twist the truth
ḥr ḏrt rf nwdw	Not destined for corruption?[31]
rḏj ṯꜣw ḥr gꜣt ḥr tꜣ	Are those designated to help folks breathe instead suffocating them?[32]
srfw	Are those designated to help folks rest
ḥr rḏjt nšp tw	Instead crushing them mercilessly?[33]
dr sꜣr {r} m wḏ	Are those designated to relieve pain
jrt=f	Instead generating it?[34]
ḫsf jw ḥr	Are those designated to punish injustice
jrt jyt	Instead promoting it?[35]

29. Parkinson ("Peasant," 78 n 27).

30. *TEP* 129–30. "The peasant here argues that a single crime can undermine the whole *standard* of justice. . . . A judge's prevarication in speech affects justice and is thus as bad as the robber's crime" (Parkinson, "Peasant," 78).

31. *TEP* 130–31. Cf. Zeph 3:7—"Surely the city will fear me, it will accept correction without losing sight of all that I have done for it. Yet they rise up early to practice corruption," and Q 11.85—"O my people! Give full measure and weigh justly. Do not 'defraud' (بخس, lit., 'reduce') people of their property, nor go about 'spreading corruption'" (فسد, lit., "making things rotten").

32. *TEP* 131. "Doing justice is breath for the nose" (*TEP* 177), and "a pauper's belongings are his breath" (*TEP* 264).

33. One of the greatest distinctions between Job and Qur'an is that the latter calls God the "most merciful of the merciful" (Q 21.83), whereas the former says "although I am innocent, I cannot answer him; instead I must appeal to my accuser for mercy" (Job 9:15) because "he is merciless" (16:13).

34. *TEP* 131–33. Sirach similarly warns his students about giving in to anxiety and stress: בני למה ואץ להרבות לא ינקה תרבה עשקך, "My son, why do you multiply your misfortunes? Stirring up your anxiety will not make you 'blameless'" (Sir 11:10; cf. Moore, *WealthWise*, 147–49).

35. *TEP* 133–34.

Corrupt Leaders Persecute the Poor

Evidently the poor hold a special place in Ḥueninpu's heart because several times he comes close to segregating poverty-induced thievery from the covetousness displayed by corrupt officials like Nemtinaḫt, often proposing that the poor in such situations should be extended "mercy" (*sft*), not punishment.[36] Unlike Nemtinaḫt, Ḥueninpu demands that Egypt's leaders fully recognize these distinctions, reminding Pharaoh that most thefts are the result of the desperately poor simply trying to stay alive. In such circumstances, he pleads:

sf nb t	Whoever has food should be merciful.
nḫt n ḫnr	Criminals are powerful,
twt ṯ3wt n jwtw jḫt=f	But it is the powerless who take things
ḫnp jḫt jn ḫnr	As possessions which criminals then re-take.[37]

If all this sounds familiar it may be because the French writer Victor Hugo powerfully elucidates the same concerns in his most famous book, *Les Misérables*, a text widely held to be the greatest novel of the 19th century.[38] In this *exposé* Hugo attacks the pretensions of haughty French society, especially its cruel mistreatment of the poor. He writes, "words intended to be insults—'beggars,' 'rabble,' 'mob,' 'populace'—indicate, alas, that the blame lies with those in charge rather than those being charged, with the privileged rather than the deprived."[39]

Like Hugo, Ḥueninpu questions whether desperate people should be punished for trying to feed their families in a world so shamelessly and violently corrupt.[40] Job expresses something similar when he chal-

36. *TEP* 152 (*DME* 224). Qur'an is very clear about treatment of the poor: "What will make you understand the 'challenging path' if not to free a slave, or share food in times of famine with an orphaned relative or a 'needy person' (مسكينا) in 'misery?'" (مذربه, from the verb ذرب, 'to cling to the dust'" [Q 90.12–16]).

37. *TEP* 153–55. N.B. the antonymous parallel between "criminals" and the "powerless."

38. Bellos (*Novel*), e.g., calls it the "novel of the century."

39. Hugo, *Les Misérables*, 1051. Hugo's "Exhibit A" is the protagonist's nineteen-year imprisonment simply for taking a loaf of bread. Cf. TJob's mention of Job's spouse's exchange of hair for bread (TJob 22.3).

40. Gerstenberger (*Theologies*, 158) notes that "in many parts of the world ethnic, cultural and religious minorities are being oppressed and their existence threatened . . . Any use of violence, even by the marginalized and oppressed, has evil consequences for those not involved . . . Probably there is no case in which terrorist attacks on the public can be approved . . . but if no democratic means are available by which an oppressed and threatened minority can improve its situation . . . then acts of resistance like boycotts, strikes and campaigns extending to armed battle must be considered."

lenges his professors to explain their rationale for punishing the innocent. Should the "arrows of Šadday" be allowed to penetrate so deeply into their hearts that they find themselves forced, like Job, to "drink their poison?"[41] Is there ever a time when academic pretentiousness should be challenged and curtailed, especially when it turns otherwise lovely people into "worthless physicians?"[42] Moreover, should the deity's actions be exempted from scrutiny? Put another way, should such scrutiny be avoided because it makes insecure teachers fearful of engaging in serious theological reflection, which might in turn lead to their being "torn apart in his wrath" and/or "trapped in his net?"[43]

Ḥueninpu's eighth speech gives full vent to such questions:

jṯw `wꜣ nḥmw	Thief! Robber! Plunderer!
srw jr.n.tw r {r} ḫsf rjyt	Magistrates are selected to suppress crime!
jbww pw n ꜣdw	And provide shelter against aggressors!
srw jr.n.tw r ḫsf r grg	Magistrates are supposed to fight falsehood![44]

Not unexpectedly, he feels outrage and disgust for "ferrymen who ferry only those who can afford the fare," for "storekeepers who refuse to let poor people shop in their store," for "hawks who feed on defenseless chicks," and for "butchers who slaughter, but never clean up the blood."[45]

Then suddenly, like Eliphaz and Bildad, he shifts the angle of perspective:

41. Job 6:4.

42. Job 13:5; 14:13. Washburn (*University*, x) poignantly argues that "the single biggest threat to the future of American higher education is the intrusion of a market ideology into the heart of academic life." In Bloom's opinion (*Closing*, 26), though, the concern is much deeper: "Openness—and the relativism that makes it the only plausible stance in the face of various claims to truth, and various ways of life . . . is the great insight of our times. The true believer is the real danger. The study of history and of culture teaches that all the world was mad in the past; men have always thought they were right, and that led to wars, persecutions, slavery, xenophobia, racism, and chauvinism. The point is not to correct the mistakes and really be right; rather it is not to think you are right at all."

43. Job 16:2, 9–14; 19:6.

44. *TEP* 327–29. Challenging King Jehoiakim, the prophet Jeremiah bluntly demands, "Are you a king because you compete in cedar? Did your father (Josiah) not eat and drink and do justice and righteousness? Then things went well for him. He judged the cause of the poor and needy, and things went well" (Jer. 22:15–16).

45. *TEP* 203–8. Cf. Parkinson ("Peasant," 66).

ḥmy m sbn dpwt=k	O Helmsman, stop guiding your ship off course. . . .
s`nḫw m rḏj mwt.tw	O Life-giver, stop letting your people die on your watch. . . .
sḥtmw m rḏj ḥtm.tw	O Destroyer, stop letting your people perish. . . .
šwyt m jr m šw	O Shade, stop blazing like the sun. . . .
jbw m rḏj jṯ msḥ	O Shelter, stop abandoning your people to the crocodiles."[46]

In short, *TEP* is a no-holds-barred attack against anyone denying the obvious distinctions between the *real* and the *ideal*, a text Parkinson dubs "a moral anecdote . . . fissured with deep irony."[47]

Retribution/Compensation Is Coming

Governmental corruption is so deep, Ḥueninpu concedes,[48] it often seems a foregone conclusion that the poor cannot receive justice in a system so broken. But can they at least be allowed to grieve? To be so punitive as to refuse even *this*, he warns, will eventually backfire against the powers-that-be, exacting from them a much higher price than would otherwise be the case:

m `wn ḥwrw ḥr jḫt=f	Do not defraud a poor man of his possessions:[49]
ṯ3w pw n m3r jḫt=f	A pauper's belongings are his breath;
dbb fnḏ=f pw nḥm st	To seize them is to suffocate him.[50]

46. *TEP* 250–55 (shifting from 3ps to 2ps).

47. Parkinson ("Peasant," 55). Pondering Job's use of the term משל ("enigma, riddle") in 17:6, Jackson ("Bully," 65) suggests that it is a "deliberate rhetorical device (in keeping with the extensive use of irony and sarcasm throughout the work) designed to provoke the reader/audience into choosing their own conclusion."

48. Egypt, of course, holds no monopoly on corruption. The Indian economist Kautilya (d. 283 BCE) proverbially muses that "just as it is impossible to know when a fish moving in water is drinking it, so is it impossible to know when government servants in charge of undertakings misappropriate money" (*Arthashastra* 2.9.33).

49. *TEP* 262–63 (Eg, *ḥwrw*, to steal, defraud"). Cf. Sirach's warning to wealthy Jews: "Do not cheat the poor of their living, nor goad them into becoming indigent, bitter souls . . . Do not reject their petitions or give them cause to curse you" (Sir. 4:1, 5; cf. Barclay, *Jews*, 1–11). Note also that Qur'an pronounces a strong "woe" on "anyone who 'defrauds' (لطف) when they 'purchase' (ستقف), and/or 'gives back little' (خسر) when they sell" (Q 83.1–3).

50. *TEP* 263–65 (lit. "to take them away is to stop up his nose"). Notably absent from *TEP* is any warning to the poor about, say, the dangers of indebtedness, like that which the מבין ("instructor") pronounces at Qumran: "Do not sell your soul for money, for it is good to be a spiritually-minded servant serving your supervisors 'without

nfr nfrt nfr r=f	The goodness of a good man lasts a long time,[51]
jw swt m3`t r nḥḥ	But M3`t lives forever.
h33=s m-a jrr sj r ẖrt-nṯr	She descends with him to the grave,[52]
jw qrs.tw=f sm3 t3 jm=f	Where earth enshrouds his corpse,[53]
n sjn.tw rn=f tp t3	She does not wipe his name from the earth,
{jw=f} jw sẖ3.tw=fḥr bw-nfr	But instead honors his piety
tp-ḥsb pw n mdw-nṯr	According to the dictates of her divine authority.
jn jwsw pw n g{r}s3.n=f	If it (the memory of the good man) is placed on hand-scales, it will not tilt;
jn mḫ3t pw n rḏj.n=s ḥr gs	If placed on vertical scales, it will not drift to the side.[54]
mk wj r jwt mk ky r jwt	So whether it be against me or someone else
wšd=k	Go ahead and prosecute![55]
m pḥ ntj n pḥ.n=f n sf	But stop oppressing those unable to defend themselves.
n=k n mn.n=k	You are obstinate and cruel
n sksk n bh3.n=k	When you refuse to engage or withdraw
n rḏj.n=k n=j ḏb3w n mdt tn nfrt	And fail to compensate me for these words of truth[56]
prrt m r3 n r` ḏs=f	Proceeding from the very mouth of Ra.[57]

You Cannot Fool the Gods

Alongside M3`t, Ḥueninpu mentions several other deities, including *R`* (Ra), *Ḥ`py* (Ḥapy), the "Lady of Plague" (*nbt y3dw*—a popular epithet

compensation' (חנם)" (4Q416.2.2.17).

51. *TEP* 337 (lit., "is good to him"; N.B. that *nfr* repeats three times).

52. *TEP* 338–39. In a similar vein Isaiah "taunts" (משל) a Babylonian king (probably Nebuchadnezzar II) with a "mock dirge" (Isa 14:4b-21; cf. Shipp, *Dirges*, 163).

53. Smelik ("Ma`at," 534) observes that she enacts "an important role in the judgment of the dead as depicted in Egyptian illustrated texts related to the Netherworld."

54. *TEP* 337–43. Wilson (*Egypt*, 121) argues that "the peasant does not stop with the concept of a blindfolded justice holding a sword and a pair of scales. M3`t cannot stop at the repair and punishment of 'falsehood' or the coldly impersonal leveling-off of the scales; M3`t involves the positive seeking-out of justice."

55. *TEP* 345 (lit. "interrogate"). Ḥueninpu imagines Nemtinaḫt's boss enacting a prosecutorial role not dissimilar to that enacted by the Joban Prosecutor.

56. *TEP* 349 (Eg, *ḏb3w*, "to compensate, reward"; "to pay for, provide," *CT* 1.163). Wilson (*Egypt*, 86) reckons that "the hope of reward and promotion in the next life" is so strong that *TEP* and other texts "leave open the possibility that the next life may even bring a change in rank."

57. *TEP* 350.

for Saḫmet), and Thoth.[58] Ra, of course, is the "lord of heaven" to whom every Egyptian is subject, the sun-deity responsible for pronouncing justice through sages like Ipu-Wer.[59] Ḥapy is the fertility deity responsible for annually flooding the Nile to prepare it for barley and other lifegiving crops.[60] As the daughter of Ra, Saḫmet is in charge of dealing with plague, pestilence, and pandemic.[61] And like Ea/Enki in Mesopotamia,[62] Thoth is responsible for addressing conflicts between warring factions, both divine and human.[63] Each of these deities plays a supportive role alongside M3`t. In fact, Ḥueninpu advises Pharaoh to "copy these three; If they are merciful, then you, too, should be 'merciful' (*sfn*)."[64] From a Joban perspective, of course, it's difficult to ignore how much these roles so clearly resemble those enacted by the Joban Advocate/Redeemer.[65]

The Dialogue of Ipu-Wer with the Lord of All

Whereas *TEP* censures a single corrupt official, *DILA* more broadly condemns the nation's capitulation to social, political, religious, and economic corruption.[66] Several traits differentiate the two texts, but one of the most obvious is the way in which each engages the poverty-wealth polarity. Both texts condemn the oppression of the poor, but *DILA* also condemns the persecution of the wealthy:

58. *TEP* 171 (Ra), 173 (Ḥapy), 151 (Saḫmet), 181 (Thoth).

59. *TEP* 171, 350 (cf. Gardiner, *Sage*, 19–94). The goal of every Egyptian is to "live like Ra every day after death" (*EBD* 38b.6). In Mesopotamia the sun-deity Šamaš is the primary "god of justice" (*CH* 1.27–49).

60. Cf. *RDEGG* 61.

61. "Spells exist that regard plagues as brought by the 'messengers' of Saḫmet. On the assumption that the goddess can ward off pestilence as well as bring it, the Egyptians adopt Saḫmet ('lady of life') as a beneficial force in their attempts to counteract illness" (*RDEGG* 139).

62. Cf. Espak, *Enki*.

63. *RDEGG* 157–59. In *DMS* 23–24, Parkinson ("Dialogue," 156) sees Thoth as one who "appeases the gods." The Canaanite deity most likely to enact this conciliatory role is El (cf. Pope, *El*, 29; Moore, *WealthWatch*, 41–46).

64. *TEP* 182–83.

65. Job 19:25 (גאל). Cf. Mowinckel ("Himmel," 207–12); Ringgren ("גאל," 350–55); Seow (*Job*, 823); and Moore ("Gyroscope," 27–355).

66. Lichtheim (*AEL* 1.149) argues that *DILA* exemplifies what she calls the "national distress" motif animating earlier texts like *CKS*. Redford ("Literature," 2243) reads *DILA* as a timely response to the "calamitous condition of human society."

When the "wealthy" (*špsw*) are woeful
The "poor" (*šwꜣ*) rejoice.[67]
Every town says,
"Let's drive out the 'powerful' (*ḳnw*) from our midst.[68]
Look! The land is spinning like a potter's wheel.
The robber now has his own riches,
And the rich man is a thief."[69]
Gold and lapis lazuli,
Silver and turquoise,
Carnelian and amethyst.
Such jewels adorn the necks of slavegirls
While their mistresses wander the land, begging,
"Give us something to eat!"[70]

Because it "laments the rise of the poor and overthrow of the rich,"[71] *DILA* more closely resembles Qohelet and Sirach than, say, 4QInstruction or the GNT Letter of James.[72]

Perhaps *DILA*'s most distinctive component is its willingness, like Job, to hold the deity accountable not only for innocent suffering,[73] but for shirking his responsibility to dispense compensation/retribution fairly and without bias.[74] Like Elijah with the Ba`al prophets, Ipu-Wer appears to make every effort to engage this issue honestly:

67. *DILA* 2.7.

68. *DILA* 2.7–8. Aristotle (*Ath. Pol.* 19.6—20.3) registers similar concern over "people rule" (δῆμος . . . κρατέω), even though he eventually comes around to accepting δημοκρατία ("democracy") as preferable to oligarchical tyranny (cf. Moore, "Associations," 149–51).

69. Gardiner (*Admonitions*, 42) suggests that "we should probably understand, with Kurt Sethe, that the times have changed, there are no men of yesterday, only *novi homines* ('upstarts')." Whether the direct quotation extends this far is not clear.

70. *DILA* 3.2–3. Hackett (*Balaam*, 52–53) sees *DA* 1.7–15 expressing a similar "topsy-turvy" sentiment, and Marlow ("Nile," 229–42) recognizes something similar in Isa 19:5–10.

71. Parkinson ("Ipuuer," 166).

72. Cf. Moore (*WealthWise*, 98–110, 130–41). Clines (*Parties*, 126–28) observes that while Job never portrays the poor realistically, neither does he depict wealth as in any way problematic.

73. In other words, Job is hardly the only ANE voice daring to question the deity's motives. "Does it seem good to you to oppress, despise the work of your hands, and favor the schemes of the wicked?" (Job 10:3).

74. Sometimes it is impossible to tell whether the target of Ipu-Wer's criticism is Ra or Pharaoh, his vicar on earth (cf. Gardiner, *Admonitions*, 79), an ambiguity much like that defining the identity of the עבד ("servant") in the biblical servant songs; e.g., Isa 52:13—53:12 (cf. Berges, "Knecht," 153–78).

Look, why does he create people
Without distinguishing between the gentle and the violent?[75]
People say, "He is the shepherd of humanity"[76] and "There is no evil in his heart."
But why did he not realize their true nature in that first batch?
Perhaps he would have then curbed their evil,
Stretching out his arm against them,
Destroying the seed of their inheritance.[77]
Where is he today? Is he asleep?[78]
We see no evidence of his power.
If we have been saddened,
Should we not be able to meet with you?[79]
Insight, Authority, and Justice are yours,[80]
But you have brought chaos into the land
Accompanied by the noise of tumult.[81]
If you would but take a taste of this anguish,
Then you might understand.[82]

75. *DILA* 11.11–12. Jeremiah raises a similar question in his first lament (Jer 12:1–4; cf. Moore, *Babbler*, 79).

76. *DILA* 12.1 (cf. Isa 53:6). As Gardiner points out (*Admonitions*, 79), the "he" here most likely refers to the sun-deity Ra. In a similar listing of divine attributes Eliphaz promises Job that the deity's care for him will be so thorough that "when you inspect your sheepfold you will find nothing missing" (Job 5:24).

77. *DILA* 12.2–3. For Gardiner (*Admonitions*, 79–80) "only one meaning can be attached to these words: if the ideal king here envisaged had known, from the very beginning of things, how wicked human nature is, he would have exterminated humanity and . . . rooted up the seed from which the present chaos and abuses have sprung." Cf. Torah's tradition of a deity "exterminating humanity" by "imposing obstacles" (Gen 2:17) and "destroying herds" (6:7).

78. *DILA* 12.5. The "sleeping deity" motif appears not only in the Elijah cycle (1 Kgs 18:27), but also in the Disappearance of Telipinu from Anatolia (cf. Moore, *Wealth-Warn*, 31–36).

79. *DILA* 12.6. Job's complaint is similar: "If I summoned him and he answered me, would he listen to my voice . . . ? He is not a mortal, as I am, that I might answer him so that we might together come to court" (Job 9:16, 32).

80. *DILA* 12.11. Translating *Sỉꜣ* as "intellectual perception" and *Ḥw* as "authoritative utterance"/"creative command," Wilson (*ANET* 443) recognizes that "kingship . . . needs the ability to comprehend a situation, the authority to meet the situation by command, and the balance of equitable justice." Gardiner (*Admonitions*, 85) points out that alongside *Mꜣ't*, *Ḥw* and *Sỉꜣ* habitually appear as a deified pair associated with the king as early as the Pyramid Texts.

81. Eg, *ḫnnw* ("tumult") denotes the disequilibrium resulting from the absence of *Ḥw* and *Sỉꜣ* (cf. המון in Isa 13:4).

82. *DILA* 13.5–6. Cf. Job 6:30, "Is there any wrong on my tongue? Cannot my taste discern calamity?"

Dialogue of a Man with His Soul

Recognizing the parallels between *DMS* and the book of Job would at first glance seem to be obvious. Technically *DMS* is a dialogue,[83] but in this case not one between separate entities. Rather it is a conversation between a man and his *ba*, an Egyptian word often translated into English as "soul."[84] With regard to *form*, *DMS* appears to be a mix of prose, poetry and something Miriam Lichtheim likes to call "symmetrically structured speech."[85] With regard to *function*, Adolf Erman labels it a tract on suicide,[86] while Katharina Lohmann rejects this as an overreaction, arguing that the *ba* in *DMS* simply enacts the *role* of "counselor/sage" in conversation with its "host."[87]

At any rate this text focuses, like Job, on the mortal dynamics of life-vs.-death.[88] Where *DMS* compresses this polarity, however, Job decompresses it. Where the *ba* celebrates life in the here-and-now, the host casts his gaze forward to a glorious afterlife, dismissing present reality as mere overture.[89] Like Job, the host laments that death is preferable to life because, as Lichtheim succinctly puts it, "those who suffer from life long for death."[90] Like Elihu, however, the *ba* warns his "host" not to be so otherworldly as to dismiss the possibility of experiencing celestial grace in the here and now: "Stop worrying! Enjoy yourself!"[91] Imagining death as a peaceful "harbor" (*dmí*) where new arrivals are treated as "sages who cannot be turned away,"

83. Redford ("Literature," 2234) calls it a "dialogue employed to stunning effect."

84. Eg *bꜣ* (*DME* 77). According to Allen (*Pyramid*, 7) the Egyptians believe that a dead individual's *ba* (individual "soul") nightly reunites with his *ka* ("individual life force") to become a fully-functioning *aẖ* ("cosmic being").

85. *AEL* 1.163. Literarily this third category looks too much like the second to merit a separate classification. Kugel (*Idea*, 302), in fact, thinks (a) that the feature commonly identified as parallelism is better understood as the rhetorical structure of seconding and closure as a way of organizing the basic elements of a poetic unit; and (b) that the wall between prose and poetry is thoroughly perforated.

86. In 1896, Erman entitled this text "Eine Gespräch des Lebensmüden mit seiner Seele" ("a dialogue of a suicidal man with his soul"). Osing ("Lebensmüden," 571–73) still refers to the protagonist as a suicidal person ("Lebensmüden," lit., "tired of life"), and Faulkner ("Tired," 21–40) calls *DMS* "The Man Who Was Tired of Life."

87. Lohmann ("Gespräch," 207–10). N.B. that the "host" envisions the afterlife as a place where it is possible for anyone to become a respected *jẖt* ("sage," *DMS* 146).

88. Allen (*Debate*, 137).

89. Parkinson ("Dialogue," 152). The protagonist in TJob also emphasizes the superiority of "heavenly things" over "earthly things" (cf. TJob 33.3–9).

90. *AEL* 1.163 (cf. Job 3:11—"Why did I not die at birth, come forth from the womb and expire?").

91. E.g., *šms hrw nfr smḫ mḥ* (*DMS* 68). Cf. ויחננו ("He extends grace to him," Job 33:24).

his unhealthy obsession with the afterlife eventually upsets his *ba* so much, he feels impelled to remind him of an inescapable truth:

jr sḫꜣ.k ḳrs nḥꜣt jb pw	Burial is a heartache which depresses
jnt rmyt pw m sjnd z	And saddens with the bringing of tears.
šdt z pw m pr.f	It is taking a man from his house
ḫꜣ` ḥr ḳꜣꜣ	And casting him onto the brow of a high hill
nn pr.n.k r ḥrw	Where no one can ascend any higher toward Ra.[92]

MESOPOTAMIAN TEXTS

Assyriologist W. G. Lambert calls wisdom "an outstanding genre of Akkadian literature, second only to the epics in literary merit and content value,"[93] and though much ink has been spilled on the subject since 1960, this remains the majority opinion.

The Babylonian Theodicy

In addition to the three Egyptian texts just discussed, two Mesopotamian texts testify to the persistence of the compensation/retribution motif-trajectory. Like the Hebrew scrolls of Qohelet[94] and Job,[95] *BT* features a "sufferer"[96] interacting with a "friend" over many of the same issues debated by Job and his "friends."[97] This begins early on in the poem when the "suf-

92. Cf. *DMS* 38, 146. Assmann (*Death*, 87) recognizes that "in death, it seems, the person of the deceased emerges in its various aspects or constituent elements, which now take on a life of their own. I call this process of emergence *dissociation*." Hollis ("Literature," 109) emphasizes that behind such dissociation lies a deep "sense of loss and disarray."

93. *BWL* v.

94. Dating the Babylonian Theodicy to c. 1000 BCE, Sneed (*Politics*, 45) follows Ebeling ("Kohelet") in dubbing it the "Babylonian Ecclesiastes."

95. N.B. Job's interaction with רעי איוב (the "friends of Job," Job 2:11) and cf. Lambert (*BWL* 63); Oshima (*Theodicy*, xiii–xv); and Moore (*Babbler*, 216–23). Salters ("Acrostics," 426) reads the Babylonian Theodicy as "the earliest example of the acrostic phenomenon in Babylonian literature," a literary technique Murphy ("Wisdom," 160) identifies as most dominant within "wisdom."

96. Oshima (*Poems*, 115) prefers the term "sceptic."

97. Cf. Sitzler (*Vorwurf*, 99–109). Job and Eliphaz display a similar dynamic (Moore, *Babbler*, 175, 216–23). Lambert (*BWL* 301) points out that the first word of *BT*, *ašiš*, is likely a ptc. of *ašāšu*, meaning (a) "to lay foundations"; (b) "to experience distress" (*Lud* 2.47); (c) "to rage" (e.g., a storm); and/or (d) "to gather, collect." Focusing on the fourth

ferer/sceptic" confesses his fear of being an *aḫurrû* ("younger child"),[98] complaining that *šimtum* ("destiny, fate")[99] has destroyed his family *zārû* ("seedgiver, progenitor")[100] after his parents abandon him for the *erṣet là târi* ("land of no return").[101]

To this the "friend" replies that sooner or later everyone (including parents) must someday "cross the river Ḫubur,"[102] and besides, not every *bukru* ("firstborn son")[103] automatically grows up to be a "prosperous . . . wealthy lord" (*ešērū*[104] . . . *bēl mešrū*).[105] Indeed, only the *nakdū* ("vigilant")[106] possess the skill-set necessary to achieve *ṭuḫdum* ("prosperity").[107] This prompts the "sufferer/sceptic" to complain:

---

option, Lambert imagines the author of *BT* as a "collector of knowledge." Evidently the first Westerner to call this text a "theodicy" is the pioneer Assyriologist Bruno Landsberger ("Theodizee," 32).

98. *BWL* 70.9 *a-ḫu-ra-[k]u-ma*. The antithetical parallel with *bukru* ("firstborn") in 70.19 recurs in *LKU* 43.13, 15.

99. *BWL* 70.9. This is perhaps the most significant *Leitwort* in Enuma Eliš; cf. *ši-mat-ka la ša-na-an*, "your destiny, (O Marduk), is unequaled" (*Ee* 4.4). In fact, Bottéro (*Mésopotamie*, 189) calls it "le terme le plus fort et le plus riche et significatif."

100. *BWL* 70.9 (cf. Heb זרע).

101. *BWL* 70.10; cf. *DI* 1 (*qaqarri l[ā târi]*); Job 16:22; *DT* §27).

102. *BWL* 70.17. "While originally the subterranean river of fertility, Ḫubur later becomes known as the river of death" (Albright, "Rivers," 171; cf. Job 33:18).

103. *BWL* 70.19. The editors of *CAD* posit that even though the cognates בכר, ܒܘܟܪܐ, بكر, and Ug *bkr* (*CAT* 1.14.6.25) all signify "first-born," there is "no indication that such is the nuance in Akkadian" (*CAD* B.310). Yet since the editors of *HAL* disagree with this assessment (*HAL* 125), it seems likely that *bukru* in line 19 counterbalances *aḫurrû* in line 9.

104. *BWL* 70.19. One of Marduk's "Fifty Names" at the end of *Enūma Eliš* is *šá ri-i-ta maš-qí-ta uš-te-eš-še-ru*, "the one who makes pasture and watering holes plentiful" (*Ee* 7.59).

105. *BWL* 70.20. N.B. the prominence of the wealth motif in Torah; e.g., in the Joseph novella (Gen 47:13–19; cf. Sadler, "Genesis," 131). In a prayer to Ištar the supplicant prays that *ša im-nu-uk-ki meš-ra-a lu-uṣ-ṣip dum-qa lu-uk-šu-da ša šu-me-lu-uk-ki*, "From your right (hand) may I receive wealth (and) from your left hand good things" (*AGH* 62.32). Lambert (*BWL* 303) reads *namrû* in 70.20 from *marā'u* ("to fatten up"; cf. מריא, Isa 1:11), taking it as "a jibe at the plumpness of the wealthy in the same spirit as when Amos calls the opulent Samaritan ladies 'cows of Bashan' (Amos 4:1)." Also the term *lamassu* in the next line (70.21) is "a common expression for being successful" (*BWL* 303).

106. *BWL* 70.22, defining this term from the root *naqādu* ("to be alert, anxious") instead of *nakādu* ("to palpitate, worry"). As a general rule the slothful do not *produce* anything. Cf. מתרפה במלאכתו אח הוא לבעל משחית, "the slacker in his 'work' is akin to a vandal" (Prov 18:9, lit., "is brother to a lord of destruction").

107. *BWL* 70.22. Von Soden (*AHw* 1393) translates *ṭuḫdum* as "*überreichliche Fülle*" ("overwhelming fullness"). N.B. that one of Marduk's "Fifty Names" is *mu-ṭaḫ-ḫi-du*

ku-ši-ri še-te-qu e-et-ti-iq mu-tu-t[i]	My success vanishes,[108] my "half-portion" disappears,[109]
ku-bu-uk-ku i-te-niš ba-ṭi-il iš-di-ḫu	(My) power dwindles,[110] (my) income fades.[111]

Dismayed by this response, the "friend" asks:

ak-kat-ti bēl pa-an ša uṣ-ṣu-bu-šú na-ḫa-šú	Does the landlord[112] building his fortune[113]
[aq-r]a-a ṣa-ri-ri i-ḫi-ṭa a-na ^{D}*ma-mi*	contribute the rarest gold to Mami?[114]

At this the "sufferer/sceptic" insists that "regular sacrifices to the goddess"[115] are foundational to his religious routine, solemnly insisting (like the "pious

---

ú-ri-sin, "the one who makes their stables prosper abundantly" (*Ee* 6.124; cf. Seri, "Names," 507–19).

108. *BWL* 72.28. Lambert (*BWL* 72.28) reads *ši-ti-qa*, but Oshima (*Theodicy*, 30) reads *še-te-qu* (with the commentary), taking it as a G stative form of *šêtu*, "to escape, vanish." That which "escapes" is *kušīru*, the final element in the traditional expression *ina še-e-ri du-un-qi ina mu-uṣ-la-li ni-me-li ina šum-še-e ku-ši-ru* ("in the morning prosperity, at noon profit, at sunset success") habitually concluding prayers to Sin, Ninurta and Marduk (Sidursky, "Prayers," 570.18′20-′).

109. *BWL* 72.28. Oshima (*Theodicy*, 30) plausibly suggests that *e-te-ti-iq* is the result of a scribe's insertion (distracted by the previous word *ši-ti-qa*) of a *ti* sign between *te* and *iq*, obscuring the "fact" that the root is *etēqu*, "to transfer, relocate" (cf. *CAD* E.384–95). Should *mu-tu-t[i]* (Oshima) be preferred over *mu-tu-r[i]* (Lambert), then what most likely "relocates" (*etēqu*) is half of the sufferer/sceptic's estate.

110. *BWL* 72.29. Erra argues that even though a few city-dwellers are *puggulat ku-bu-ku-uš* ("mighty in power"), they hardly compare to the rugged, self-sustaining power of field-dwellers (*Erra* 1.55). N.B. the *enēšu/lapānu* word-pair for "poverty" in *BWL* 74.71.

111. *BWL* 72.29. A business which is *išdiḫu* ("income-producing, profitable") is by definition proactively engaged in *šadāḫu* ("moving forward").

112. *BWL* 74.52. If *bēl pa-ni* is equivalent to *bēl makkūri* (NÍG-GA), as Lambert suggests (*BWL* 74), then "landlord" is preferable to "*nouveau riche*" (*BWL* 75.52) or "rich man" (Oshima, *Theodicy*, 19).

113. *BWL* 74.52. One of Marduk's "Fifty Names" includes the epithet *mu-na-ḫiš da-ád-me*, "the one who enriches humanity" (*Ee* 7.66).

114. *BWL* 74.53. On *ḫâṭu* cf. *kaspa ša ina pāniya ana PN kî a-ḫi-ṭu la taddissu*, "you did not give PN the silver at my disposal after I had it 'weighed out'" (*BIN* 1.94.37). Elsewhere this deity is called *tab-sú-ut ili*^{MEŠ} *e-ri-iš-tam* ^{D}*ma-mi . . . ba-ni-a-at a-wi-lu-ti*, "Wise Mami, midwife of the gods . . . humanity's creator" (*Atr* 1.193).

115. *BWL* 74.55, (*[ak-]ru-ub sat[tu]k-kē*^{e} *il-tim-ma*). Most of these offerings are agrarian in nature. Cf. *suluppē . . . ana* SÁ.DUG4 *ša Šamaš ana Ebabbar bēlu liddin*, "May the lord give dates as an 'offering' for Šamaš at (his temple in) Ebabbar" (*YOS* 3.102.9).

sufferer" in *Ludlul* and the namesake character of *Tobit*)[116] that whatever his flaws, religious infidelity is not one of them.[117]

Then the "friend" warns:

gi-šim-ma-ru iṣ [ma]š-re-e a-ḫi aqr[u]	O date-palm, tree of wealth,[118] esteemed brother. . . .
gi-riš ina u^{4}-um la ši-ma-ti i-qa-am-me-šu ma-al-ku	The king tends to burn at the stake[119]
gi-is maš-re-e bel pa-ni ša qur-ru-nu ma-ak-ku-ru	Any landlord who recklessly stockpiles his wealth.[120]
gi-ir-ri an-nu-tu-ú i-ku-šu a-la-ka taḫ-ši-iḫ	Do you wish the same fate?
gi-mil du-um-qí ša ili da-ra-a ši-te-'-e	If not, then compensate the gods adequately![121]

116. Tob 1:6–8 (cf. Moore, *WealthWarn*, 142–55).

117. *[ak-]la-ma-a nin-da-ba-a*, "[D]o I hold back offerings?" (*BWL* 74.54). Contrast this with the satirical comment of a "slave" to his "master" on how to treat one's deity: *ila tu-lam-mad-su-ma ki-i kalbi arki-ka it-ta-na-lak*, "Can you teach your god to trot behind you like a dog?" (*BWL* 148.60).

118. *BWL* 74.56. Citing Borger ("Weihe," 171, 176), Jiménez (*Poems*, 193) contends that "according to Mesopotamian tradition, the palm is the king of the trees," and that its symbolism is strong enough to provide Sennacherib the title, "date palm of Aššur," not to mention its association with Ištar who in one NA hymn is called "palm tree, daughter of Nineveh, stag of the lands" (Livingstone, *Poetry*, text #7). In the annals of Sargon II the ^{GIŠ}*immaru* is called *balti nagišunu*, "the wealth of their region" (cf. Lie, *Sargon*, 335; Porter, *Trees*, 18), and Giovino (*Tree*, 135) finds it significant that *BWL* 74.63 "links the Akkadian words *mašrû/mešrû* ('wealth/prosperity') with the palm tree."

119. *BWL* 74.64. The "friend" compares this punishment to that doled out to wild donkeys trampling village crops and carnivorous lions devouring village livestock (lines 59–62). Citing a line from the Instructions of Šuruppak (NI-ZUḪ PIRIĜ NA-NAM UL-DAB5 SAĜ NA-NAM, "the thief is a lion, and when caught, is actually a slave"), Oshima (*Theodicy*, 34) proposes that the "lion"-saying here "refers to the fact that when livestock is stolen," the ancients "view the big cats not only in terms of their strength, but also in terms of their thieving acts" (cf. Alster, *Wisdom*, 62).

120. *BWL* 74.63. The noun *makkūru* derives from *makāru* ("to do business, buy"; a *bīt makkūri* is a "house of business/treasury"). Some of the Hittite *išḫiul* texts illustrate this "taxation" mentality more overtly. Should the "royal granary" (LUGAL-*wa-aš* ARÀḪ-*an*) be burglarized, e.g., it is the "men of the city" (LÚ^{MEŠ} URU-*LÌ*) who must "compensate" (*šar-ni-in-kán-zi*) the king for his loss (*KUB* 13.9 + 40.62.3–10).

121. *BWL* 74.66 (lit., "eternal ones"). On *gimillu* as "compensation," cf. *[aš]šum gimil dumqi epē* [*ša*] *tīda*, "for you know what it means to receive compensation" (*KAR* 297.8 + 256.9). On Akk *dārû* as "eternal" cf. Ug *dr* (*DULAT* 279–80), Heb דור (*HAL* 209), Syr ܕܘܪ, Arab دور (Wehr 299).

Finally the "sufferer/sceptic," like Job,[122] scolds his "friend" for succumbing to a worldview so naïve:

il-lu nu-us-su-ku mi-lik-ka d[am-qu]	Dear friend, you do share profitable advice,[123]
il-te-en zik-ra mut-ta-ka lut-t[i-ir]	But let me remind you that sometimes even
il-la-ku ú-ru-uḫ dum-qí la muš-te-'-u ì-l[i]	Those who are prosperous neglect the god,[124]
il-tap-ni i-te-en-šú muš-te-mi-qu šá ì [l-ti]	While those petitioning the goddess remain homeless.[125]

Acknowledging his friend's naïveté,[126] the "sufferer/sceptic" begins to wonder (a) whether he is "yoked to state service like a slave,"[127] and (b) whether this slavery might reflect the "deity's decision to impose poverty on him instead of wealth."[128] To this the "friend" replies that even though he generally finds him to be "sane" (*kina ra-áš*), he now wonders whether the burden of pain and suffering has driven him into "irrational fantasy" (*la mur-qa*),[129] or worse, convinced him to resist "the gods' cosmic plans"

122. E.g., Job 21:17, 20.

123. That is, the "sufferer/sceptic" rarely allows his setbacks to push him beyond the point where he can no longer distinguish that which is "profitable" (*dumqu*) from that which is not. Socioeconomic notions rooted in and correlating with Akk *dumqu* permeate *BT* (cf. *CAD* D.180–83).

124. *BWL* 74.70. This complaint occurs often in the speeches of "pious sufferers"; e.g., Jeremiah challenges Yhwh: מדוע דרך רשעים צלחה ("Why does the way of the wicked prosper?" Jer 12:1).

125. *BWL* 74.71. Citing several parallels, Lambert (*BWL* 303) argues that *ītenšu* in *BWL* 74.71 and *itnušu* in *BWL* 74.275 "are not expressions for physical weakness, but for impecuniosity." The list of compliant birds attacking violent ones (*DA* 1.7–9), and Jeremiah's first lament (Jer 12:1–7) attest to the probability that topsy-turvy scenarios are one of the primary tools used to challenge the "old wisdom" establishment (cf. Assmann, *Ma'at*, 72; Kruger, "Scenarios," 59–61).

126. *BWL* 76.72 (Akk *ligimû*). This term recurs in 76.128.

127. *BWL* 76.74 (*il-ku ša la né-me-li a-šá-aṭ ab-šá-nu*). Likely this is a roundabout reference to taxation.

128. *BWL* 76.75 (*il-ta-kan* DINGIR *ki-i maš-re-e ka-tu-ta*).

129. *BWL* 76.78 (lit., "non-sensical").

altogether.[130] Cloaking himself in the mantle of asceticism,[131] the "sufferer/sceptic" then confides to his "friend" that a more radical response lurks on the horizon:

bi-i-ta lu-ud-di	I will abandon my home;
bi-šá-a a-a aḫ-ši-iḫ	I will no longer crave possessions.[132]

He ponders whether he should

bé-e-ra lu-up-ti a-ga-a lu-maš-šèr	Open the mountain passes and release the water,[133]
bi-it-bi-ti-iš lu-ter-ru-ba lu-ni-'i bu-bu-ti	Drive hunger away from every house,[134]
bi-r-iš lu-u-te-e'-lu-me su-le-e lu-ṣa-a-[a-ad]	And though famished, still patrol the streets.[135]

Like the mythical king Gilgamesh,[136] he begins to imagine a future where he can

bi-ir-ta lu-ul-lik né-sa-a-ti lu-ḫu-uz	Take to the road and travel great distances,[137]

130. *BWL* 76.79 (*ú-ṣur-ti i-li ta-na-ṣu*). Lambert (*BWL* 77) reads "blaspheme against your god's designs." Noting that Akk *uṣurtu* often translates Sum GIŠ-ḪUR, Farber Flügge (*Inanna*, 183) notes that GIŠ-ḪUR closely parallels ME, the Sum *Leitwort* denoting the fundamental elements of the cosmos Enki transfers to Inanna, who then tries to smuggle them down into the Netherworld (*ID* 13–63; cf. Moore, *WealthWarn*, 12).

131. Oshima (*Theodicy*, xlvii) thinks that *BT* "offers a degree of consolation for unrewarded piety," but Lambert's (*BWL* 65) reading focuses on the theological question: "Both 'sufferer' and 'friend' begin by assuming that the gods are responsible for maintaining justice among men. They end by admitting that these very same gods make men prone to injustice. In a sense the real problem is shelved."

132. *BWL* 76.133–34. The *bītu/bīšu* ("house/possessions") word-pair occurs elsewhere; e.g., in the apodosis *ana bītim šuāti še'am kaspam u bīšam inaddin*, "let him pay for the house with grain, silver, or personal possessions" (*CH* L67+a; Richardson, *Laws*, 66).

133. *BWL* 78.138. Like *ašîš* in 70.1, *bēru* is another polysemantic term, meaning (a) "choice, select"; (b) "remote, distant"; and/or (c) "mile/measure of distance" (*CAD* B.207–11). Cf. *ḫuršāni be-ru-ti ša GN kīma qê luselliṭ*, "I made a cut through the distant mountains (like) a taut string" (*Tn* 30.17.31).

134. Cf. the proverb *bi-ru-ú-um bit a-gur-ri i-pal-la-aš*, "A starving man will break into a solid brick house" (*BWL* 235.19–20).

135. *BWL* 78.140. Guillaume (*Finance*, 99) contends (*a là* Albertz, "Theodizee," 349–72) that this text "uses the *topos* of the hunger of the poor and attributes it to the rise of a new rich class."

136. George, *Gilgamesh*, 91–137.

137. *BWL* 78.137 (cf. *GE* 9.1–4; Moore, *WealthWatch*, 71).

be-e-ra ki-di šar-ra-qiš [lu-u]r-tap-pu-ud Roaming[138] the countryside like a bandit.[139]

Victor Hurowitz wonders whether the "friend's" response to the "sufferer/sceptic" betrays a bit of cautious agreement.[140] Maintaining that the "law of rich and poor" has guided the cosmos "since ancient times,"[141] the "friend" nevertheless wonders whether the gods Enlil,[142] Enki,[143] and Mami[144] might in some way be responsible for endowing humanity with "twisted speech" (*itguru dabābu*)[145] in order to "flatter the fortunes of the wealthy" (*ša šarî idabbubū dumqišu*) while "humiliating the poor like thieves" (*šarraqiš ulammanū dunnumâ amēlu*).[146] Whether this explanation satifies the "sufferer/sceptic," however, is as difficult to ascertain as whether or not the whirlwind speeches "satisfy" Job.[147]

Takayoshi Oshima, on the other hand, suggests that the message of the "friend" basically boils down to three points: (a) human beings do not (indeed, cannot) understand the gods' plans;[148] (b) every creature must

138. *BWL* 78.139. Near the end of *GE* the protagonist (Gilgamesh) reverts to an Enkidu-like role as a "roamer (*rapādu*) of the wilderness (*ṣēru*)"—the so-called "Robin Hood option" (Hilton, "Origins," 197–210). This phrase, repeated ten times on tablet 10, reprises the prostitute Šamḫat's words to Enkidu (*GE* 1.208). Cf. the *satan's* "roaming" in Job 1:7; 2:2.

139. Cf. the similar fatalistic tone in the proverb *lu-uš-kun ik-ki-mu lu-ut-tir-ma man-nu i-nam-din*, "If I put things in storage, I shall be robbed. If I squander, who will give to me?" (*BWL* 241.45–47).

140. Hurowitz ("Theodicy," 778). Krüger ("Poems," 186) prefers to call this "concession," not "agreement."

141. *BWL* 80.198. Lambert (*BWL* 81) offers no translation, but von Soden ("Weisheitstexte," 153, followed by Oshima, *Theodicy*, 37) reads "ein Gesetz seit jeher sind Reichtum ebenso wie Armut" ("a law in which wealth means just as much as poverty").

142. *BWL* 88.276. According to the ancient commentary on *BT*, ^{D}Narru is equivalent to ^{D}Enlil (cited in Hurowitz, "Theodicy," 777).

143. *BWL* 88.277. According to the god-list found in CT 25.33.16 (published by Civil, "Chariot," 9) ^{D}KA^{ZU}-LUM-GAR^{MÁR} = ^{D}É-*a*.

144. *BWL* 88.278 (cf. *Atr* 1.193).

145. *BWL* 88.279. N.B. that "twisted speech" is also condemned in *TEP* 129–30 and Prov 8:8.

146. *BWL* 88.281, 283. Lambert (*BWL* 89.283) reads "they harm a poor man like a thief"; Oshima (*Theodicy* 25.283) reads "they treat the pitiable (man) badly like a thief." That "twisted speech" might originate from divine sources is anathema to texts like *DILA* and, to a somewhat lesser extent, Job.

147. Job 38:1—41:34. Schifferdecker (*Whirlwind*, 2) argues that Yhwh's whirlwind speeches "provide an answer to Job's situation," just not the answer he wants to hear.

148. Cf. the proverb *ṭe$_4$-im ili ul il-lam-mad mim-mu ili a-na a-*. . ., "The will of a god cannot be understood; the way of a god cannot be (known)" (*BWL* 265.7–8).

nevertheless seek divine blessing through ritualistic prayer and sacrificial offering; and (c) wealth achieved through godlessness never lasts.[149] On this last point *BT* resonates with Job's "farewell speech":

הכי אמרת יהבו לי	Have I ever said, "Give me something?"
ומכחכם שחדו בעדי	Or, "From your wealth offer me a bribe?"[150]
אם אשמח כי רב חילי	If I were to celebrate my great wealth,
הוא עון	That would be wrong.[151]

The Poem of the Pious Sufferer

Another parallel from Job's world is the Babylonian "Poem of the Pious Sufferer," a text often identified by its first line: *Ludlul bēl nēmeqi*.[152] Likely written by an *awīlum* ("gentleman") named Šubši-mešre-šakkan,[153] it (a) recounts the "slings and arrows" deemed responsible for his suffering, while (b) imagining their ultimate origin in the enigmatic will of his divine patron, Marduk.[154] The text begins with an opening hymn to Marduk depicting him as an aloof monarch caught up in the throes of *Sturm und Drang*,[155] a capricious deity whose personality, in Hermann Spieckermann's

149. Oshima (*Theodicy*, xxii–xxv). On the problem of "wicked wealth," cf. Prov 13:22; Sir 4:27–5:8; 1 En. 94.8–10; Luke 6:43–45; Jas 5:1–5.

150. Job 6:22.

151. Job 31:25, 28 (cf. Neville, "Ethic," 181–200).

152. "Let us praise the lord of wisdom" (cf. *BWL* 21–62; Annus and Lenzi, *Ludlul*; Foster, *Muses*, 392–409; Oshima, *Poems*, 3–5). Lambert ("Wisdom," 31) suggests that ^{D}*Ši-du-ri* . . . ^{D}XV *ni-me-qí* ("Šiduri . . . goddess of wisdom") in *Šur* 2.173 refers to the barmaid who counsels Gilgamesh not to despair over Enkidu's death (OB *GE* 10.1).

153. *Lud* 3.44, 4.111, and 119. This name means "Gather up the wealth, O Šakkan" (Šakkan is the deity of domestic livestock; cf. Foster, *Agade*, 154; Nolan and Lenski, *Macrosociology*, 154). Noting its trifold appearance here, Lambert ("Wisdom," 34) suggests that this "extremely rare" name refers to "an historical figure under Nazimurattaš," probably a Kassite official "important enough to have his messenger fed at state expense."

154. Krüger ("Poems," 184) finds it "more plausible" that the "speaker assumes that he himself has made a mistake out of ignorance than to assume that the gods do not act properly." Leick (*Mesopotamia*, 22) observes that "towards the end of the second millenium Marduk assumes many of the functions performed by Ea/Enki (the old wisdom deity) without replacing him."

155. *Lud* 1.1–40 ("storm and stress," a phrase associated with von Klinger's play *Sturm und Drang*, first performed in Hamburg in 1777). Lenzi ("Marduk," 483) thinks that Marduk is hardly "the divine equivalent of the cat that toys with the mouse before devouring it. Rather, he ultimately shows mercy to frail and imperfect humans who anger him. Šubši-mešre-šakkan has experienced this mercy and is intent upon telling others what Marduk has done for him."

view, "rhythmically" oscillates between "wrath and mercy."[156] Opening hymn completed, the "gentleman" then goes on to list several attacks he has been forced to repel,[157] including (a) the abandonment of "my prosperity spirit" ([D]ALAD *dum-qí*),[158] (b) the "expulsion from my house" (*uš-te-ṣi ina* É-*ia*),[159] and (c) the king's reluctance to bestow upon him "redemption"

156. Spieckermann, "Wrath," 6. Whether Marduk *subordinates* his mercy to his wrath, however, is not as clear as Spieckermann would suggest. N.B. the summary statement *ka-bat-ta-šu muš-ne-šat* ("his temper is benevolent," *Lud* 1.34) alongside the jussive proclamation, *libbaka liṭib ka-bat-ta-ka liḫdu* ("May your heart be content, your temper positive," *BBRel* 31–37.30). For comparison, N.B. that lines 176–85 of the Šamaš Hymn, as Foster recognizes (*Muses*, 627), "consider the alternately harsh and tender qualities" of the sun-god Šamaš (cf. Moran, "Marduk," 255–60; Albertz, "Mardukfrömmigkeit," 25–53; Collins, "Wrath," 67–77; and Moore, *WealthWise*, 38–42).

157. Assyrologists debate whether *Ludlul* more likely resembles a lament psalm or a thanksgiving psalm, but as Weinfeld ("Parallels," 217–18) points out, both *Ludlul* and the Sumerian poem "A Man and His God" (*COS* 1.179.573–75) contain a recounting of the protagonist's troubles *as well as* praise of the divine, so it is more likely, in Oshima's opinion (*Poems*, 32), that "the main intention of these texts is to demonstrate the gratitude of the sufferers for their redemption, not to draw the gods' attention to their sufferings."

158. *Lud* 1.45. Both good and evil [D]*šêdū* ("daemons") densely populate the occult world of the ancient Near East. An Assyrian prayerbook references both side-by-side within the same prayer: [D]*šêdu ḫa-a-a-ṭu al-lu-ḫap-pu ḫab-bi-lu gal-lu-u râbiṣu ilu limnu*, the *Šêdu*, the 'Lookout,' the 'Snatching Net," the *Gallu*, the *Rabiṣu*, the evil god" (*KAR* 2.58.42) . . . [D]*šêdu na-ṣi-ru ilu mu-šal-li-mu*, "the protecting *šêdu*, the healing god" (*KAR* 2.58.47). So ingrained is the notion of a "protecting [D]*šêdu*" in Mesopotamia, "pious sufferers" find it vexing when *il-la-ku ú-ru-uḫ dum-qí la muš-te-ʾ-u ì-li*, "those who neglect (their) god experience prosperity," *BWL* 75.70). In the Sum "A Man and His God" (*COS* 1.485), the deity restores his devotee with [D]UDUG SIG5 KA-E EN-NU-UJ3 MACKIM MU-UN-DA-AN-TAB [D]LAMMA, "a protective spirit who stands guard at the mouth as a divine guardian." Eventually the [D]LAMMA ("divine guardian") and [D]ALAD ("protective spirit") return to support Šubši-mešre-šakkan (*Lud* 4.56).

159. *Lud* 1.50.

(*pa-ṭā-ru*).[160] Reacting to the prosecutorial plotting of Marduk's priestly "attendants" (*nanzazū*),[161] he sharply criticizes them:[162]

na-piš-ta-šu u-šat-bak-šu	"Let's make him surrender his rations;[163]
ú-šat-bi te-er-tu-šú	Let's deduct his commission;[164]
qip-ta-šú a-tam-ma-aḫ	Let's confiscate his loan;[165]
er-ru-ub É-uš-šu	Let's impound his house."[166]

Then he laments:

160. *Lud* 1.56. Akk *paṭaru* (lit., "to unravel," *CAD* P.286) is cognate to Ug *pẓr*, Heb פשׁר, Syr ܦܫܪ, and Arab فسر ("to explain, interpret," Wehr 713) and serves as a major motif in the Hittite *išḫiul* texts. Given the appearance in 4.45 of the phrase *e'-il-ti ip-pa-ṭir* ("my debt is redeemed"; cf. *šumma awīlam e'iltum iṣbassuma*, "If a debt brings about the seizure of a man . . . ," *CH* §117), it may be that what the king refuses to "redeem" is an outstanding debt like, say, a pledged field (cf. *CAD* P.294–95; cf. Job 29:25; van der Toorn, "Theodicy," 78).

161. *Lud* 1.57. Oshima (*Poems*, 81) reads "courtiers." Cf. the king's סרכין ("tacticians," Theo τάκτικοι) who try to find in Daniel some sign of שׁלו ("neglect"; Theo πρόφασις, "pretext," Dan 6:5). On the standards expected of royal assistants N.B. the proverb *na-da-nu šá šarri ṭú-ub-bu šá šá-qi-i na-da-nu šá šarri dum-mu-qu šá a-ba-rak-ku*, "Giving pertains to a king, doing well to a cupbearer. Giving pertains to a king, showing favor to a steward" (*BWL* 259.5–8).

162. Cf. the similar prosecutorial tactics of גבריא אלך הרגשו ("the troublemakers") who conspire against Daniel (Dan 6:16; cf. van der Toorn, "Lions," 626–40).

163. *Lud* 1.59. Oshima (*Poems*, 81) reads "I shall make him spill his life." Like Heb נפשׁ, the root meaning of Akk *napištu* is "life," but in some contexts it can mean "livelihood, provisions, sustenance" (*CAD* N/1.302). N.B. the designation *É na-pi-iš-tim* in an OB letter ("house of provisions," *PBS* 7.125.32) and the phrase *É-iš-šu* ("his house") in *Lud* 1.62.

164. *Lud* 1.60. Oshima (*Poems*, 81) reads "I will make him lose his post." Akk ***têrtum*** means "assignment" (*AHw* 1350), but N.B. that at Mari a *bēl têrtum* ("commissioner," *ARM* 1.61.29) works in a *bīt têrtum* ("house of commissions/tollbooth," *ARM* 2.76.31).

165. *Lud* 1.61. Annus and Lenzi (*Ludlul*, 32) read "I will seize his office," but N.B. the phrase *šūtma la ana qí-ip-tim addiššina*, "I did not give them (the textiles) on loan" (*BIN* 6.26.17; cf. *CAD* Q.261).

166. *Lud* 1.62 (lit., "I will enter his house"; the next logical step after "expulsion," 1.50). The same epithet occurs in the Šamaš Hymn (*a-na bīti-šú ul ir-ru-bu šu-nu aḫḫu*^{MEŠ}*-šu*, "nor will his brothers take over his estate," *BWL* 132.117). Cf. *ina qāt qēberiya marra īkim*, "he took the spade from the hand of the one who wished to bury me" (cited in Cohen, *Wisdom*, 34.168.43').

ana ṣi-in-di u bir-ti ú-za-'i-zu mim-ma-a	They (re)distribute my property to commoners and riff-raff;[167]
pi-i ÍD-ia u-man-ṭi-ṭù sa-ki-ka	They silt up the channels in my canals,[168]
ina qer-bé-ti-ia ú-ša-as-su-ú a-la-la	They drive the work-song from my fields,[169]
par-ṣi-ia u-šal-qu-u ša-nam-ma	They let others process my commission,[170]
ù ina pil-lu-de-e-a a-ḫa uš-ziz-zu	They appoint a stranger to my office.[171]

These are serious charges, of course, but in spite of their gravity he still hopes to embrace "prosperity" (*da-me-eq-tum*) someday,[172] grounding his hope on the specious presumption that "prosperity" (*išartu*) always increases[173] whenever "wickedness" (*zapurtu*) decreases.[174]

167. *Lud* 1.99. Oshima (*Poems*, 85) reads "the gang and the riff-raff." On the term *mimmu* ("property, possessions") cf. the Amarna reports *ul la ḫalqu mi-im-mi šarri*, "the property of the king is not lost" (*EA* 96.20) and *kali mi-im-mi* PN, "all the property of PN" (105.25).

168. *Lud* 1.100. One of the complaints of the Igigi-gods is that they have to do "canal duty"; i.e., restore commercial traffic by "digging out the canals" (*i-ḫer-ru-ú nara*, "dredging the river," *Atr* 1.23).

169. *Lud* 1.101. Pecchioli Daddi ("Song," 559–60) examines an antiphonal work-song sung by LÚ^{MEŠ} ^{GIŠ}TUKUL-*uš* ("workers"; lit., "men of the tool/weapon") in a Hittite ritual text (*KBo* 37.68; cf. also the princely warning to noblemen to stop oppressing their "workers" in *KBo* 1.22.3′). Gilgamesh laments the death of Enkidu by listing those who will most likely miss him, including the "farmer" (^{LÚ}*ikkaru*) who reflects upon his "sweet work-song" (*a-la ṭa-a-bi*, *GE* 8.23–24). On *qerbetu* ("field") cf. *nam-maš-še-e* ^{D}*šakkan lik-tamme-re . . . ina qir-bé-te*, "let Šakkan's creatures be gathered into the field" (*BWL* 170.19).

170. *Lud* 1.103 (Akk *parṣu*). Reacting to the multiple nuances embedded in Sum ME and GARZA (*ID* 127–63), *DI* 44–62 compresses them down into the Akk administrative term *parṣu* (cf. *Lud* 4.61).

171. *Lud* 1.104. The word-pair *parṣu/pilludû* ("commission/office") is not uncommon (cf. *Ee* 5.67; *BWL* 78.135).

172. *Lud* 1.119. Akk *dumqu* ("prosperity") appears earlier on the tablet (1.45) in the "prosperity daemon" epithet (^{D}ALAD *dum-qí*; cf. above).

173. *Lud* 2.3. Cf. ^{D}*Ea* ^{D}*Šamaš u* ^{D}*Marduk yâši ruṣannima ina annikunu i-šá-ru-tam lullik*, "Help me, O Ea, Šamaš and Marduk, and give me your blessing so that I may enjoy my prosperity" (*KAR* 267.4′).

174. *Lud* 2.3. This presumption underlies the words of the "friend" in *BT* when he says, *n[a]-ak-di pa-li-iḫ* ^{D}*ištar u-kam-mar ṭuḫ-[da]*, "the humble person who fears Ištar will accumulate wealth" (*BWL* 71.22; *contra* the "sufferer/sceptic's" words in 75.70–71). Von Rad (*Theology* 1.425) depicts this polarized thinking as "old wisdom," what economists today would call "zero-sum" theory (Thurow, *Zero-Sum*, 3–25; Hornborg,

Accused by the *nanzazū* of forsaking his religious duties,[175] he insists that "the day of worship . . . brings delight to my heart,"[176] not so much for religious reasons, but because it affords him an opportunity to remember "the day of Ištar's procession"[177] as a "day of profit and wealth."[178] His detractors fail to see this because they tend to be fickle adolescents accustomed to "reaching up to their god" (*i-ša-an-na-na* DINGIR-*šin*)[179] in times of "compensation" (*i-šib-ba-a-ma*),[180] but fleeing the prospect of "Netherworld descent" (*a-rad ir-kal-lu*) during seasons of "distress" (*ú-táš-šá-šá-ma*).[181]

Eventually securing Marduk's "redemption" (*paṭāru*), Šubši-mešre-šakkan begins the arduous task of "reintegrating into society."[182] Ascertaining what this implies is difficult,[183] yet it hardly seems coincidental that the

---

Exchange, 6–26; Rachman, *Zero-Sum*, 261–78), the socioeconomic cousin to what contemporary theologians call "health-and-wealth" religion (cf. Fee, *Disease*; Bowler, *Blessed*).

175. *Lud* 2.12–24. Caring for the humanoid statues of the gods is an expensive enterprise prone to all sorts of problems (cf. Ep Jer 10–11; Walker and Dick, *Induction*, 3–31).

176. *Lud* 2.25. Markter (*Ezechiel*, 67) documents how deeply the "heart" operates in ANE thinking as a "central notion" (*Zentralbegriff*).

177. *Lud* 2.26, UD-*mu ri-du-ti* ^{D}*ištar*. In light of *a-rad ir-kal-la* ("descending to the Netherworld," 2.47) a few lines down, it's difficult to avoid wondering how much *ri-du-ti* ^{D}*ištar* resonates (intentionally or otherwise) with the "descent" motifs in *ID/DI* (cf. Moore, *WealthWarn*, 4–17).

178. *Lud* 2.26, *ne-me-li ta-at-tur-ru*. Akk *nēmelu* often appears in word-pairs; cf. *ni-me-lu/išdiḫa*, "profit/income" (*BAM* 315.2.7); and *nēmelu/kušīru*, "profit"/"success" (Sidursky, "Prayers," 570.19 ′20-′). Annus and Lenzi (*Ludlul*, 35) read "wealth and weal."

179. *Lud* 2.45 (Akk *šanānu*); cf. *ši-mat-ka la ša-na-an*, "your (Marduk's) destiny is untouchable" (*Ee* 4.4, 6).

180. *Lud* 2.45 (Akk *šebû*); cf. *āšib ali lu rubû ul i-šeb-bi akla*, "the prince who dwells in the city is never satisfied with food" (*Erra* 1.52), and Heb שׂבע (Exod 16:3; Ruth 2:18).

181. *Lud* 1.47. Cf. *la ta-šu-uš u*$_4$*-me-šam-ma*, "You (Šamaš) are not distressed during the day" (*BWL* 129.41). Acknowledging Marduk's success in sparing him from the "pit" (*ḫaštu*, 4.4–5), Šubši-mešre-šakkan is grateful (4.29). In fact, an Akkadian prototype of *Ludlul* at Ugarit shows him praising Marduk for *ultu erṣēti ušēlânni*, "raising me out of the Netherworld" (cited in Cohen, *Wisdom* 168.41). Qur'an also recognizes this all-too-human behavior, noting that when "the Lord is generous" (ربه فاكرمه), this triggers the belief that "he is honoring me" (اكرمن), but when he "tests by restricting provisions" (ابتلاه فقدر عليه رزقه), this leads to the fear that "the Lord 'is disgracing me'" (اهانن, Q 89.15–16).

182. Lenzi ("Gates," 734). Spieckermann (*Theologie*, 106) imagines this reintegration process to be "kultische."

183. When attempting to locate the sociohistorical context of this or any other wisdom text it is critical that readers learn to accept, in Beaulieu's words ("Wisdom," 6), that "the sapiential tradition of ancient Mesopotamia" is not designed to convey historical detail, but "tell us something important about the purpose of wisdom teachings . . . foundational to civilized life."

ritualization of his *paṭāru*-"redemption" involves (a) passing through several "gates," one named "Productivity" (*ḫé-gál-la*),[184] another "Gifts" (*šul-ma-na*),[185] and (b) donating several of his own "gifts" to a now-placated Marduk, including *irbu*,[186] *ṭa'tu*,[187] and *igisû*[188] comprised of "fatted bulls" (*le-e ma-re-e*) and "prized sheep" (*šap-ṭi*).[189] Sociologically the ritual's purpose is to create a recognizable vehicle for individuals to recommit themselves to the Marduk cult.[190] Why is this important? Because, as Jack Barbalet recognizes, "both the micro- and the macro-power structures in any given society are inevitably accompanied by . . . resistance."[191]

Unlike, say, the Mesopotamian "Dialogue of a Man with His God"[192] or the Egyptian "Complaints of Khahkheperre-sonb,"[193] *Ludlul bēl nēmeqi* manipulates several well-worn motifs about *work*, *productivity*, and *wealth*

184. Lud 4.39. Akk *ḫé-gál-lu* (from Sum ḪÉ.GÁL) occurs in one of Hammurabi's titles: *bābil* ḪÉ.GÁL *ana* É.GIŠ.NU$_X$.GAL, "the one who makes the temple (of Sin named) Egišnugal productive" (*CH* 2.20). This term can signify abundance, productivity, or fertility. Cf. ^{D}IM *šārik* ḪÉ.GÁL *ana mati*, "Adad, who gives fertility to the land" (OIP 2.112.7.87, cited in *CAD* Ḫ.168).

185. *Lud* 4.41, 49. Cf. *šul-ma-ni babbanu ana Bēl inandin*, "he (the king) should give an exceptional gift to Bel" (*ABL* 1431.8′). One of the "Prescriptions of Queen Ašmunikkal to the Guardians of the Mausoleum" reads "a dog barks, but when he arrives he is silent" (*KUB* 13.8.7), a proverb Collins ("Animals," 242) attributes to "zealous bureaucrats who 'bark' for payment of a debt they cannot collect from exempted (dead) persons, and so fall silent."

186. *Lud* 4.53. Akk *irbu/erbu* is the nominal form of the verb *erēbu* ("to come in, enter"). Thus *erbu* means "that which comes in"; i.e., "income." Cf. *šumma la išqulu ana bīt* PN *e-re-bu*, "If he does not pay up he will enter into the house of PN" (i.e., "debtor's house," *TCL* 6.68.14; cf. Matt 18:30).

187. *Lud* 4.53. In some lexical lists Sum KADRA is equivalent not only to Akk *ṭa-a-tum* ("purpose gift"), but also to *kadrû* ("bribe") and *šulmānu* ("recompense, reward"; *MSL* 13.113.12; 116.42; *AHw* 1382). Cf. the recurring use of שלם in Job.

188. *Lud* 4.53 (IGI.SÁ). Cf. *igisê*^{e} *šul-ma-ni u-šá-bi-lu šu-nu ana sá-a-šu*, "they (the gods) bring him (Marduk) gifts and presents" (*Ee* 4.134).

189. *Lud* 4.54. Olyan (*Ritual*, 8) acknowledges that even "though we have no access to historically-situated ritual practice, we do have literary representations of texts" in which the "literary representations of rites must also have had some relationship to contemporary practice in order to resonate with their intended audiences."

190. Cf. Sommerfeld (*Aufstieg*, 185–212). Al-Rawi and George ("Sippar," 135–36) publish a NB epistle addressed to Hammurabi's son Šamšu-iluna condemning any priesthood foolish enough to hold itself in higher esteem than the priests of Marduk. Finn (*Marduk*, 37–41) discusses how many times Marduk's statue is violently taken from his temple (Esagila), and the impact of these thefts on Babylonian life.

191. Barbalet ("Power," 532).

192. Cf. Foster (*Muses*, 148–50); Sitzler (*Vorwurf*, 61–71).

193. *AEL* 1.145–49.

in order to produce a text designed to show how challenging it can be to find a theological balance between retribution and reality.[194]

SUMMARY

The book of Job ardently contrasts compensation/retribution with disinterested piety, a recurring polarity which suggests that this "great text" is not so much polyphonic as it is dimorphic.[195] The questions preoccupying the ANE texts above much resemble those preoccupying Job's "friends," but it remains difficult to find a single text, apart from the Joban Prologue, which clearly features the disinterested piety motif. Why? Is it because punishment is always easier to dispense than forgiveness? For Mark Hamilton the book of Deuteronomy is the "linchpin of the Old Testament,"[196] but the book of Job may well be (to borrow an image from Robert Frost) a "masque of revolt"[197] against the "simplistic Deuteronomistic view of historical process."[198]

Nevertheless Joel Kaminsky is wise to caution against over-marginalizing "key aspects of the Bible's understanding of the economy of divine recompense" because the issue is "quite a bit more complex than commonly asserted by many contemporary interpreters."[199] In point of fact the principles of (deutero)nomistic law demand far less energy to process than the issues debated in the dialogical wisdom texts generally and Job in particular. James Kwon emphasizes that "the book of Job prominently portrays the motif of the pious sufferer in Job's confrontations with 'friends' enamored of the retribution principle" and that "these distinct features . . . may reflect a critical and belittling idea of Deuteronomic Torah." However, in no way do they "deny the entire concept of Torah and traditional laws about divine judgment."[200]

194. This is not the only way to read this text, of course. Focusing on Šubši-mešre-šakkan's desire to praise Marduk and the community's desire to "welcome him back," Oshima (*Poems*, 28–34) explains the poem's *raison d'être* from a purely cultic perspective.

195. *Pace* Newsom (*Job*, 1).

196. Hamilton ("Deuteronomy," 207).

197. Terrien (*Presence*, 361); cf. Frost ("Masque," 473–90).

198. *CMHE* 344. For Koch ("Gibt es ein Vergeltungsdogma," 1; ET = "Is There a Doctrine of Retribution"), "it is when scepticism gains the upper hand that there is a radical reassessment of the concept that there is a powerful sphere of influence in which the built-in consequences of an action take effect." Job and Qohelet are the predominant Tanak texts responsible for maintaining such healthy scepticism.

199. Kaminsky ("Recompense," 303).

200. Kwon ("Job," 49).

5

The Compensation/Retribution Motif in Early Joban Tradition

Mark Larrimore observes that the (post)modern age is "the only period in history where Job is widely available in translations without commentary and marketed on its own as a freestanding book," and that this explains why so many view the book today as "implicitly self-sufficient."[1] Close examination of the book itself, however, reveals that it is not all that "clearly defined" or "self-interpreting."[2] Every generation finds in Job something of value, even when important aspects of its theological profile are overlooked.

Second Temple sages, moreover, tend to "endorse a reward and punishment theodicy of the kind articulated by Job's counselors,"[3] so given the opaque complexities of rabbinic tradition, it comes as no surprise that discussion about the early Joban tradition often occurs in the shadow of a dark, blurry cloud.[4] Rabbinic readers tend to avoid anything which might

1. Larrimore (*Job*, 26–27).

2. Cf. Schniedewind (*Book*, 3); and Fishbane ("Job," 86–98). Citing Bakhtin, Newsom (*Job*, 263) warns about the "danger of trying to summarize an (ongoing) conversation."

3. Mittleman ("Job," 26). According to R. Ami, e.g., "there is no death without sin and no suffering without transgression" (*b. Šabb.* 55a). Curiously, Job himself seems to side with his counselors, esp. in his farewell speech (e.g., Job 30:1–8; cf. Hamilton, "Elite," 69–89). Magdalene ("Job," 23) accurately concludes that "the theological idea that human disability, disease, and disaster stem from human sin is very ancient and continues to hold sway in some theological circles." According to John 9:1–3 the Nazarene sage rejects this association outright.

4. Schiffman (*Traditions*, 1) notes that "the historian of Judaism faces a special challenge in that the very resources which must be used to trace the complex history of Jewish civilization are, at the same time, not only witnesses to that history but reflections of it." Cf. Moore (*WealthWatch* 168–70).

be construed as "sanctifying" Job's character because of "his attitude of defiance towards God. Rather than justifying God's ways, even when morally unintelligible, Job requires that God justify them to him.[5] This claim on God, as Job himself learns, has its limits. It is not, in a tradition as polyphonic as Judaism, *ipso facto* wrong. But neither is it *ipso facto* right."[6]

Painstakingly working his way through the midrashim,[7] Dov Weiss comes to a similar conclusion, noting that while most rabbis refuse to criticize their heroes, some do, even when "no such criticism appears in Scripture."[8] Christian exegetes, on the other hand, tend to reject *any* criticism of their biblical heroes, sometimes to the point of postulating that "protests against God cannot occur."[9] As noted above, Pohl's dissertation contests this approach because (a) Job's lament in chapter 3 is as much a "protest speech" as it is a Jeremianic lament,[10] so (b) the "submission-protest" polarity cannot capture the full impact of this "great text."[11]

Second Temple reactions to Job come in several shapes and sizes, but the pages below will not examine them all. Instead the focus will be delimited to two major texts: the Targum of Job (TgJob) and the Testament of Job (TJob). The first is an early semitic response to MT Job[12] while the second, like OG Job,[13] is prototypically Hellenistic.[14]

5. Cf. Job 42:4.

6. Mittleman ("Job" 26–27). N.B. that Job makes two demands of God: (a) that "you take your hands off me" (כפך מעלי הרחק); and (b) that "I will speak, and you will answer me" (אדבר והשיבני; Job 13:20–22).

7. To make matters more complex Kalman ("*Iyov*," 77–81) notes how difficult it can be to distinguish tannaitic from amoraic texts (cf. Wiggins, *Tannaim*).

8. Weiss ("Protesting," 391–92).

9. Weiss ("Protesting," 392).

10. *Pace* Linafelt ("Black," 1–5).

11. Pohl (*Job*, 129).

12. Mangan (*Job*, 5) observes that "the targum of Job is one of the most enigmatic of targums: while a targum of the book of Job was discovered among the Dead Sea Scrolls (11QtgJob), this text bears little resemblance to the later Rabbinic targum known to us from the printed editions of the Bible." Klein (*Essays*, 50) notes that "with the discovery of fragments of three targumic texts at Qumran (4QtgLev, 4Qtg Job, and 11QtgJob) there is no longer any doubt about *written* targums as early as the 1st century CE," but Muraoka ("Qumran," 425–43) pushes the date back to 250–150 BCE on linguistic grounds. Weiss (איוב, ix) and Mangan (*Job*, 5–8) argue that in its final form TgJob is likely to be a composite of various targums written over several periods, and Shepherd (*Job*, 259–86) recognizes the stylistic and linguistic differences to be considerable.

13. Gammie ("Job," 30–31) challenges Gerleman's (*Job*, 14–17) hypothesis that the Greek translator of Job and the Greek translator of Proverbs are the same person or come from the same scribal community.

14. Cf. Gray ("Septuagint," 331–50); Schaller ("Hiob," 377–406); Haas ("Perseverance," 151–52); Hengel (*"Hellenization"*); Haag (*Zeitalter*); and Spittler ("Job," 829–68).

TARGUM JOB

Early in the sixteenth century (CE) a medieval rabbi named Ya`akov ibn Chaviv compiled an abridged Talmud,[15] doubtless for the same reason that contemporary editors still publish abridged texts—to make unwieldy seminal texts more accessible to a larger readership.[16] Abridgements, however, come with pros and cons. On the one hand they introduce readers to unabridged texts without overwhelming them, while on the other hand this very convenience often vaccinates them against any desire to engage the original texts themselves. At any rate, one passage in Chaviv's abridged Talmud preserves a childhood memory of R. Yose ben Yehuda:

> Once on a visit to Tiberias my father found R. Gamaliel sitting at the table of R. Yoḥanan holding a Job scroll written in Aramaic. Thereupon my father said to him, "I remember the time when I met your grandfather standing on the steps of the Temple mound when a Job scroll written in Aramaic was brought to him, whereupon he told the builder to bury the scroll beneath the Temple mound." Upon hearing this R. Gamaliel ordered the Aramaic scroll on R. Yoḥanan's table to be buried.[17]

Ben Yehuda cites this story in a Talmudic debate over what to do with sacred texts translated into languages other than the "holy tongue" (Hebrew).[18] Should they be "rescued from the fire" or "buried?"[19] Some rabbis lean toward the first option while others, like R. Gamaliel and Yose ben Yehudah, lean toward the second.[20]

TgJob Prologue

Whatever its religious status, however, TgJob is one of the most important contributors to the early Joban tradition. With the Prosecutor's question in Job 1:9, for example, TgJob reads:

15. Finkel, *Yaakov*.

16. Karl Barth's *Dogmatik in Grundriss*, e.g., is a one-volume abridgment of his fourteen-volume *Kirchliche Dogmatik*.

17. *b. Šabb.* 115a (cf. Finkel, *Yaakov*, 112).

18. לשון קודש (*b. Šabb.* 115a). According to the psalmist every language except Hebrew is לעז ("strange, unintelligible, foreign," Ps 114:1).

19. *m. Šabb.* 16.1.

20. Even the most nominal comparison between MT Job and TgJob shows why R. Gamaliel and R. Yose hesitate to revere the latter.

ואתיב סטנא קדם יי ואמר	The *satan* returned an answer before Yhwh,[21] saying,
האפשר די למגן איוב דחל קדם יי	"Is it possible that Job's fear of Yhwh comes without compensation?"[22]
הלא מימרך טללתא אמטולתיה	Has your Memra not built a protective shelter around him,[23]
ואמטול ביתיה ואמטול כל די ליה	A protective shelter around his household,[24] and a protective shelter around everything he has?"[25]

Later, at the second meeting of the divine council the heavenly Judge again invites the Prosecutor to assess Job's piety, noting that in spite of his suffering,

הוא מתקף בשלימותיה עוד כדון	He still holds fast to his integrity,
וגרית ביה וסלעמותיה מגן	Though you incited my Memra against him to destroy him "for no reason."[26]

Near the end of the Prologue, however, Job's spouse forwards an alternative suggestion:

21. TgJob 1.9a. N.B. that TgJob assigns to this council meeting a specific time; viz., "on the day of judgment at the first of the year . . . at the place of judgment before Yah" (TgJob 1.6). In fact, as Mangan (*Job*, 25) points out, TgJob "usually makes explicit Hebrew's 'one day'—here to New Year's day when good and evil deeds are brought before the Lord to be judged."

22. TgJob 1.9b. Aram מגן translates MT חנם. In Talmud מגן describes the importance of paying physicians for their services because אסיא דמגן במגן מגן שוא, "a physician who heals 'at no compensation' (במגן) is useless" (שוא, *b. B. Qam.* 85a). N.B. the trifold repetition of מגן here in parallel with the adjective שוא ("useless, in vain").

23. TgJob 1.10. In contrast to MT הלא אתה שׂכת בעדו ("have you not put a hedge around him"), TgJob omits the personal pronoun for the deity, inserting instead the buffering term מימר (Memra; lit., "word"; from ימר, "to speak") in a common rabbinic technique for "obviating anthropomorphism" (*DTTM* 775). Another example occurs in TgJob 1.11 (MT ידך, "your hand" becomes מחת ידך, "plague of your hand"). Mangan (*Job*, 6–7) lists several more examples while Klein (הגשמת, 135–39) and Cook ("Targums," 104) recognize that 11QtgJob tends to go out of its way to avoid circumlocutions for the deity (cf. discussion in Shepherd, "Job," 401–4).

24. TgJob 1.10 (lit., "his houses").

25. TgJob 1.10. N.B. the trifold use of the nominal form אמטול (from Aram טלל, "to cover over") denoting Job's three losses in reverse order.

26. TgJob 2.3. N.B. (a) another buffering insertion of מימר, particularly in reference to divine anger (McCarter, "Temper," 78–91), and (b) that TgJob again translates MT חנם with Aram מגן, a term which, like MT חנם, can semantically straddle the economic—non-economic divide.

עד כדון את מתקף בשלימותך	Are you still stumbling over your integrity?[27]
בריך מימרא דיי ומית	Curse the Memra of Yhwh and die![28]

To this her husband retorts:

היכמא די ממללן חדא מן נשיא דעבדין	Why do you jabber on like some silly servant-girl,
קלנא בבית אבהתהון	Shaming the house of your ancestors?[29]
הכדין את ממללא לחוד טבא נקבל מן קדם יי	Since we deem it expedient to receive a good word from the Presence of Yhwh,
וית בישא לא נקבל	Should we not also accept the bad?[30]

TgJob Dialogues

TgJob Prologue does not stray far from MT Prologue, but things begin to change in the Dialogues. In Eliphas' first speech, for example, TgJob inserts the names of several celebrities in what appears to be a pastel shellacking of Eliphas' retribution theology.[31] For example, the rhetorical questions in MT Job 4:7 now read:

אדכר כדון מן דזכי כאברהם הובדו	Who among the innocent—like Abraham—ever perishes?
האן תריצין כיצחק ויעקב אתכחדו	Who among the upright—like Isaac or Jacob—suffers ruin?[32]

27. TgJob 2.9 נקף ("to stumble"). MT reads חזק ("to cling").

28. TgJob 2:9. Tg follows MT in the deployment of ברך ("to bless"; so also Mangan, *Job*, 26), but whether or not this is a circumlocution remains unresolved in spite of the fact that (a) the majority of ETs read with Syr ܓܕܦ ("to revile, curse"); and (b) there are other examples of circumlocution in TgJob (Noegel, "Janus," 315).

29. TgJob 2.10.

30. TgJob 2.10 (cf. Shepherd, "Targum," 401–4). Doubtless TgJob preserves the words uttered by Job in MT Job 2:10 in order to retain the primacy of the "disinterested piety" motif.

31. This is not an isolated incident. In this targum (like all targums) the line between history and hagiography can sometimes be blurry. In TgJob 32.2, e.g., Elihu is the son of Barachel the Buzite from the clan of Abraham, not Ram.

32. TgJob 4.7. Inserting the names of these Torah celebrities makes Eliphas look much less naive than the character in MT Job 4:7.

The "predator-prey" imagery which follows continues this celebrity name insertion strategy:

אכליות דעשׂו דמתיל לאריא טרפא	The roar of Esau[33] is like that of a young lion over its prey
וקלא אדם דמתיל לשחלא	The growl of Edom[34] is like that of a fierce lion.
מרתיחין כדביא בחטופיהון	Like that of wolves stalking their victims.[35]
ורברבנוי דמתילין לליתא מתפרשׁין למבז בזתא	These leaders[36] accumulate spoil like lions,
היכמה דאריה יהובד מדלית עדאה	But just as the lion starves without spoil,
היכדין יהובד ישמעאל מדלית זכותא	So also does Ishmael perish without significance
ובנוי לסטיא אתפרשׁו מן אורחין תריצין	As his thieving sons forsake the honorable paths.[37]

Louis Ginzberg lists several reasons why rabbinic texts insert celebrity names,[38] but the names here appear to be inserted for a specific reason; viz., to temper and soften the harshness of Eliphas' payback perfectionism.[39]

More celebrity names appear in Eliphas' second speech:

לחוד אברהם דסיב ויצחק דקשׁישׁ בנא	Now Abraham, who is grey, and Isaac, who is old, have mentored us,
ויעקב דרב מאבוך יומיא	As well as Jacob, a man much older than your father.[40]

33. TgJob 4.10 (some mss read שׂעיר, "Seʿir"). Gen 36:33–34 assigns to Jobab the kingship of Edom and TJob 1.6 shows Jobab descending from the sons of Esau (cf. Bartlett, *Edomites*, 23–35).

34. TgJob 4.10 (some mss omit).

35. TgJob 4.10, reading כ ("like/as") + דב ("wolf").

36. TgJob 4.10 (lit., "great ones"; cf. Eg *wr* in *TEP* 144).

37. TgJob 4.11. Mangan (*Job*, 31) reads Aram לסטיא as a transliteration of Gk λῃστής ("thief"; cf. 5.5).

38. Ginzberg (*Legends* 5.381–84). Tropper (*Simeon*, 114) documents the insertions of celebrity names into several rabbinic texts while Noam (*Images*, 32–58) discusses the significance of their omission.

39. Dunham (*Sage*, 13–14) prefers the phrase "theological legalism."

40. TgJob 15.10 (some mss omit these names; others read the names of Job's three "friends" in MT—Eliphaz, Bildad, and Zophar). In Q 15.54, Ibrahim asks whether the three visitors announcing Sarah's pregnancy (Gen 18:1–15) are there to take advantage of his الكبر, "old age" (lit., "greatness [of years]).

Other names pop up as well.[41] In a lengthy passage describing the fate of the wicked, for example, Eliphas makes a bold comparison:

לא יתעתד ולא יתקים עתריה דקרח	They will not accumulate wealth, for the riches of Korah will not last,
ולא יתמחת לארעא מנהון ומהלין טבתא דדתן ואבירם	But will be driven off the land with the possessions of Dathan and Abiram.[42]

As Ginzberg observes, there are several ways to explain the insertion of celebrity names into the targums, but the most likely rationale here seems to be that they help temper this professor's legalism. In TgJob 15.31, for example, the Aramaic translator inserts a term expressly designed to reinforce this intention:

לא יהימין בבר נש דבשקרא	The wicked trust none who wallow in deceit
תעי ארום שקרא תהי פרוגיה	For deceit is their "compensation."[43]

This strategy continues into the speeches of Baldad. For example, Bildad's infamous "your-children-died-because-they-deserved-it" remark now reads:

אפשר דאלהא יעקם דינא	Is it possible for God to circumvent the law?
ואם שדי יקלקל צדקא	Or for Šadday to pervert justice?[44]

41. E.g., Lot, Egypt, Israel, Pharaoh, Amalek, Balaam, Midian, Sihon, Og, and the Flood generation. TgJob 4.8 even includes דרא דטובענא עבדי שקרא ופלחי לעות ישתלמין ("the generation of the Flood, servants of deceit and worshipers of vain idols"). Mangan (*Job*, 14) dutifully observes that in spite of its dramatics this last example "completely misses the point of the Hebrew text" because it replaces the ploughing-sowing-reaping sequence in MT with "another reality"; viz., "the moralistic interpretation of the targumist" (*Gen. Rab.* 26.7 unapologetically continues this line of "interpretation").

42. TgJob 15.29. MT Job 15.29 reads simply ולא יטה לארץ מנלם ("and they will not plant their possessions in the land"); cf. Syr ܠܐ ܢܥܬܪ؛ ܘܠܐ ܢܩܘܡ ܩܢܝܢܗ ܘܠܐ ܢܫܡܠܐ ܥܠ ܐܪܥܐ ("they are not rich, their wealth will not endure, and they will not fully develop the land"); OG οὐ μὴ βάλῃ ἐπὶ τὴν γῆν σκιὰν ("they will not cast a shadow upon the land"); Vg *nec mittet in terra radicem suam* ("they will not plant their roots in the land").

43. TgJob 15.31. Aram פירוג ("compensation, price") translates MT תמורה ("substitute, exchange"). Cf. Syr ܫܘܡܠܝܗ ("his growth"); OG κενὰ γὰρ ἀποβήσεται αὐτῷ ("for emptiness will be his result"); Vg *redimendus sit* ("are redeemed"). The fact that TgJob so frequently gravitates to Aram פירוג ("compensation"; cf. TgDeut 23.19) is more than a little significant. N.B. how it is used to translate MT מרה ("rebellion," Job 17:2), תמורה ("exchange," 15:31; 20:18), and מחיר ("price," 28:15).

44. TgJob 8.3 (קלקל, lit., "to disorder, disarrange"). MT repeats the same verb in each line (עות, "to bend, falsify"), but TgJob uses a pair of synonyms because, as Mangan

אין בניך חבו קדמוי	If your children sinned against him
ושדרינון באתר מרדיהון	He dispatched them for their rebellion.[45]

Maintaining the (in)digestion metaphor,[46] Sophar continues this shellacking over strategy:

יהי ימםלי כרסיה יגרי ביה תקוף רוגזיה	To fill their belly to the full God will stir his anger into them,
בשלדיה דפרוגי עלוי מטרין ויחת	Releasing onto their corpses the rains of "recompense."[47]

As indicated above, Elihu's second speech in MT focuses on three concerns: (a) defending the deity's "honor"; (b) defending the integrity of the "righteous"; and (c) defending the need for a Righteous Judge to maintain order over a chaotic cosmos.[48] With regard to the last of these points TgJob reads:

והוא ישדיך ומן יחיב	If the heavenly Judge is silent who will convict?
ויסלק שכנתא ומן יסכניה	If he removes the Šekinah[49] who will despair
ומסער חובא על עמא	When he imposes guilt on both community
ועל בר נש כחדא	And individual alike?[50]

(*Job*, 14) points out, "one of the features of the parallelism of the poetry of the Book of Job is the exact repetition of the same word in the two parts of the verse," whereas "the targumist . . . translates these differently."

45. TgJob 8.4. MT reads ביד פשעם וישלחם ("he drafted them into the power of their transgression"; so OG, Vg, and Syr). Gordis (*Job*, 88) emends MT ביד ("into the hand") to בעד ("after, behind") in what appears to be an attempt to spotlight TgJob's shellacking over of MT Job.

46. Crenshaw (*Job*, 105) recognizes that the (in)digestion metaphor dominates Zophar's thinking.

47. TgJob 20.23 (cf. Ezek 37:1–14). TgJob here uses Aram פרוג ("compensation," see above) to translate the common Heb term לחם ("bread, food"). Rather than translating לחם with a similarly common Aram term like, say, אוכל ("food"), it instead goes out of its way to choose a term designed to echo the "compensation/retribution" motif.

48. To review, MT Elihu here responds to Job's increasingly angry critique of the deity's job performance.

49. TgJob 34.29. Replacing MT פנים ("face") with שכנתא ("the Šekinah") is another instance of Tg's desire to "obviate anthropomorphism" (*DTTM* 775; Ginzberg, *Legends*, 2.260). Wolfson ("Shekinah," 8312–13) reports that שכנה "is derived from the root שכן, which means 'to dwell, to abide,' and thus is functionally synonymous with כבוד, the Heb term most often used to designate divine 'glory,' the revelatory aspect of God that assumes material form—most often of a luminous nature—in relation to the people of Israel." Cf. Ezek 1:1—10:18.

50. TgJob 34.30 (lit., "the people and the son of man"). Cf. the individual (*TEP*) vs. community (*DILA*) focus in Egyptian wisdom.

ממני מלכא בר נש דילטור	If he establishes a human king as prosecutor[51]
מטול תקליא די בעמא	Over a wayward populace
אפשר די מעמך ישלמנה	Do you think his compensation/retribution will depend on your permission?[52]

Summary

Like MT Job, the "compensation/retribution" motif plays a significant role in TgJob. In light of the examples just cited, this seems most likely to be because of TgJob's desire to temper—not reject, only temper—the retributional thinking of Job's counselors, doubtless to help his Aramaic-speaking audience develop a theological understanding of the book less clear-cut than the original.[53]

TESTAMENT OF JOB

Unlike TgJob, TJob is not a translation or a commentary, but a text belonging to a specialized literary genre called διαθήκη ("testament").[54] The characters wear the same names as those in MT Job, but the roles they enact are very different, as is the plotline. As Pieter van der Horst puts it, the story in TJob relies on "little more than the framework of the biblical story."[55]

51. TgJob 34.30. As Mangan (*Job*, 37) points out, דילטור is probably a transliteration of the Gk word δηλητήρ ("destroyer," *LSJ* 384). Noting its repeated appearance in TgJob 8.13; 13.16; 15.34; 17.8; 20.5; 27.8; 34.30; and 36.13, she consistently translates it as "accuser" (*DTTM* 299, "informer, sycophant"), but whether דילטור refers to an historical individual or reflects, however subtly, the Prosecutor's activity in the Joban Prologue are questions needing further investigation.

52. TgJob 34.33.

53. Gordon (*Versions*, xxx) recognizes the "moralizing tendencies of the Targums" with regard to theological concerns, especially "reward (and) retribution," and Scarlata (*Eden*, 118–19, 223) discusses the ins and outs of "haggadic expansion" in the targums generally.

54. Charlesworth ("Introduction," 773) argues that

> no binding genre is employed by the authors of the testaments, but one can discern among them a loose format: The ideal figure faces death and causes his relatives and intimate friends to circle around his bed. He occasionally informs them of his fatal flaw and exhorts them to avoid certain temptations, (and) typically instructs them regarding the way of righteousness.

In a careful study of the Coptic and Slavonic versions of TJob, Haralambakis (*Job*, 37) observes that neither version entitles the book "The Testament of Job," nor does the term διαθήκη ("testament") appear in the title of every Greek manuscript.

55. Horst ("Women," 93). The whirlwind speeches, e.g., do not appear in TJob at all,

This pseudepigraphal text does not even allude to the disinterested piety motif, but instead focuses on whether the "athlete of endurance" (Job)[56] has enough spiritual strength to withstand the evil machinations of Satan (capital "S"),[57] the antagonist who operates not as a courtroom prosecutor, but as ὁ διάβολος (the Devil). As John Collins puts it, the TJob story "is no longer one of passive suffering, but of active conflict between Satan and Job."[58] Unlike the MT protagonist, the protagonist in TJob never has to fumble about in the dark looking for an explanation for his suffering.[59] Instead, as Susan Garrett observes, his "existential crisis in the face of suffering is completely eliminated" because now he "understands precisely what is happening to him."[60] Overstating the issue only slightly, Berndt Schaller calls TJob "the most important and most comprehensive witness to the haggadic Job tradition in ancient Judaism."[61]

TJob is a Hellenistic novella designed to fill in the gaps and smooth out the wrinkles in MT Job,[62] doubtless to refashion it into something more

---

even though they are what McKeating ("Job," 244) calls the "dramatic climax" of MT Job.

56. TJob 4.8. "I am your father Job, fully engaged in "patient endurance" (ὑπομονή; cf. TJob 1.5; Rev 13:10; 14:12).

57. TJob 3.6. Other names describing this character are "the devil" (ὁ διάβολος, TJob 3.3; 26.6), "the evil one" (ὁ πόνηρος, 7.1; 20.2; cf. Brock, *Iobi, ad loc.*), "the wretched one" (ὁ πενιχρός, 27.1), and "the enemy" (ὁ ἐχθρός [47.10]).

58. Collins ("Testaments," 349).That Joban tradition so quickly defaults to a Satan-vs.-God polarity like the one here in TJob helps explain why so many translators read השׂטן in MT Job 1:6 as the PN "Satan." Whether consciously or not, the dualistic allure is "simply" too strong to resist. Cf. Frey ("Dualismus," 3–46); Kinet ("Ambiguity," 30–35); Duhaime ("Dualism," 215–20); Qimron ("Dualism," 195–202); Stuckenbruck ("Dualism," 145–68); and Schäfer (*Gods*).

59. Haralambakis (*Job*, 19). Rahnenführer ("Hiob," 70) surveys some of the ways in which TJob deviates from MT.

60. Garrett ("Job," 56).

61. Schaller ("Hiob," 377). Recognizing several parallels between TJob and Tobit, Trotter ("Job," 450) notes (a) that "each text highlights the righteousness of its protagonist, particularly by including an exceptional emphasis on his charity before and after his afflictions; (b) that there are striking correspondences in the testaments given by Job and Tobit in their basic structure and their exhortation to charity; and (c) that the wives in each story have to work in order to provide for their husbands during the periods of their afflictions, a circumstance that eventually results in a confrontation between each husband and his wife."

62. Alter (*Canon*, 27) thinks that had the Aramaic and Greek translations of Job been available to the canonizers, "it is rather unlikely that they would have felt impelled to put (it) in the Bible." One of the most obvious examples of a contemporary retelling of biblical narrative is *The Da Vinci Code*, author Dan Brown's sensationalized take on the Christian story from a postmodern, agnostic perspective.

palatable to a Greek-speaking audience.[63] Introducing the protagonist as a dying patriarch named Job(ab),[64] the story begins with a pronouncement of his last will and testament in a format quite different from that housing the ANE dialogical literature.[65] The action starts in earnest when Job, in response to a mysterious nocturnal voice,[66] asks "the Lord" (ὁ κύριος) for the "authority" (ἐξουσία)[67] to "purge" (καθαρίζω) an "idol" (εἴδωλος) from a nearby shrine called "the place of Satan" (ὁ τόπος τοῦ σατανᾶ).[68] This action triggers all the action which follows, as Satan responds to Job(ab)'s purge by seizing his possessions, killing his children, humiliating his spouse, and afflicting him with boils.[69]

After a few more introductory remarks the next chapters show Job(ab) reflecting on the successes of his life, particularly his philanthropy, his hospitality, his charities, his piety, even his musicianship,[70] particularly his custom of playing the ten-string guitar for the widows in his care at their daily

63. Guffy ("Job," 215–16) tries to go a step further: "The Testament of Job has sometimes been thought an anemic little book. It appears to flatten all the delicious ambiguity and tension of the book of Job, especially with respect to questions of theodicy." Yet "the Testament of Job attempts to resolve the tensions of the book of Job over questions of theodicy by appealing to philosophical training in patience and culminating in contact with the divine through mystical transformation."

64. TJob 2.1 reads, 'Εγὼ γαρ εἰμι Ιωβαβ πρὶν ὀνομάσαι με ὁ κύριος Ιωβ ("I was Jobab before the Lord named me Job"). Whether this Jobab is related to the Edomite king in Gen 36:33 seems likely, if not absolutely certain. Cf. Spittler ("Job," 831–32); Kolenkow ("Testament," 259–67); and Collins ("Literature," 268–85).

65. Bloch ("*Aseneth*," 1–28) notes how Greek novellas like Joseph and Aseneth (*OTP* 2.177–247) often retell biblical stories from expository perspectives beyond the parameters of conventional midrashic expectation.

66. TJob 3.1. Cf. Eliphaz's "night spirit" in Job 4:15, about which Crenshaw (*Wisdom*, 102) remarks, "Eliphaz refers to God's spirit that whispers within the ear as sufficient directive."

67. TJob 3.6. Satan later returns the favor by asking for "authority" (ἐξουσία) over Job's possessions (TJob 8.2).

68. TJob 3.6; 5.2; 4.4. In 3.6 the text reads ὁ τόπος τοῦ σατανᾶ ἐν ᾧ ἀπατηθήσονται οἱ ἄνθρωποι ("the place of Satan in which people are deceived"; cf. συναγωγῆς τοῦ σατανᾶ, "synagogue of Satan" in Rev 2:9; 3:9).

69. TJob 4.4–5 (in an order, again, differing from that found in MT/OG/Syr/Vg). In 4.4 the Lord warns Job that "if you put your hand to purge the place of Satan" (ἔαν ἐπιχειρήσεις καθαρίσαι τὸν τόπον τοῦ Σατανᾶ), he "will rise up against you with wrath for battle" (ἐπαναστήσεταί σοι μετὰ ὀργῆς εἰς πόλεμον. Cf. Enlil's infliction of drought, famine, plague and flood [*Atr* 1.352-end; Longman and Walton, *Flood*, 55–59]).

70. TJob 9–15. Spittler ("Job," 842) calls this "typical midrashic embellishment . . . magnifying the pious generosities of Job," and Gregory (*Generosity*, 291–94) spotlights similarly typical embellishment at the beginning of Tobit (Tob 1.6–9).

meal.[71] What's significant about this is that already in this early aside TJob reflects the influence of the "compensation/retribution" motif. To curtail the widows' habit of "contemptuous grumbling" (τῆς ὀλιγωρίας τοῦ γογγυσμοῦ), for example, he daily ministers to them via performances he matter-of-factly calls "the wages of compensation" (τὸν μισθὸν τῆς ἀνταποδόσεως).[72]

Job and Satan

After the destruction of his shrine Satan disguises himself as a pauper, marches over to Job's house, knocks on the front door, and begs for bread.[73] Prior to this Job tells his servants not to let anyone disturb him, but feeling pity for this "beggar" the doormaid opens the door anyway. Always willing to feed the poor,[74] Job then gives her a burnt loaf for the beggar,[75] but as she takes it out to him she suffers a panic attack of "shame" (αἰδέομαι)[76] powerful enough to persuade her to replace Job's stale burnt loaf with a fresh unburnt loaf from her own pantry. Rather than thanking her for her generosity, Satan seizes on her behavior to accuse her of disobedience, to the point of calling her a κακὴ δουλή ("evil servant").[77] Technically his accusation is correct: she *has* disobeyed her master. But context is everything. To criticize this servant so harshly right after receiving her help spotlights one of this "beggar's" most sinister roles—*prosecutor*.[78] Unlike, say, the words of the risen Christ to the Laodiceans, he has no interest whatsoever in "disciplining" (παιδεύω) her in a spirit of "love" (φίλια).[79]

Susan Garrett presumes that all female characters in TJob are intentionally drawn to look like Eve in that each obsesses over things "earthly"

71. TJob 14.2 (τὸ τρέφεσθαι τὰς χήρας, "the feeding of the widows").

72. TJob 14.4. Herodotus (*Hist.* 1.18) uses the root of this term (ἀποδείκνυμι) to describe how the Chians support the Milesians in their war against the Lydians because the Milesians stood by them earlier in their conflict with the Erythraeans.

73. TJob 6.1–6.

74. Cf. Portier-Young ("Job," 14–27).

75. TJob 7.3. Job gives him food because he "does not want to be accused of not providing for a begging enemy" (TJob 7.11; cf. Prov 25:21a; Rom 12:20). That is, he does not want to be convicted of wrongdoing on a technicality.

76. TJob 7.5.

77. TJob 7.7–8.

78. For a literary parallel, N.B. that Inspector Javert in *Les Misérables* (p. 1190) kills himself because of his inability/unwillingness to accept Valjean's forgiveness.

79. Rev 3:19. N.B. that Elihu, "inspired by Satan" (ἐμπνευσθεὶς ἐν τῷ σατανᾷ), speaks "insulting words" (λόγους θρασεῖς) to Job in TJob 41.5–6. Just as MT Job stereotypes Job's spouse, so TJob stereotypes Elihu.

instead of "heavenly."[80] Imagining chapters 44–53 as material based on an underlying source different from the one underlying chapters 1–43, van der Horst excludes Job's daughters from this assessment,[81] but Garrett argues convincingly that their exclusion has nothing to do with source criticism, but with the fact that the hearts of Job's daughters have already "changed" (ἀλλοιόω)[82] to "another heart (ἄλλην καρδίαν) . . . detached from worldly things" (ἀφισταμένη τῶν κοσμικῶν).[83]

The question here, however, is twofold: (a) What causes her to feel ashamed? and (b) Why is Satan's response to criticize her after receiving her gift? From the perspective of the present study the answer by now should be obvious. Rather than overlooking her disobedience in response to her overlooking his "helplessness," Satan instead undermines her because it is his basic nature—he is always looking for "chinks in the armor." Like Inspector Javert in *Les Misérables*, nothing in his nature resonates on any level with the reality of *grace*.[84] As Miroslav Volf puts it, "Not all people who experience forgiveness are transformed by it. After having been forgiven, Javert cannot forgive because the rules to which he has bound himself do not allow him to be merciful."[85] On the contrary, graceless characters sometimes view pain as an invitation to complain. In *The Problem of Pain*, C. S. Lewis reveals a deeply empathetic understanding of this reality: "I am not arguing that pain is not painful. Pain hurts. That is what the word means. I am only trying to show that the old Christian doctrine of 'being made perfect through suffering' is not incredible."[86] *Question:* Is Satan's prosecution of the doormaid a one-time occurrence or does it not reflect something alluded to in MT Job; viz., the prosecutorial spirit displayed by Job's Prosecutor, spouse, and "friends?" One need only glance at the MT Dialogues to see that because of this spirit these characters make no effort whatsoever to help him navigate

80. TJob 36.3. Bergant (*Wisdom*, 41–42) cautions against turning Job into an insensitive chauvinist, pointing out that his impatience extends to his "friends" as well as his spouse. Garrett ("Job," 70), however, finds the nameless doormaid and Job's wife to be "agents of Satan" because he uses each to accomplish his will.

81. Horst ("Women," 93–116).

82. Garrett ("Job," 57), e.g., Kasia (TJob 49.1), and Amaltheia's Horn (50.2).

83. TJob 50.2 (Bergant, *Wisdom*, 41–42).

84. Hugo, *Misérables*, 1190. By contrast, Heb חסד ("grace, loyalty, kindness") stands at the very heart of Boaz's actions toward the widows Naomi and Ruth (cf. Moore, "Ruth," 303–5; Sakenfeld, *Ḥesed*, 233–40).

85. Volf (*Free*, 204).

86. Lewis (*Pain*, 105, 107, citing Heb 2:10). Cf. MT Elihu's understanding of "grace" (חנה) as a first step toward healing (Job 33:24), a motif conspicuously absent in TJob's brief reference to him.

the worst crisis of his life, but choose instead to accuse him of arrogance and wickedness.

Job and His Wife

Whereas MT minimizes the activity of Job's wife, TJob maximizes it. Opinion is divided over why this is so, as well as the exact nature of the sequential relationship between Dinah and Sitis (Job's two wives),[87] but Dianne Bergant imagines the purpose of her character to be something of a "literary device accentuating the quality of Job's moral disposition"; i.e., an "alter ego."[88] Not to be overlooked, however, is the fact that TJob depicts her as a major character driven by a preferential awareness of the "compensation/retribution" motif. Examining how the narrative does this, Russ Spittler identifies three events: (a) compensation of food from a nobleman (her employer); (b) compensation of food from Satan (her nemesis); and (c) celebratory lament.[89]

Compensation of Food from a Nobleman

After his health is crippled and he moves to the κοπρία ("city dump"),[90] Job sees something one day which "stabs" him in the heart.[91] Having once served as a ruler in Egypt,[92] he now finds himself witnessing the humiliation of his queen as she moves into the workforce, serving as a "water-carrier" (ὑδοφοροῦσα);[93] i.e., a "maidservant" (παιδίσκην) assigned the most menial

87. TJob 2.9; 25.1. Legaspi ("Job," 77) identifies two traditions about Job's wife. "One tradition, known from rabbinic literature (*b. B. Bat.* 15b; *y. Sot.* 5.6.2; TgJob 2.9; and *LAB* 8.7–8), identifies the wife of Job with Jacob's daughter Dinah (Gen 34:1–14). A second (Greek) tradition . . . identifies Job's wife with an 'Arabian woman' (γυναῖκα Ἀράβισσαν, OG Job 42:17)." TJob "creatively combines both traditions in an attempt to offer a clearer understanding of Job's background, to provide a solution to lingering questions concerning his relation to ethnic Israel, and to elaborate on themes in the book of Job in a way that vindicates the role of women."

88. Bergant (*Wisdom*, 41).

89. Spittler ("Job," 848).

90. TJob 21.1 (cf. κοπραγωγέω, "to carry dung").

91. TJob 21.3 (κατανυκτικός, from κατανύσσω, "to stab, gouge"). In the GNT Acts of the Apostles Peter's Pentecost sermon is said to "stab" his audience "in the heart" (κατενύγησαν τὴν καρδίαν, Acts 2:37).

92. TJob 28.7 (ὁ τῆς Αἰγύπτου ὅλης βασιλεύων, "the one ruling over all Egypt").

93. TJob 21.2 (ὕδορ + φορέω, "water" + "carry").

tasks in the "house of a certain nobleman" (οἶκος τινὸς εὐσχήμονος).[94] This continues for eleven years, after which her employer cuts her wages so drastically, she can no longer afford to purchase enough food to keep her husband alive. Job's response to this pressure is to castigate the town council for allowing it to happen,[95] but when this elicits no response she finally hits rock-bottom, begging for food in the ἀγορά ("marketplace/town square").

Compensation of Food from Satan

It is at this rock-bottom moment that one of the dealers in the marketplace—that is, someone disguised as a dealer[96]—ramps up his sales-pitch: "You can have whatever you want for the right price," he says, to which she retorts, "And where would I get the money? Are you oblivious to the evils which have befallen us?"[97] To this the "dealer" then replies in words much like Bildad's:

Εἰ μὴ ἄξιοι ἦτε τῶν κακῶν	Had you not deserved the evils,
Οὐκ ἂν ἀπελάβετε αὐτά	You would not have received them.[98]

To compensate Satan for this food she then permits him to cut off her hair, publicly, in the town square.[99] For Garrett, "allowing her hair to be exposed, loosed, and then cut off in public view would not be construed by early readers of TJob as a noble act of largesse . . . but as a shameless forfeiture of the dignity and sexual modesty appropriate to one of her station."[100] Doubtless

94. TJob 21.2.

95. TJob 21.3; 22.3. He asks the council, πῶς χρῶνται τῇ γαμετῇ μου ὡς δουλίδι ("How can you treat my spouse as a slave?").

96. Disguised characters are not uncommon in ancient literary texts; e.g., the goddess Ninšubur disguises herself as a mourner (*ID* 39), the archangel Raphael disguises himself as a traveler (Tob 5:4), the warrior Odysseus disguises himself as a beggar (*Od.* 17), and Satan disguises himself as both a beggar and a salesman (TJob 23.1).

97. TJob 23.3–4.

98. TJob 23.6. In MT Job 8:4, Bildad says, "If your children sinned against him he gave them over to the power of their sin" (see above). In other words, Satan's reply to Job's wife in TJob is a close copy of Bildad's reply to Job in MT Job.

99. Several sources attest to the perceived shamefulness of women who shear off their hair (*m. Naz.* 4.5; 1 Cor 11:5–6). Commenting on the Ritual of the Soṭah (Num 5:18), Philo (*Spec. Laws* 3.56) explicitly uses the word αἴδος ("shame"—cf. ἀιδέομαι in TJob 7.5) to translate פרע ("to expose, dishevel"; cf. OG ἀποκαλύπτω, "to reveal"; Vg *discoperiet caput eius*, "he will discover her head"; Syr ܦܪܥ, "to expose/shave off").

100. Garrett ("Sex," 62–63).

this is true as far as it goes, but it is critically important that her motivation not be misconstrued; viz., her desire to keep her spouse from starving.[101]

Celebratory Hymn

In another major shift from MT Job, TJob inserts a celebratory hymn to help readers reflect more purposefully upon *her* victory. Chapters 24 and 25 preserve complementary reactions to her behavior, the first prosaic and the second poetic. In chapter 24 she admits that the public shearing off of her hair is indeed ἀτίμως ("dishonorable"),[102] but instead of focusing on the ramifications of this "dishonor," the hymn expounds a "how-the-mighty-have-fallen"[103] theme structured around a six-fold refrain: "Now she ____ her hair for bread," each refrain featuring a synonym for "compensation." Where once it was a joyful privilege to visit her beautiful, well-appointed home, for example, she now "exchanges (καταλλάσσω)[104] her hair for bread." Where once she shipped food on camels to the hungry, she now "hands over (ἀντιδίδωμι)[105] her hair for bread." Where once she fed the poor from seven tables in her dining room, she now "sells (καταπιπράσκω)[106] her hair for bread." Where once she washed her feet in gold and silver basins, she now "exchanges (ἀντικαταλλάσσω)[107] her hair for bread." Where once she wore clothes woven with gold and linen, she now "exchanges (ἀντικαταλλάσσω)[108] her hair for bread." Where once she lounged on couches fashioned from gold and silver, she now "sells (πιπράσκω)[109] her hair for bread." With each refrain the poet identifies another aspect of her beleaguered status. Even though she admits to having done something "dishonorable," she now laments how difficult it is to resume a social status approximating that of an אשת חיל ("honorable wife").[110]

101. In her final remarks Sitis admits that "the weakness of my heart has crushed my bones" (TJob 25.10), but whether this refers to the shaving of her head or general "wretchedness" (πανάθλιος, TJob 24.4) is not clear.

102. TJob 24.10.

103. Cf. Isa 14:4–16.

104. TJob 25.3.

105. TJob 25.4.

106. TJob 25.5.

107. TJob 25.6.

108. TJob 25.7.

109. TJob 25.8.

110. Prov 31:10. Yoder ("Woman," 427–47) and Ben Zvi ("Wife," 27–49) highlight the socioeconomic aspects of the "honorable wife" in Prov 31:10–31. In TJob she eventually returns to her "despotic boss" (ὁ δεσπότικος αὐτῆς ἄρχων, 40.7) before finally

Job and the Three Kings

The three "kings" who visit Job in his distress are Eliphas, Baldad, and Sophar, each name a Greek transliteration of the Hebrew names אליפז, בלדד, and צופר (as they appear in OG).[111] Unlike Eliphaz, however, Eliphas makes no effort to connect with Job on a theological plane. Instead he laments the loss of his "wealth" (πλοῦτος).[112] Further, just like the hymn celebrating Job's wife, this one structures itself around a simple refrain: "Where now is the 'splendor' (δόξα) of your throne?" The first of these reads:

> *Σὺ εἶ ὁ τὰ ἑπταχισλία πρόβατα ἐκτάξας εἰς τὴν τῶν πτωχῶν ἔνδυσιν*
> Are you the one who selected 7,000 sheep to clothe the poor?
>
> *ποῦ οὖν τυγχάνει ἡ δόξα τοῦ θρόνου σου*
> Where now is the splendor of your throne?[113]

The tenth (and final) refrain reads:

> *Σὺ εἶ Ιωβ ὁ τὴν μεγάλην δόξαν ἔχων*
> Are you the great and glorious Job?
>
> *ποῦ οὖν τυγχάνει ἡ δόξα τοῦ θρόνου σου*
> Where now is the splendor of your throne?[114]

Like the hymn for Job's spouse, this passage avoids any reference to the theological notions of justification or creation or theodicy or disinterested piety, but instead focuses on Job's loss of worldly wealth.

When Job chides Eliphas for wallowing in such materialism, Baldad steps in to ask, in light of his circumstances, whether his mind is still *καθίστημι* ("anchored, stable").[115] To this Job answers "yes," then explains:

> *Ἐν μεν τοῖς γηίνοις οὐ συνέστηκεν*
> My heart[116] is not fixed on earthly things[117]

---

walking into a field, lying down, and dying. When word of her death reaches the village, the townsfolk (esp. the poor) issue a *μυκήματος κλαυθμοῦ* ("bellowing cry") as they bury her body next to the graves of her children (TJob 40.6–9).

111. OG Job 2:11 (Ελιφας, Βαλδαδ, and Σωφαρ).

112. TJob 32.1–12 (cf. Moore, *WealthWise*, 117–23).

113. TJob 32.2.

114. TJob 32.12.

115. TJob 36.2 (lit., "set down, fixed, steady"). In other words, "Are you still sane?"

116. TJob 36.3a. Since *συνέστηκεν* is 3ps, it cannot have a 1ps subject, but more likely references the same subject in 36.3b, *καρδία μου* ("my heart").

117. Aristotle (*Metaph.* 1049a20) distinguishes γῆ ("earth" in the next line) from the relatively rare term deployed here, *γηίνος* ("earthly").

> ἐπεὶ ἀκατάστατος ἡ γῆ καὶ οἱ ἐνοικοῦτες ἐν αὐτῇ
> For the earth and all who dwell on it are unstable.
>
> ἐν δὲ τοῖς ἐπουρανίοις συνέστηκεν ἡ καρδία μου
> Instead my heart is fixed on heavenly things,[118]
>
> διότι οὐχ ὑπάρχει ἐν ουρανῷ ταραχή
> For there is no instability in heaven.[119]

Accepting Job's depiction of the earthly-heavenly polarity as more-or-less orthodox, Baldad then poses what looks to be a straightforward theological question, "In whom do you hope?" To this question Job responds by affirming that his hope lies in God, knowing full well that his profession of faith doubtless *does* look "insane"[120] to those who refuse to accept the fact that a truly sovereign deity, by definition, both *gives* and *takes*.[121] When Baldad asks whether such divine behavior is "unjust" Job concludes the conversation with a question of his own: "Who are we to busy ourselves with 'heavenly matters,' seeing that we are naught but dust and ashes?"[122] Afterwards, when Sophar offers to have his "physicians" (ἰατροί) examine him,[123] Job declines the offer because of his conviction that God alone is the only true Healer.[124]

SUMMARY

Whereas TgJob begins the process of translating and interpreting MT Job for Aramaic-speaking audiences, TJob transforms the book into something more palatable to Greeks. Unlike MT Job, the TJob protagonist says nothing about "worthless physicians" or "miserable comforters." Nor does he

118. Cf. the repetitive use of ἐπουράνιος in Eph 1:3; 2:6; 3:10; 6:12.

119. TJob 36.3. In 33.3, Job goes only so far as to declare that "My throne is in the 'upper world' (ὑπερκόσμιος)." Here he goes a step further.

120. Baldad wonders whether Job's mind is properly "put together" (συνίστημι, 38.3), so Job assures him that he is both καθίστημι ("stable") and συνίστημι ("put together").

121. TJob (cf. MT Job 2:10). In the opening hymn to Marduk in *Lud* 1.1–34, Babylon's patron deity is depicted as a capricious god whose mind "rhythmically" oscillates between "wrath and mercy" (Spieckermann, "Wrath," 6). Cf. *a-na-ki-igaṣ-ṣu* GIŠ.TUKUL.MEŠ-*šu ka-ba-ta-šú muš-neš-šat*, "though his hand is heavy, his heart is merciful" (*Lud* 1.34). In Qur'an the deity "tests" (لون, lit., "twists") his "submitted ones" (*muslims*) with both الحسنت ("the good") and السيات ("the bad") "in the hope that they might someday return" (Q 7.168).

122. Careful readers will note that "dust and ashes" are Job's final words in the canonical book.

123. TJob 38.7.

124. TJob 38.6–8.

demand that his wife and "friends" admit that a sovereign deity, by definition, both *gives* and *takes*. Instead TJob softens the theological edges of the canonical book in order to challenge its Greek-speaking readership to decide whether heavenly matters are more important than earthly matters, thereby continuing the cosmic dialogue begun in MT Job.[125]

125. Witte ("Deuteronomy," 56) recognizes that "the idea that justice brings fulfilled life and that religious, moral and social integrity brings blessing cannot just be pushed away (Deut 30:16). The one like Job, who tries this, and for whom the equation of deuteronomic theology is no longer an option, falls into a double trap: if he denies the association between God's justice and the fate of the human being, he appears as an evildoer, who is threatened by a bad life (Job 15; 18; 20; cf. Deut 28:15–67), but if he follows these thoughts further, he gets into a maelstrom of self-justifications which end with the conviction that God is not just. The poet lets Job fall into both traps, and eventually lets him break free with God's intervention. By this means the poet shows the borders, if not the dead-end paths, of a one-dimensional theology of justice."

6

Concluding Remarks

It's a sunny May morning and I am sitting in an ER cubicle waiting to learn the results of the CAT scan on my wife's leg. Having endured over thirty surgeries on this leg, she has had the knee joint prosthetically replaced several times, the necrotic bone tissue surgically removed, the broken ankle reset with permanent titanium screws, the femur replaced, and the hip replaced. To retard the spread of osteoporosis she has injected herself with a powerful drug every day for two years, and to stem the advance of MRSA and other bugs she has repeatedly submitted to antibiotic infusions several times a day for months at a time.[1] The most recent surgery is what plastic surgeons call a "muscle flap," a rather desperate "last stand" procedure in which a healthy section of calf muscle is cut from the back of the calf and transplanted over the prosthetic knee joint. If the flap "takes," then the next step is to suture a skin graft over the wound and redress it until it heals.

The hardest part for me is having to watch her suffer—physically, mentally, emotionally, socially, and yes, spiritually.[2] It's one thing to sit next to panicky parishioners in an ICU waiting room; it's quite another to have to listen to a loved one groan in pain for meds which are almost always late.[3] Not daring to compare my "suffering" with hers, it's still agonizing to feel so . . . helpless. Beyond the physical agony, her suffering is a reminder of how

1. The acronym MRSA stands for Methicillin Resistant Staphylococcus Aureus.

2. Due to several factors—the problems with her leg, the COVID-19 pandemic, and the fact that she suffers from no less than three different immuno-suppressive conditions—the only safe way my wife can attend church is online.

3. This is less the fault of floor nurses than their administrators, particularly those refusing to hire enough staff to cover the legitimate needs of the patients they claim to want to serve; cf. Geyer and Mngomezulu, "Concerns," 92–94.

pain can twist otherwise good-humored adults into crabby children, once self-reliant spirits into skeletal ghosts, once vibrant voices into cold silence.[4] Paul Brand's description of pain as "the gift nobody wants" is doubtless correct in many cases,[5] but sometimes, frankly, it is impossible to imagine pain as a "gift."[6] Granted, not all alcoholics turn into abusive drunks, nor do all dementia-stricken grandparents regress into testy toddlers.[7] But such stereotypes exist for a reason. Pain is relentless. Pain takes no prisoners.[8] If the statistics are right,[9] about half the readers of this book will either personally experience chronic pain or find themselves caring for someone who is.

More to the point, pain raises disturbing theological questions. Like the character of Job, what happens to faith when pain strikes? Does it recede? Does it survive? Does it grow?[10] Can a chronic sufferer maintain a healthy holistic faith without expecting reward or fearing judgment? Valerie Pettys recognizes that "when human suffering exceeds the boundary between what can be imagined and the unthinkable, meaning gives way. The world as it has been known collapses."[11] To anyone unacquainted with this reality it can look disingenuously easy to suggest, with Elihu, that pain can be a first step toward "redemption,"[12] or to preach with the apostle Paul that "suffering produces endurance, endurance produces character, and character produces hope."[13] Reality is usually quite different from the ideal. As

4. Terrien (*Presence*, 362) understatedly describes Job as someone in whom "the poison of pain may at times vitiate his judgment."

5. Yancey and Brand (*Pain*, 72–86) come to this conclusion after Brand discovers that lepers can become easy prey for hungry rats nibbling on their digits at night while they sleep, totally unable to feel pain.

6. Sorge's (*Pain*, 79) proposition that the purpose of Job's pain "is to glorify God by changing him and bringing him to a higher spiritual inheritance" is doubtless well-intended, but this still looks like a positivistic campaign slogan.

7. Jarvik and Small (*Parentcare*, 252) list four of the greatest problems facing the elderly: disease, disability, debility, and death.

8. Cf. Elihu's well-meaning description of what pain can do (Job 33:19–22).

9. Roy, *Pain*, 16–28. Cole (*Pain*) defines pain management in four stages: *crisis, fix-it, management, and rebuilding*. Chaitow (*Pain*) describes several types of pain therapies, some more realistic than others. Cf. Shelly and Seigler, *Pain*, 19–42.

10. The protagonist in M. Night Shyamalan's film *Signs* is a pastor suffering the loss of his faith after witnessing the death of his wife in a freak accident. Cf. Moore, *Faith*, 15–28.

11. Pettys, "Darkness," 90.

12. Job 33:24–28 (see above).

13. Rom 5:3–4. For the apostle Paul the ideal response to suffering is to "boast" in it (καυχάομαι, 5:3). In Qur'an, moreover, Mohammed is not to surrender to infidels because "we sent messengers before you to the nations upon whom we have inflicted 'adversity' (الباسا) and 'suffering' (الضرا) in the hope that they might be humbled" (Q 6.42). In Hasan's opinion (*Pain*, 39), Qur'an teaches that "hardship is the core of the

Daniel Simundson puts it, "some biblical passages deal with suffering less as an intellectual problem . . . than as a process of coping with terrible reality."[14]

For Yosefa Raz, however, "the book of Job asks us to consider a different set of questions: How does the experience of pain change people? How does it influence the self in terms of its (d)evolution? What is the relationship between pain, language, and power?[15] What value does pain have, whether religious, aesthetic or moral?"[16] Hans-Peter Müller sees in the Dialogues of Job two questions: (a) What are the discernible differences between the attitudes of Eliphaz, Bildad, and Zophar? and (b) How does Job's attitude change toward them?[17] Based on the pages above, however, the following pages will attempt to read Job through lenses shaped and contoured by two other questions:[18] (a) How does Job theologically process what C. S. Lewis calls "the problem of pain?"[19] and (b) How do Job's wife and "friends" respond to it?[20]

JOB AND HIS PAIN

Job's opening speech is one of the most gut-wrenching passages of the Bible.[21] The amount of spiritual energy poured into this lament far exceeds that poured into the laments of, say, David or Naomi.[22] William Pohl is doubtless correct to classify it as a "protest speech,"[23] but from a comparative form-critical perspective Job's first speech is a *lament*,[24] and as such is

---

earthly journey."

14. Simundson, "Suffering," 220.

15. Cf. Pyper, "Pain," 234–55.

16. Raz, "Job," 77.

17. Müller, *Hiob*, 73.

18. L. Wilson's (*Job*, 8) warning is well taken, however, when he cautions contemporary readers not to expect answers from Job "that it never intends to give."

19. Lewis (*Pain*, 86) justifiably presumes that "the possibility of pain is inherent in the very existence of a world where souls can meet."

20. Cf. Morris, *Illness*, 190–217; and Stull, *Pain*, 1–19. Merton (*Seeds*, 25) contends that "created things do not bring us joy, but pain. Until we love God perfectly, everything in the world will be able to hurt us. And the greatest misfortune is to be dead to the pain they inflict on us, and not to realize what it is."

21. Job 3:1–26.

22. Cf. 2 Sam 12:15–20 (death of Bathsheba's first child) and Ruth 1:20–21 (Naomi changes her name to Mara). The lament psalms deserve to be studied separately; cf. Westermann, *Lament*; Kynes, "Weeping"; and Pemberton, *Lament*.

23. Pohl, *Job*, 248.

24. Cf. Knierim, "Form," 123–65; Holbert, "*Klage*"; Westermann, "Klage," 44–80; and Barton, "Form," 838–41.

subject to comparison with other ANE laments.[25] One of the most obvious intratextual parallels, for example, occurs in the final lament of Jeremiah,[26] a text with features so close to those in Job, some see a legitimate case for literary dependence.[27] Where Job laments the day of his birth, so does Jeremiah.[28] Where Job laments that he does not immediately die after *exiting* the womb, Jeremiah laments that Yhwh does not "make me die" while still *in* the womb.[29] Where Job finds life "troubling" and "weary," Jeremiah finds it "sorrowful" and "shameful."[30]

Intertextual parallels occur as well. In Babylon, e.g., the mother-goddess Mami deploys similar "curse-the-day" language to lament the day she decides to support Enlil in his plan to destroy the earth via flood:

u-mu-um li-id-da-i-im	Let that day become dark!
li-tu-ur li-ki-il	Let it turn again to gloom![31]

Further, where Job rejoices in Death as a resting place able to take in weary souls and silence oppression,[32] the Egyptian "host" in *DMS* similarly imagines it as a place of "rest in the West," a "peaceful "harbor" where newly arrived immigrants become "tenured professors" as the scent of "lotus flowers" fills the air.[33]

But it is in the Greek literature where one of the most powerful parallels occurs. Alfonse de Lamartine proposes that "Job is the Prometheus of the word, raised to the heavens still shrieking, still bleeding, in the very claws of the vulture gnawing at his heart. He is the victim become judge, by the sublime impersonality of reason, celebrating his own torture and, like the Roman Brutus, casting up to heaven the drops of his blood."[34] Apart from Prometheus, however, Medea's decision to kill her own children comes

25. Cf. Roberts, "Weeping," 132–42; Michalowski, *Lamentation*, 39–61.

26. Jer 20:7–18. Contemporary students of Jeremiah prefer to describe the material in Jer 11:18—12:6; 15:10–21; 17:14–18; 18:18–23; and 20:7–18 as "laments" rather than "confessions" (cf. Moore, *Babbler*, 58–80). Lundbom ("Curse," 590) recognizes that "Jeremiah's words have a striking parallel to Job chaps. 3 and 10."

27. Dillman (*Hiob*, xxxii–xxxiii), e.g., argues that Jeremiah is dependent on Job, while Greenstein ("Jeremiah," 102) finds Job's dependence on Jeremiah more likely.

28. Job 3:1–12; Jer 20:7–18.

29. Job 3:10; Jer 20:17–18. Cf. Dawson, "Womb," 435–68.

30. Job 3:17; Jer 20:18. Cf. discussion in Fuchs, "Klage," 215–23.

31. *Atr* 3.3.34–35 (cf. Job 3:9). Jacobsen and Nielsen ("Day," 187–204) discuss other parallels.

32. Job 3:17–19.

33. *DMS* 51, 134–35.

34. De Lamartine, *Littérature*, 2.441.

more immediately to mind.[35] Betrayed by her husband Jason,[36] who leaves her for another woman,[37] she strikes back where she knows it will most hurt. Like the ANE patriarchs Kirta and Abraham,[38] his deepest desire is to ensure the survival of his children so that they might perpetuate his legacy.[39] So she decides to remove them from the picture.[40] As the plan formulates in her mind she soon finds herself conflicted when her "heroic self requires the killing of the children" as her "maternal self" simultaneously "defends them":[41]

βροτων οἵτινές εἰσιν πάμπαν ἄπεροι	Mortals who have absolutely no experience
μηδ' ἐφεύτευσαν παῖδας	With children (having never had any),
προφείρεν εἰς ἐντυχίαν τῶν γεναιμένων	Maintain a fortunate advantage over those who do.
οἱ μὲν ἄτεκνοι δι' ἀπειροσύνην	For the childless, because they do not have children,
εἴθ' ἡδὺ βροτοῖς εἰτ' ἀναριὸν παῖδες τελέθους' οὐχὶ	And do not know whether children are a blessing or a vexation,
πολλῶν μόχθων ἀπέχονται	Vaccinate themselves against many hardships.[42]

35. *Eur. Med.* 214–447; cf. Hershkowitz, *Madness*, 31–35. Euripides (d. 406 BCE) is not the first to write about Medea. Literary mention of her goes all the way back to Hesiod (*Theog.* 956–62; 992–1002; cf. Foley, "Medea," 63).

36. This is the same Jason who sails with his Argonauts to recover the Golden Fleece; Wood, *Search*, 78–139.

37. The other woman is Creusa, daughter of Creon, king of Corinth.

38. Cf. Moore, *WealthWatch*, 124–27.

39. Cf. Moore, "Abraham," 2. Ovid (*Metam.* 7.74) links Medea to the sorceress deity Hecate; cf. Bömer, "Ovidius," 74.

40. "How wretched am I in my stubbornness! It was all in vain, I see, that I brought you up, all in vain that I was wracked with toils in labor, enduring the harsh pains of childbirth. Truly, many were the hopes that I, poor fool, once had in you children, that you would tend me in my old age and when I died dress me for burial with your own hands, an enviable fate for mortals. But now this sweet imagining is over, for bereft of you I shall live out my life in pain and grief" (*Eur. Med.* 1028–39). Medea here enacts a role not unlike that enacted by the Joban Prosecutor.

41. Foley, "Medea," 62–63. Lest her behavior be deemed "extremist," Liebman ("Extremism," 75) thinks that in Western culture "extremism is the religious norm. It is not religious extremism, but religious moderation which requires explanation."

42. *Eur. Med.* 1090–97. In the book of Job the children die from a hand other than their mother's, but Job still expresses his pain through tortuous maternal images.

Without mentioning Job by name, C. S. Lewis discusses the problem of pain in straightforward language sensitive to the gap separating Job's world from the (post)modern world.[43] For example, one of Job's most persistent questions is, "Why do I suffer so much if I do not deserve it?"[44] Recognizing how much this question still puzzles people today, Lewis is quick to point out that retribution and revenge are not the same thing. Whereas the latter has no place on the biblical deity's agenda, the former must be taken seriously because if not, there can be no justice.[45] Challenging his readers to think clearly about this matter, he warns that "some enlightened people would like to banish all conceptions of retribution . . . from their theory of punishment and place its value wholly in the deterrence of others or the reform of the criminal himself. They do not see that by so doing they render all punishment unjust. What can be more immoral than to inflict suffering on me for the sake of deterring others if I do not deserve it?[46] And if I do deserve it, you are admitting the claims of 'retribution.'"[47] Anticipating criticism of this position, he adds: "When our ancestors refer to pains and sorrows as God's 'vengeance' they are not necessarily attributing evil passions to God," but "until the evil man finds evil unmistakably present in his existence, in the form of pain, he is enclosed in illusion."[48]

So to review: (a) the book of Job engages the natural conflict between the motifs of disinterested piety and compensation/retribution; (b) the problem with Job's counselors is not that they hold retribution to be important, but that they hold it to be *all* important; and (c) addressing this theological polarity is just as difficult now as it was then.

43. Lewis, *Pain*, 86–109.

44. Job asks Eliphaz, "Is there any wrong on my tongue? Cannot my taste discern calamity?" (Job 6:30), and to the deity he asks, "If I do sin, so what? How does that harm you?" (7:20).

45. Ḥueninpu (*TEP* 97, 93, 94, 98, 122, 223, 136) and Ipu-Wer (*DILA* 13.5–6) say basically the same thing, upbraiding the Pharaoh for acting as if retribution is unnecessary. For Tsevat ("Job," 98), "Where the principle of retribution has no validity, there can be no injustice."

46. Lewis, *Pain*, 92–92. As these lines strike the page the news is breaking that Naomi Judd, the mother of Wynona and Ashley Judd, has just committed suicide, an ironic occurrence since she recently published a book on how to survive toxic abuse (Judd, *River*). Sexually abused by a close relative as early as the age of three, beaten and raped by a heroin-addicted boyfriend at twenty-two, she suffered from clinical depression most of her life in spite of all the fame and fortune she received as one-half of The Judds.

47. Lewis (*Pain*, 91–92) speaks of "the universal human feeling that bad men ought to suffer," and that "it is no use turning up our noses at this feeling, as if it were wholly base. On its mildest level it appeals to everyone's sense of justice."

48. Lewis, *Pain*, 93.

JOB'S SPOUSE AND "FRIENDS" ON HIS PAIN

Not everyone responds to pain the same way, nor does Job respond to it at the end of his journey the same way he does at the beginning. The same is true of his wife and "friends." Granted, it is tempting to censure these characters for not behaving like a 21st century pastor comforting a troubled parishioner, but such "interpretation" has little to do with the book's ANE context, and can easily overlook the following questions: (a) Why does Job's wife presume that cursing God is theologically appropriate? and (b) Why do Job's "friends" presume that retributional censure is always appropriate?[49]

Why Does Job's Wife Presume That Cursing God Is Theologically Appropriate?

In some ways this is a trick question. Job's wife may or may not presume that "cursing God" is theologically appropriate. Unfortunately the text is silent. But whatever she *does* presume, the question itself may be directed not only to her, but to the "host" in *DMS*, the sufferer/sceptic in *BT*, and even to contemporary suicide advocates promoting a life-choice which, to be honest, attracts chronic sufferers much more than non-sufferers.[50] Job's wife may say, "Curse God and die" (a) because she is tired of watching her husband try to maintain his "integrity" (תם) in the face of relentless pain;[51] or (b) because she is completely undone by her loss of status;[52] or (c) because she is simply tired of having to do everything to keep the family afloat.[53]

49. Hawley, "Condemnation," 459–78.

50. Nicol and Wylie (*Dying*, 2) attribute the living will and the right to refuse resuscitation (DNR—*do not resuscitate*) to pathologist Jack Kevorkian's movement to legalize assisted suicide, but Albright ("Suicide," 89–94) and Smith ("Suicide," 54–62) challenge this practice from both a nursing and a legal perspective.

51. Job 2:9.

52. TJob 21–25.

53. Good (*Job*, 200) lists several other possibilities (see above), but Gately and Ladin ("Caregivers," 111) recognize that "the provision of care is often complex, time-consuming, and without financial remuneration, (and) can affect the physical and mental health, financial savings, productivity, and well-being of the caregiver."

Why Do Job's "Friends" Presume That Retributional Censure Is Theologically Appropriate?

John[54] suffered a debilitating stroke at the age of thirty-five, effectively ending his ability to work. The aphasia in particular was so bad, only a few people could understand him. Within a year he lost his well-paying job as a first-class technical consultant for an international corporation. Pushed into poverty, he soon discovered that his wife and daughter wanted nothing more to do with him. When they sued for the house he had built for them, the settlement forced him to move into a rickety mobile home at the edge of town. Diagnosed a diabetic, he had to undergo daily kidney dialysis treatment. Eventually reduced to sitting in a soiled diaper all day, he finally came to the decision that he could "no longer live like this" and that after the Christmas holidays he planned to discontinue his dialysis treatments. At this news one of his adult siblings immediately censured him for deciding to "commit suicide," even at the funeral.

Caring for the sick is not easy. Some, like Job's "friends," respond to it by turning all their attention to theological discussions designed to defend God's honor against "arrogant rebels" like Job. Whether such a response might on some level be appropriate, the sickbed of a "pious sufferer" is usually not the place for it.[55] Unwilling to walk with John through his pain they choose instead to respond to him in language more familiar to *them* than to *him*.[56] Each "friend" takes a slightly different approach, but all try to convince him that (a) suffering is the result of (unconfessed) sin; (b) retribution is the only way to deal with it; and (c) once forgiven, he should look forward to regaining his health. In short, they try to convince Job that the pristine doctrine of *retribution* is preferable to the murky business of dealing with *reality*.

Others, like Job's spouse, simply want things to end; that is, to throw off the shackles of what is perceived to be an unjust situation.[57] No one steps up to serve Job as he is, but as they think he should be. Therefore the deity steps in, his goal being to lead Job and his "friends" into a more

54. Not his real name.

55. Metaxas (*Letter*, 1–4) censures many American churches for behavior disturbingly similar to that enacted by the German Evangelical Church in the 1930s.

56. O'Connor (*Job*, 102) convincingly argues that the book of Job's "primary concern" is not so much "the suffering of the innocent, but the larger question of human relationship to God in the midst of suffering."

57. TJob responds to this by depicting Sitis as a caregiver willing to go so far as to shave her head to ensure her husband's survival.

holistic understanding of *reality*.[58] Through it all Job does not sin, nor does he surrender his integrity. In the film *Rudy*, a young college student asks a priest why God does not open a door for him to enroll at Notre Dame and play football for the Fighting Irish.[59] He asks whether he has worked hard enough. He asks whether he has prayed hard enough. He asks whether he has done something wrong or failed to do something right. Finally the priest responds, "Son, in thirty-five years of religious studies, I've come up with only two incontrovertible facts: (a) there is a God, and (b) I'm not him."

Job's response to *his* teacher (Yhwh) is not dissimilar:

ידעתי כי כול תוכל	I know that you can do all things,
ולא יבצר ממך מזמה	And that no purpose of yours can be thwarted.
לכן הגדתי ולאאבין	That is why I spoke of things I do not understand,
נפלאות ממני ולא אדע	Things too incredible for me to comprehend.[60]
על כן אמאס ונחמתי על עפר ואפר	So I accept my decline onto dust and ashes.[61]

58. Boda and Baines ("Wisdom's Cry," 57) ask, "What is the purpose of these speeches? By ignoring the plight of the human Job and speaking instead of Yhwh's activity especially throughout the non-human world, Yhwh is showing Job, first, that he is indeed at work maintaining justice throughout his creation, and second, that Job's plight is not the center of the universe."

59. Based on the true story of Daniel Eugene Ruettiger, the only Notre Dame player ever to be carried off the field on the shoulders of teammates.

60. Job 42:2–3.

61. Job 42:6 is a classic *crux* for which several interpretations are proposed. Vg's reading of *ago paenitentiam* ("I do penance") influences most ETs to read the polysemantic term נחם as "repent." Fontaine ("Hero," 70–85), however, reads "I recant and change my mind concerning dust and ashes." Good (*Tempest*, 375–78) reads "Therefore I despise and repent of dust and ashes." Curtis ("Response," 497–511) reads "Therefore I feel loathing contempt and revulsion (toward you, O God) and I feel sorry for frail man." Attending more directly to the honor-shame polarities governing Middle Eastern culture, Muenchow ("Dust," 597–611) reads "Therefore I despise myself and sink down into the dust and the dirt." Whichever translation is adopted, Sherwood ("Job," 115) observes that "scholarship has generally understood the Book of Job in one of three ways: (a) the world is governed by a predictable causality, in which case suffering can be understood as punishment for sin and Job's prosperity in the Epilogue is seen as a result of his piety; or (b) the world is governed by an unpredictable causality, in which case faith in God is required since humans are incapable of fully understanding how suffering and prosperity results; or (c) causality plays no governing role in the world." Sherwood's conclusion is that "by maintaining the belief that causality is a governing principle of existence the first two views remain entrapped within the theory of divine retribution, and therefore fail to explain adequately the events of the Epilogue."

Bibliography

Adams, Jim W. *The Performative Dimensions of Rhetorical Questions*. LHBOTS 622. London: T. & T. Clark, 2020.

Adams, Samuel L. "Wisdom Literature in Egypt." In *The Wiley Blackwell Companion to Wisdom Literature*, edited by S. Adams and M. Goff, 310–27. WBCR. Hoboken, NJ: Wiley, 2020.

Aimers, Geoffrey J. "'Give the Devil His Due': The Satanic Agenda and Social Justice in the Book of Job." *JSOT* 37 (2012) 57–66.

———. "Theodicy in an Ironical Sense: The Joban Wager and the Portrait of Folly." *JSOT* 43 (2019) 359–70.

al-Rawi, Farouk N. H., and Andrew F. George. "Tablets from the Sippar Library III. Two Royal Counterfeits." *Iraq* 56 (1994) 135–48.

Albertz, Rainer. "*Ludlul bēl nēmeqi*—eine Lehrdichtung zur Ausbreitung und Vertiefung der persönischen Mardukfrömmigkeit." In *Ad bene et fideliter seminandum: Festgabe for Karlheinz Deller*, edited by Gerlinde Mauer and Ursula Magen, 25–53. AOAT 220. Neukirchen-Vluyn: Neukirchener, 1988.

———. "Der sozialgeschichtliche Hintergrund des Hiobbuches und der 'Babylonischen Theodizee.'" In *Die Botschaft und die Boten: Festschrift für Hans Walter Wolff*, edited by Jörg Jeremias and Lothar Perlitt, 349–72. Neukirchen-Vluyn: Neukirchener, 1981.

Albright, Angela. "Nursing: Against Suicide." In *Contemporary Perspectives on Rational Suicide*, edited by James L. Werth Jr., 89–94. Series in Death, Dying, and Bereavement. Philadelphia: Brunner/Mazel, 1999.

Albright, William F. "The Mouth of the Rivers." *AJSL* 35 (1919) 161–95.

Allen, James P. *The Debate between a Man and His Soul: A Masterpiece of Ancient Egyptian Literature*. CHANE 44. Leiden: Brill, 2011.

———. "The Discourses of the Eloquent Peasant." In *Middle Egyptian Literature: Eight Literary Works of the Middle Kingdom*, 229–326. Cambridge: Cambridge University Press, 2015.

———. "The Dispute of a Man and His Soul." In *Middle Egyptian Literature: Eight Literary Works of the Middle Kingdom*, 327–60. Cambridge: Cambridge University Press, 2015.

———. *The Pyramid Texts*. WAW 23. Atlanta: SBL, 2005.

Alonso Schökel, Luis. "Toward a Dramatic Reading of the Book of Job." *Sem* 7 (1977) 45–61.

Alster, Bendt. Tiamat." In *DDD* 867–69.

———. *Wisdom of Ancient Sumer*. Bethesda, MD: CDL, 2005.

Alt, Albrecht. "Die Weisheit Salomos." *TLZ* 76 (1951) 139–48.

Alter, Robert. *The Art of Biblical Narrative*. 2nd ed. New York: Basic, 2011.

———. *Canon and Creativity: Modern Writing and the Authority of Scripture*. New Haven: Yale University Press, 2000.

———. *The David Story: A Translation with Commentary of 1 and 2 Samuel*. New York: Norton, 1999.

Andersen, Francis I. *Job: An Introduction and Commentary*. TOTC. Downers Grove, IL: InterVarsity, 1976.

Andersen, Ragnar. "The Elihu Speeches: Their Place and Sense in the Book of Job." *TynBul* 66 (2015) 75–94.

Anderson, Jeff S. *The Blessing and the Curse: Trajectories in the Theology of the Old Testament*. Eugene, OR: Cascade Books, 2014.

Andrew, Christopher. "In the Beginning: Spies of the Bible and Ancient Egypt from Moses to the Last Supper." In *The Secret World: A History of Intelligence*, 13–26. New Haven: Yale University Press, 2018.

Annus, Amar, and Alan Lenzi. *Ludlul bēl nēmeqi: The Standard Babylonian Poem of the Righteous Sufferer*. SAACT 7. Helsinki: The Neo-Assyrian Text Corpus Project, 2010.

Apt, Naphatali. "Die Hiobserzählung in der arabischen Literateur." PhD diss., University of Heidelberg, 1913.

Arneth, Martin. *"Sonne der Gerechtigkeit": Studien zur Solarisierung der Jahwe-Religion im Lichte von Psalm 72*. BZABR 1. Wiesbaden: Harrassowitz, 2000.

Assmann, Jan. *Death and Salvation in Ancient Egypt*. Translated by D. Lorton. Ithaca, NY: Cornell University Press, 2005.

———. *Ma`at. Gerechtigkeit und Unsterblichkeit im alten Ägypt*. Munich: Beck, 1990.

Audet, J. P. "Origines comparées de la double tradition de la loi et de la Sagesse dans le Proche-Orient ancien." *International Congress of Orientalists* 1 (1964) 352–57.

Augustine. *Expositions of the Psalms*. In *The Works of St. Augustine*, translated by M. Boulding, 3.15–20. Hyde Park, NY: New City, 2000.

Avrahami, Yael. *The Senses of Scripture: Sensory Perception in the Hebrew Bible*. LHBOTS 545. London: T. & T. Clark, 2012.

Bachvarova, Mary R. *From Hittite to Homer: The Anatolian Background of Ancient Greek Epic*. Cambridge: Cambridge University Press, 2016.

Bailey, Clinton. *Bedouin Culture in the Bible*. New Haven: Yale University Press, 2018.

Baines, John, and Norman Yoffee. "Order, Legitimacy, and Wealth in Ancient Egypt and Mesopotamia." In *Archaic States*, edited by G. Feinman and J. Marcus, 199–260. Santa Fe, NM: School of American Research, 1995.

Bakhtin, Mikhail. *Problems of Dostoevsky's Poetics*. Translated by C. Emerson. 1929. Reprint, Minneapolis: University of Minnesota Press, 1984.

Bakon, Shimon. "The Enigma of Elihu." *Dor-le-Dor* 12 (1984) 217–28.

Baldwin, Susanna. "Miserable but Not Monochrome: The Distinctive Characteristics and Perspectives of Job's Three Counselors." *Themelios* 43 (2018) 359–75.

Balentine, Samuel E. "Ask the Animals and They Will Teach You." *WWSup* 5 (2006) 3–11.

———. *Have You Considered My Servant Job? Understanding the Biblical Archetype of Patience*. SPOT. Columbia: University of South Carolina Press, 2015.

Bales, Kevin. *Disposable People: New Slavery in the Global Economy*. Berkeley, CA: University of California Press, 2004.

Ball, Charles J. *The Book of Job: A Revised Text and Version*. Oxford: Clarendon, 1922.

Balla, Ibolya. "The Relationship between Husband and Wife according to Sirach 25–26, 36." In *Family and Kinship in the Deuterocanonical and Cognate Literature*, edited by A. Passaro, 107–26. Berlin: de Gruyter, 2013.

Barbalet, Jack M. "Power and Resistance." *BJSoc* 4 (1985) 531–48.

Barclay, John M. G. *Jews in the Mediterranean Diaspora: From Alexander to Trajan (323 BCE–117 CE)*. Berkeley, CA: University of California Press, 1996.

Barnett, Ronald, and Søren S. E. Bengsten. *Knowledge and the University: Reclaiming Life*. London: Routledge, 2020.

Barone, Diane. "Myths about 'Crack Babies.'" *EL* 52 (1994) 67–68.

Barré, Michael L. "'Fear of God' and the World View of Wisdom." *BTB* 11 (1981) 41–43.

Barth, Karl. *Dogmatik in Grundriss*. Zürcher: Theologischer, 1987.

Bartlett, Anthony. *Signs of Change: The Bible's Evolution of Divine Nonviolence*. Eugene, OR: Cascade, 2022.

Bartlett, John R. *Edom and the Edomites*. JSOTSup 77. Sheffield: Sheffield Academic, 1989.

Barton, George W. "The Composition of Job 24–30." *JBL* 30 (1911) 66–77.

Barton, John. "Form Criticism, Old Testament." In *ABD* 2:838–41.

Batto, Bernard. *Slaying the Dragon: Mythmaking in the Biblical Tradition*. Louisville: Westminster John Knox, 1992.

Beaulieu, Paul-Alain. "The Social and Intellectual Setting of Babylonian Wisdom Literature." In *Wisdom Literature in Mesopotamia and Israel*, edited by R. J. Clifford, 3–19. SBLSS 36. Atlanta: SBL, 2007.

Beckerath, Jürgen von. *Handbuch der Ägyptischen Königsnamen*. MÄS 49. Mainz: Deutscher Kunstverlag, 1999.

Beckman, Gary M. "The Hittite Assembly." *JAOS* 102 (1982) 435–42.

Beilby, James K., and Paul Rhodes Eddy, eds. *Justification: Five Views*. Downers Grove, IL: InterVarsity, 2011.

Bellos, David. *The Novel of the Century: The Extraordinary Adventure of "Les Misérables."* New York: Farrar, Straus, and Giroux, 2017.

Benjamin, Don C. *Deuteronomy and City Life: A Form Criticism of Texts with the Word CITY (עיר) in Deuteronomy 4:41—26:19*. Lanham, MD: University Press of America, 1983.

Ben Zvi, Ehud. "The 'Successful, Wise, Worthy Wife' of Prov 31:10–31 as a Source for Reconstructing Aspects of Thought and Economy in the Late Persian/Early Hellenistic Period." In *The Economy of Ancient Judah in Its Historical Context*, edited by M. L. Miller et al., 27–49. Winona Lake, IN: Eisenbrauns, 2015.

Bergant, Dianne. "An Historico-Critical Study of Anthropological Traditions and Motifs in Job." PhD diss., St. Louis University, 1975.

———. *Israel's Wisdom Literature: A Liberation-Critical Reading*. Minneapolis: Fortress, 1997.

Berge, Kåre. "Cities in Deuteronomy: Imperial Ideology, Resilience, and the Imagination of Yahwistic Religion." In *Deuteronomy in the Making: Studies in the Production of דברים*, edited by Diana Edelman et al., 77–96. Berlin: de Gruyter, 2021.

Berges, Ulrich. "Die Knechte im Psalter. Ein Beitrag zu seiner Kompositionsgeschichte." *Bib* 81 (2000) 153–78.

Berne, Eric. *Games People Play: The Psychology of Human Relationships*. New York: Penguin, 173.

Beuken, Willem A. M., ed. *The Book of Job*. BETL 114. Leuven: Leuven University Press, 1994.

Bewer, Julius A. *The Literature of the Old Testament in Its Historical Development*. New York: Columbia University Press, 1922.

Bingöl, Tugba Yilmaz. "The Predictive Role of Self-Efficacy, Gender, and Cyber Victimization on Cyber Bullying in Adolescents." *UJER* 6 (2018) 2478–83.

Birzer, Michael L. "Crime Scene Search." In *Introduction to Criminal Investigation*, edited by M. Birzer and C. Roberson, 35–46. London: CRC, 2012.

Black, Edwin. *Rhetorical Questions: Studies of Biblical Discourse*. Chicago: University of Chicago Press, 1992.

Black, Susan. "Drug-Exposed Children." *EE* 15 (1993) 23–25.

Blenkinsopp, Joseph. *Wisdom and Law in the Old Testament: The Ordering of Life in Israel and Early Judaism*. Oxford: Oxford University, 1983.

Bloch, René. "*Joseph und Aseneth*: Ein früher jüdische Liebesroman." In *Jüdische Drehbühnen: Biblische Variationen im antiken Judentum*, 1–28. Tria Corda 7. Tübingen: Mohr Siebeck, 2013.

Bloom, Allan. *The Closing of the American Mind: How Higher Education Has Failed Democracy and Impoverished the Souls of Today's Students*. New York: Simon and Schuster, 1987.

Boda, Mark J., and Shannon E. Baines. "Wisdom's Cry: Embracing the Vision of Justice in the Old Testament Wisdom Literature." In *The Bible and Social Justice: Old Testament and New Testament Foundations for the Church's Urgent Call*, edited by C. L. Westfall and B. R. Dyer, 35–63. Eugene, OR: Pickwick, 2015.

Bodner, Keith, and Ellen White. "Some Advantages of Recycling: The Jacob Cycle in a Later Environment." *BibInt* 22 (2014) 20–33.

Boettke, Peter J., and Kaitlyn Woltz. "Economics and Ethics within the Austrian School of Economics." In *The Oxford Handbook of Economics and Ethics*, edited by M. D. White, 229–47. Oxford: Oxford University Press, 2019.

Bömer, Franz. *P. Ovidius Naso: Metamorphosen, Vols. 3–4 (Books 6–7, 8–9)*. Heidelberg: Universitätsverlag Winter, 1976–77.

Borger, Rykle. "Die Weihe eines Enlil-Priesters." *BO* 30 (1973) 163–76.

Bottéro, Jean. "Le 'Dialogue de Pessimiste' et la transcendance." *RTP* 16 (1996) 4–24.

———. *La plus vieille religion. En Mésopotamie*. FH 82. Paris: Gallimard, 1998.

Botterweck, G. Johannes. "ידע." In *TDOT* 448–81.

Bowler, Kate. *Blessed: A History of the American Prosperity Gospel*. Oxford: Oxford University Press, 2013.

Boyd, J. Oscar. Review of *Handbooks for Bible Classes and Private Students: The Book of Job*, by James Aitken. *PTR* 6 (1908) 305–6.

Brand, Paul, and Philip Yancey. *Pain: The Gift Nobody Wants*. Grand Rapids: Zondervan, 1993.

Breitkopf, Alexander W. "Hermann Gunkel: The Father of Form Criticism." In *Pillars in the History of Biblical Interpretation*, edited by S. E. Porter and Z. K. Dawson, 3.34–65. Eugene, OR: Pickwick, 2021.

———. *Job: From Lament to Penitence*. HBM 92. Sheffield: Sheffield Phoenix, 2020.

Breytenbach, Cilliers, and Peggy L. Day. "Satan." In *DDD* 726–32.

Brock, Sebastian P. *Testamentum Iobi*. PVTG 2. Leiden: Brill, 1967.

Brooke, George J. Review of *The Role of the Solar and Lunar Calendars in the Redaction of the Psalms*, by Michael Chyutin. *JSOT* 31 (2007) 107–8.

Brown, Dan. *The Da Vinci Code*. New York: Doubleday, 2003.

Brown, Jeannine K. *Scripture as Communication: Introduction to Biblical Hermeneutics*. Grand Rapids: Baker, 2007.

Brown, Ken. *The Vision in Job 4 and Its Role in the Book: Reframing the Development of the Joban Dialogues*. FAT 75. Tübingen: Mohr Siebeck, 2015.

Brown, William P. *Character in Crisis: A Fresh Approach to the Wisdom Literature of the Old Testament*. Grand Rapids: Eerdmans, 1996.

Brunner, Helmut. *Grundzüge einer Geschichte der altägyptischen Literatur*. Darmstadt: Wissenschaftliche Buchgesellschaft, 1986.

Budde, Karl. *Das Buch Hiob, übersetzt und erklärt*. GHK 2/1. Göttingen: Vandenhoeck und Ruprecht, 1913.

Burnett, Richard E. "Wholly Other." In *The Westminster Handbook to Karl Barth*, edited by R. E. Burnett, 220–22. Louisville: Westminster John Knox, 2013.

Burnight, John D. "Does Eliphaz Really Begin 'Gently?' An Intertextual Reading of Job 4:2–11." *Bib* 95 (2014) 347–70.

———. *The Book of Job as Proto-Satire*. Forthcoming.

Butler, Christopher. *Postmodernism: A Very Short Introduction*. Oxford: Oxford University Press, 2002.

Buttenweiser, Moses. *The Book of Job*. New York: Macmillan, 1925.

Cagni, Luigi. *L'Epopea di Erra*. Roma: Istituto di Studi del Vicino Oriente, 1969.

Cahana-Blum, Jonathan. "Sophia." In *The Oxford Handbook of New Testament, Gender, and Sexuality*, edited by B. Dunning, 469–84. Oxford: Oxford University Press, 2019.

Calmet, Augustin. *Commentaire literal sur tous la livre de L'Ancien et du Nouveau Testament. X. De Livre de Job*. Paris: Emery, Saugrain, and Martin, 1722.

Carenga, Maulana. *Ma`at, the Moral Ideal in Ancient Egypt: A Study in Classical African Ethics*. London: Routledge, 2004.

Carr, David M. *The Formation of the Hebrew Bible: A New Reconstruction*. Oxford: Oxford University Press, 2011.

Carson, Donald A. *Divine Sovereignty and Human Responsibility: Biblical Perspectives in Tension*. Grand Rapids: Baker, 1994.

Ceresko, Anthony R. *Job 29–31 in the Light of Northwest Semitic: A Translation and Philological Commentary*. Rome: Biblical Institute, 1980.

Cernucan, Michael A. "From Sorrow to Submission: Overlapping Narrative in Job's Journey from 2:8 to 2:10." PhD diss., Hebrew Union College/Jewish Institute of Religion, 2016.

Chaitow, Leon. *How to Overcome Pain: Natural Approaches to Dealing with Arthritis, Anxiety, and Back Pain to Headaches, PMS, and IBS*. London: Watkins Media, 2017.

Charlesworth, James H. "Introduction." In *OTP* 1:773.

Chase, Steven. *Job*. Belief: A Theological Commentary on the Bible. Louisville: Westminster John Knox, 2013.

Childs, Brevard. *Biblical Theology in Crisis*. Philadelphia: Westminster, 1970.

Chirichigno, Gregory C. *Debt-Slavery in Israel and the Ancient Near East*. JSOTSup 141. Sheffield: Sheffield Academic, 1993.

Cho, Paul Kang-Kul. "The Integrity of Job 1 and 42:11–17." *CBQ* 76 (2014) 230–51.

Churnai, Varunaj. *Beyond Justice: Death, and the Retribution Principle in the Book of Job*. Carlisle: Langham, 2018.

Civil, Miguel. "Išme-Dagan and Enlil's Chariot." *JAOS* 88 (1967) 3–14.

Clifford, Richard J. "Isaiah 40–66." In *HBC* 573.

Clines, David J. A. "The Arguments of Job's Three Friends." In *Sitting with Job: Selected Studies in the Book of Job*, edited by R. Zuck, 265–78. Grand Rapids: Baker, 1992.

———. "False Naivety in the Prologue to Job." In *On the Way to the Postmodern: Old Testament Essays, 1967–1998*, 2.735–44. Sheffield: Sheffield Academic, 1998.

———. *Interested Parties: The Ideology of Writers and Readers of the Hebrew Bible*. Sheffield: Sheffield Academic, 1995.

———. *Job 1–20*. WBC 17. Dallas: Word, 1989.

———. "Putting Elihu in His Place: A Proposal for the Relocation of Job 32–37." *JSOT* 29 (2005) 243–53.

Cohen, Yoram. "The Problem of Theodicy: A Mesopotamian Perspective." In *Colères et repentirs divins*, edited by J.-M. Durand et al., 243–70. OBO 278. Göttingen: Vandenhoeck & Ruprecht, 2015.

———. *Wisdom from the Late Bronze Age*. WAW 34. Atlanta: SBL, 2013.

Cole, Debra S. *Pain Management Solutions: Managing Pain in Stages*. Bloomington, IN: iUniverse, 2012.

Collins, Billie Jean. "Animals in Hittite Literature." In *A History of the Animal World in the Ancient Near East*, edited by B. J. Collins, 237–50. Leiden: Brill, 2002.

———. "Divine Wrath and Divine Mercy of the Hittite and Hurrian Deities." In *Divine Wrath and Divine Mercy in the World of Antiquity*, edited by R. Kratz and H. Spieckermann, 67–77. FAT 33. Tübingen: Mohr Siebeck, 2008.

Collins, John J. "The Testamentary Literature in Recent Scholarship." In *Early Judaism and Its Modern Interpreters*, edited by R. Kraft and G. Nickelsburg, 268–85. Atlanta: Scholars, 1986.

———. "Testaments." In *Jewish Writings of the Second Temple Period*, edited by M. E. Stone, 325–56. Philadelphia: Fortress, 1984.

Coogan, Michael David. "Job's Children." In *Lingering over Words: Studies in Ancient Near Eastern Literature in Honor of William J. Moran*, edited by T. Abusch et al., 135–48. HSS 37. Cambridge: Harvard University Press, 2018.

Cook, Daniel Thomas. "Childhood Is Killing 'Our' Children: Some Thoughts on the Columbine High School Shootings and the Agentive Child." *CGJCR* 7 (2000) 107–17.

Cook, Edward. "The Interpretation of the Hebrew Bible in the Targums." In *A Companion to Biblical Interpretation in Early Judaism*, edited by M. Henze, 92–117. Grand Rapids: Eerdmans, 2003.

Cooper, Alan. "Reading and Misreading the Prologue to Job." *JSOT* 46 (1990) 67–79.

Corley, Bruce, et al. *Biblical Hermeneutics: A Comprehensive Introduction to Interpreting Scripture*. Nashville: Broadman, 2002.

Cornill, Carl H. *Einleitung in das Alte Testament*. 4th ed. Leipzig: Mohr, 1913.

Couturier, Guy. "La vie familiale comme source de la sagesse et la loi." *ScEs* 32 (1980) 177–92.

Crenshaw, James L. *Defending God: Biblical Responses to the Problem of Evil*. Oxford: Oxford University Press, 2005.

———. "Job, Book of." In *ABD* 3:858–67.

———. *Old Testament Wisdom: An Introduction*. Louisville: Westminster John Knox, 2010.
———. *Reading Job: A Literary and Theological Commentary*. Macon, GA: Smyth & Helwys, 2011.
———. Review of *Job: A New Translation*, by E. Greenstein. *RBL* 3 (2021).
———. Review of *Wisdom in Revolt*, by Leo G. Perdue. *RSR* 20 (1994) 232.
———. "Theodicy." In *ABD* 6:444–47.
Cross, Frank Moore. *Leaves From an Epigraphist's Notebook: Collected Papers in Hebrew and Northwest Semitic Paleography and Epigraphy*. Winona Lake, IN: Eisenbrauns, 2003.
Curtis, J. B. "On Job's Response to Yahweh." *JBL* 98 (1979) 497–511.
Dahood, Mitchell J. "Chiasmus in Job: A Text-Critical and Philological Criterion." In *A Light unto My Path: FS Jacob Myers*, edited by H. Bream et al., 118–30. Philadelphia: Temple University Press, 1974.
———. "Some Rare Parallel Word-Pairs in Job and in Ugaritic." In *The Word in the World: Essays in Honor of F. L. Moriarty*, edited by R. Clifford and G. MacRae, 19–34. Cambridge: Weston College Press, 1973.
Dandamaev, Muhammad A. *Slavery in Babylonia from Nabopolassar to Alexander the Great*. Dekalb, IL: Northern Illinios University Press, 1984.
D'Andrade, Kendall. "Bribery." *JBE* 4 (1985) 239–48.
Davidson, Andrew B. *The Book of Job*. Cambridge Bible. Cambridge: Cambridge University Press, 1889.
Davies, Eryl W. *Narrative Ethics in the Hebrew Bible: Moral Dilemmas in the Story of King David*. LBS. London: T. & T. Clark, 2022.
Davis, Ellen F. *Opening Israel's Scriptures*. Oxford: Oxford University Press, 2019.
Dawson, Kirsten. "'Did Not He Who Made Me in the Belly Make Him, and the Same One Fashion Us in the Womb?' (Job 31:15): Violence, Slavery, and the Book of Job." *BI* 21 (2013) 435–68.
Day, Peggy L. *An Adversary in Heaven:* sāṭān *in the Hebrew Bible*. HSM 43. Atlanta: Scholars, 1988.
de Jong, Irene J. F. "Between Word and Deed: Hidden Thoughts in the Odyssey." In *Modern Critical Theory and Classical Literature*, edited by I. de Jong and J. Sullivan, 27–50. MBCBSup 130. Leiden: Brill, 1994.
de Joode, Johan. *Metaphorical Landscapes and the Theology of the Book of Job*. VTSup 179. Leiden: Brill, 2019.
de Lamartine, Alphonse. *Cours familier de littérature*. Paris: Rue de la Ville L'Évêque, 1856.
Delekat, Lienhard. "Zum hebräischen Wörterbuch." *VT* 14 (1964) 7–66.
Delitzsch, Franz. *Das Buch Hiob. Neu übersetzt und kurz erklärt*. Leipzig: Hinrichs'sche, 1902.
Dell, Katherine. *The Book of Job as Sceptical Literature*. BZAW 197. Berlin: de Gruyter, 1991.
———. "Job." In *ECB* 337–63.
———. Review of *Defending God: Biblical Responses to the Problem of Evil*, by James Crenshaw. *JTS* 57 (2006) 616–18.
Denning Bolle, Sara. *Wisdom in Akkadian Literature: Expression, Instruction, Dialogue*. Mededelingen en verhandelingen van het Vooraziatisch-Egyptisch Genootschap "Ex Oriente Lux" 28. Leiden: Ex Oriente Lux, 1992.

Dever, William G. "Artifacts, Ecofacts, and Textual Facts: How Archaeology Today Can Illuminate the Bible." In *Recent Archaeological Discoveries and Biblical Research*, 3–36. Seattle: University of Washington Press, 2011.

———. *Beyond the Texts: An Archaeological Portrait of Ancient Israel and Judah*. Atlanta: SBL, 2017.

Dhorme, Édouard Paul. *Le livre de Job*. Paris: Gabalda, 1926.

Dick, Michael B. "The Legal Metaphor in Job 31." *CBQ* 41 (1979) 37–50.

Diewert, David A. "The Composition of the Elihu Speeches: A Poetic and Structural Analysis." PhD diss., University of Toronto, 1991.

Dillman, August. *Das Buch Hiob*. KHAT. Leipzig: Hirzel, 1891.

Dion, Paul E. "Formulaic Language in the Book of Job: International Background and Ironical Distortions." *Studies in Religion* 16 (1987) 187–93.

Dobbs-Allsopp, F. W. "The Syntagma of בת Followed by a Geographical Name in the Hebrew Bible: A Reconsideration of Its Meaning and Grammar." *CBQ* 57 (1995) 451–70.

Doetoevsky, Fyodor. *The Brothers Karamazov*. Translated by A. R. MacAndrew. 1880. Reprint, New York: Bantam, 1970.

———. *Crime and Punishment*. Translated by R. Pevear and L. Volokhonsky. 1866. Reprint, New York: Vintage, 1992.

———. *Demons*. Translated by R. Pevear and L. Volokhonsky. 1872. Reprint, New York: Vintage Books, 1994.

———. *The Idiot*. Translated by R. Pevear and L. Volokhonsky. 1868. Reprint, New York: Vintage, 2002.

———. *Notes from Underground*. Translated by R. Pevear and L. Volokhonsky. 1864. Reprint, New York: Vintage, 1994.

Drinkard, Joel F. "East." In *ABD* 2:248.

Driver, Samuel R., and George B. Gray. *A Critical and Exegetical Commentary on the Book of Job*. ICC. Edinburgh: T. & T. Clark, 1921.

Duhaime, Jean. "Dualism." In *EDSS* 215–20.

Duhm, Bernard. *Das Buch Hiob*. HKAT 16. Freiburg: Mohr Siebeck, 1897.

Dunham, Kyle C. *The Pious Sage in Job: Eliphaz in the Context of Wisdom Theodicy*. Eugene, OR: Wipf & Stock, 2016.

Eagleton, Terry. *The Illusions of Postmodernism*. Oxford: Blackwell, 1996.

Eaton, John H. *Job*. 1985. Reprint, London: T. & T. Clark, 2004.

Ebach, Jürgen. "Ist es 'umsonst' das Hiob gottesfürtig ist? Lexicographische und methodologische Marginalien zu חנם im Hi 1,9." In *Die Hebräische Bibel und ihre zweifache Nachgeschichte. FS Rolf Rendtorff*, edited by E. Blum, 319–35. Neukirchen-Vluyn: Neukirchener, 1990.

Ebeling, Erich. "Ein babylonischen Kohelet." *BBK* 1 (1922) 1–12.

Edenburg, Cynthia. "The Book of the Covenant." In *The Oxford Handbook of Biblical Law*, edited by P. Barmash, 157–76. Oxford: Oxford University Press, 2019.

Eisen, Robert. *The Book of Job in Medieval Jewish Philosophy*. Oxford: Oxford University Press, 2004.

Eissfeldt, Otto. *The Old Testament: An Introduction*. Translated by P. Ackroyd. 1934. Reprint, New York: Harper and Row, 1965.

Eller, Jack D. *Cultural Anthropology 101*. London: Routledge, 2015.

Ellis, Nicholas. *The Hermeneutics of Divine Testing: Cosmic Trials and Biblical Interpretation in the Epistle of James and Other Jewish Literature*. WUNT 396. Tübingen: Mohr Siebeck, 2015.

Emerton, John. Review of *Wisdom and the Book of Proverbs: An Israelite Goddess Redefined*, by B. Lang. *VT* 37 (1987) 127.

Endo, Yoshinobu. *The Verbal System of Classical Hebrew in the Joseph Story: An Approach from Discourse Analysis*. Assen: Van Gorcum, 1996.

Erman, Adolf. "Gesprach des Lebensmüden mit seiner Seele." *APAW* (1896) 1–77.

———. *The Literature of the Ancient Egyptians*. Translated by A. M. Blackman. 1923. Reprint, London: Methuen & Co., 1927.

Ernst, Carl W. *Following Muhammad: Rethinking Islam in the Contemporary World*. Chapel Hill, NC: University of North Carolina Press, 2003.

Eshel, Ḥanan. "The Damascus Document's 'Three Nets of Belial': A Reference to the *Aramaic Levi Document*?" In *Heavenly Tablets: Interpretation, Identity, and Tradition in Ancient Judaism*, edited by L. LiDonnici and A. Lieber, 243–55. JSJSup 119. Leiden: Brill, 2007.

Eskola, Timo. *Messiah and the Throne: Merkabah Mysticism and Early Christian Exaltation Discourse*. Tübingen: Mohr Siebeck, 2001.

Estelle, Bryan D. *Echoes of Exodus: Tracing a Biblical Motif*. Downers Grove, IL: InterVarsity, 2018.

Espak, Peeter. *The God Enki in Sumerian Royal Ideology and Mythology*. Philippika: Altertumswissenschaftliche Abhandlungen/Contributions to the Study of Ancient World Cultures 87. Wiesbaden: Harrassowitz, 2015.

Ewald, Georg Heinrich August von. *Commentary on the Book of Job*. Translated by J. F. Smith. 1852. Reprint, London: Williams and Norgate, 1882.

Farber Flügge, Gertrud. *Der Mythos "Inanna und Enki" unter besonderer Berücksichtigen der Lister der ME*. SP 10. Rome: Biblical Institute, 1973.

Farook, Mohammad Omar. *Toward Our Reformation: From Legalism to Value-Oriented Islamic Law and Jurisprudence*. Abridged by W. Krause. Herndon, VA: International Institute of Islamic Thought, 2015.

Faulkner, Raymond O. "The Man Who Was Tired of Life." *JEA* 42 (1956) 21–40.

Fee, Gordon D. *The Disease of the Health and Wealth Gospels*. Vancouver: Regent College, 1996.

Finkel, Abraham Yaakov. *Ein Yaakov: The Ethical and Inspirational Teachings of the Talmud Compiled in the 16th Century by Rabbi Ya`akov ibn Chaviv*. New York: Rowman and Littlefield, 1999.

Finn, Jennifer. *Much Ado about Marduk: Questioning Discourses of Royalty in First Millennium Mesopotamian Literature*. Studies in Ancient Near Eastern Records 16. Berlin: de Gruyter, 2017.

Fishbane, Michael. *Biblical Myth and Rabbinic Mythmaking*. New York: Oxford University Press, 2005.

———. "The Book of Job and Inner-Biblical Interpretation." In *The Voice from the Whirlwind: Interpreting the Book of Job*, edited by L. G. Perdue and W. C. Gilpin, 86–98. Nashville: Abingdon, 1992.

Floyd, Michael H. Review of *The Book of Job: A Contest of Moral Imaginations*, by C. Newsom. *ATR* 87 (2005) 158, 160.

———. "Welcome Back, Daughter of Zion!" *CBQ* 70 (2008) 484–504.

Fohrer, Georg. *Das Buch Hiob*. KAT 16. Gütersloh: Gerd Mohn, 1963.

———. "Form und Funktion in der Hiobdichtung." *ZDMG* 109 (1959) 31–49.

Fokkelman, Jan P. *Major Poems of the Hebrew Bible at the Interface of Prosody and Structural Analysis*. Vol. 4, *Job 15–42*. Assen: Van Gorcum, 2004.

Foley, Helene. "Medea's Divided Self." *ClAnt* 8 (1989) 61–85.

Fontaine, Carol A. "Arrows of the Almighty (Job 6:4): Perspectives on Pain." *ATR* 66 (1984) 243–48.

———. "Folktale Structure in the Book of Job." In *Directions in Biblical Hebrew Poetry*, edited by E. R. Follis, 205–32. JSOTSup 40. Sheffield: Sheffield Academic, 1987.

———. "Wounded Hero on a Shaman's Quest." In *The Voice from the Whirlwind: Interpreting the Book of Job*, edited by L. Perdue and C. Gilpin, 70–85. Nashville: Abingdon, 1992.

Forsyth, Neil. *The Old Enemy: Satan and the Combat Myth*. Princeton: Princeton University Press, 1987.

Foster, Benjamin R. *The Age of Agade: Inventing Empire in Ancient Mesopotamia*. London: Routledge, 2016.

———. *Before the Muses: An Anthology of Akkadian Literature*. Bethesda, MD: CDL, 2005.

———. "In Search of Akkadian Literature." In *Before the Muses: An Anthology of Akkadian Literature*, 1–47. Bethesda, MD: CDL, 2005.

———. "A Sufferer's Salvation." In *COS* 1.486.

Fox, Michael V. "God's Answer and Job's Response." *Bib* 94 (2013) 1–23.

———. "The Meanings of the Book of Job." *JBL* 137 (2018) 7–18.

———. "Three Theses on Wisdom." In *Was There a Wisdom Tradition? New Prospects in Israelite Wisdom Studies*, edited by M. Sneed, 69–86. AIL 23. Atlanta: SBL, 2015.

Franke, Judith. "Nippur." In *ABD* 4:1119–22.

Frankl, Razelle. *Televangelism: The Marketing of Popular Religion*. Carbondale IL: Southern Illinois University Press, 1987.

Fredriksen, Paula. "Paul's Letter to the Romans, The Ten Commandments, and Pagan 'Justification by Faith.'" *JBL* 133 (2014) 801–8.

Freedman, David Noel. "The Elihu Speeches in the Book of Job." *HTR* 61 (1968) 51–59.

Frey, Jörg. "Dualismus: Zur frühjüdischen Herausbildung und zur neutestamentlichen Rezeption dualistischer Weltdeutung." In *Dualismus, Dämonologie, und diabolische Figuren: Religionshistorische Beobachtungen und theologische Reflexionen*, edited by J. Frey and E. Popkes, 3–46. WUNT 2/484. Tübingen: Mohr Siebeck, 2018.

Fried, Richard M. *Nightmare in Red: The McCarthy Era in Perspective*. Oxford: Oxford University Press, 1990.

Frisch, Amos. "The Portrait of Solomon in the Book of Kings." In *Characters and Characterization in the Book of Kings*, edited by K. Bodner and B. Johnson, 50–64. London: T. & T. Clark, 2020.

Frost, Robert. "A Masque of Reason." In *The Poetry of Robert Frost*, edited by E. C. Lathem, 473–90. 1923. Reprint, New York: Holt and Company, 1969.

Frow, John. *Genre: The New Critical Idiom*. London: Routledge, 2006.

Frymer-Kensky, Tikva. *In the Wake of the Goddesses: Women, Culture, and the Biblical Transformation of Pagan Myth*. New York: Free Press, 1992.

Fuchs, Gisela. "Die Klage des Propheten. Beobachtungen zu des Konfessionen Jeremias im Vergleich mit den Klagen Hiobs." *BZ* 41 (1997) 22–28.

———. *Mythos und Hiobdichtung. Aufnahme und Umdeutung altorientalischer Vorstellungen*. Stuttgart: Kohlhammer, 1993.

Fullerton, Kemper. "*Double Entendre* in the First Speech of Eliphaz." *JBL* 49 (1930) 320–74.

Fyall, Robert S. *Now My Eyes Have Seen You: Images of Creation and Evil in the Book of Job*. NSBT 17. Downers Grove, IL: InterVarsity, 2002.

Gabriel, Gösta. *"Enūma Eliš"—Weg zu einer globalen Weltordnung. Pragmatik, Struktur und Semantik des Babylonischen "Lieds auf Marduk."* ORA 12. Tübingen: Mohr Siebeck, 2014.

Gabriel, Joseph M. "Damage." In *Rethinking Therapeutic Culture*, edited by T. Aubrey and T. Travis, 24–33. Chicago: University of Chicago Press, 2015.

Gammie, John G. "The Septuagint of Job: Its Poetic Style and Relationship to the Septuagint of Proverbs." *CBQ* 49 (1987) 14–31.

Gamper, Arnold. *Gott als Richter im Mesopotamien und im Alten Testament. Zum Verständnis eines Gebetsbitte*. Innsbruck: Universitätsverlag Wagner, 1966.

Gaon, Saadiah. *The Book of Theodicy: Translation and Commentary on the Book of Job*. Translated by L. Goodman. 1938. Reprint, New Haven: Yale University Press, 1988.

Gardiner, Alan H. *The Admonitions of an Egyptian Sage*. Leipzig: Hinrichs'sche Buchhandlung, 1909.

———. *Egyptian Grammar*. 3rd ed. Oxford: Griffith Institute, 1957.

Garrett, Susan. "The 'Weaker Sex' in the Testament of Job." *JBL* 112 (1993) 55–70.

Gaster, Theodore H. "Satan." In *IDB* 4.224–28.

Gately, Megan, and Keren Ladin. "Family and Other Caregivers." In *Chronic Illness Care: Principles and Practice*, edited by T. P. Daaleman and M. R. Helton, 111–20. New York: Springer, 2018.

Gault, Brian P. "Job's Hope: Redeemer or Retribution." *BSac* 173 (2016) 147–65.

Geiger, Abraham. *Urschrift und Übersetzungen der Bibel*. Breslau: Verlag von Julius Heinauer, 1857.

Geller, Stephen A. Review of *The Idea of Biblical Poetry: Parallelism and Its History*, by James Kugel. *JBL* 102 (1983) 625–26.

———. "'Where Is Wisdom?' A Literary Study of Job 28 in Its Settings." In *Judaic Perspectives on Ancient Israel*, edited by J. Neusner et al., 155–88. Minneapolis: Fortress, 1987.

Gemser, Berend. "The ריב—or Controversy-Pattern in Hebrew Mentality." VTSup 3 (1955) 120–37.

George, Andrew R. *The Babylonian Gilgamesh Epic*. 2 vols. New York: Oxford University Press, 2003.

Gerhards, Meik. *Der undefinierbare Gott: Theologische Annäherrungen an alttestamentliche und altorientalische Texte*. RTS 24. Berlin: LIT, 2011.

Gerleman, Gillis. "Die Wurzel שלם." *ZAW* 85 (1973) 1–14.

———. *Studies in the Septuagint I: The Book of Job*. Lund: Gleerup, 1946.

Gersonides. ספר מלחמות השם *(The Book of the Wars of the Lord)*. Translated by S. Feldman. 1560. Reprint, Philadelphia: Jewish Publication Society of America, 1984–89.

Gerstenberger, Erhard S. *Theologies in the Old Testament*. Translated by J. Bowden. Minneapolis: Fortress, 2002.

———. "ענה." In *TDOT* 11:230–52.

Gese, Hartmut. "Die Frage nach dem Lebenssinn. Hiob und die Folgen." *ZTK* 79 (1982) 161–79.

Geyer, Nelouise, and Thembi Mngomezulu. "Ethical Concerns in Relationships between Nurses, Their Employing Authorities, and Trade Unions." In *Ethics in Heath Care*, edited by S. A. Pera and S. van Tonder, 82–96. Landsowne: Juta Academic, 2005.

Ghantous, Hadi. "Was Job 'Patient?' Is God 'Just?'" *TR* 33 (2012) 22–38.

Gibson, John C. L. *Job*. DSBS. Philadelphia: Westminster, 1985.

Gilkey, Langdon. "Power, Order, Justice, and Redemption: Theological Comments on the Book of Job." In *The Voice from the Whirlwind: Interpreting the Book of Job*, edited by L. Perdue and W. C. Gilpin, 159–71. Nashville: Abingdon, 1992.

Ginzberg, Louis. *Legends of the Jews*. 1925. Reprint, New York: Cosimo Classics, 2005.

Giovino, Mariana. *The Assyrian Sacred Tree: A History of Interpretations*. OBO 230. Göttingen: Vandenhoeck & Ruprecht, 2007.

Goedicke, Hans. *The Report about the Dispute of a Man with His Ba*. Baltimore: John Hopkins University, 1970.

Goldsmith, Robert H. "The Healing Scourge: A Study of Suffering and Meaning." *Int* 17 (1963) 1–27.

Goldingay, John. *Isaiah*. UBCS. Grand Rapids: Baker, 2001.

———. *Job for Everyone*. Louisville: Westminster John Knox, 2013.

———. *Old Testament Theology*. 3 vols. Downers Grove, IL: InterVarsity, 2006.

Good, Edwin M. *In Turns of Tempest: A Reading of Job with a Translation*. Stanford: Stanford University Press, 1990.

———. "Job and the Literary Task: A Response." *Soundings* 56 (1973) 470–84.

Gordon, Cyrus H. "The Story of Jacob and Laban in Light of the Nuzi Tablets." *BASOR* 66 (1937) 25–27.

Gordon, Robert P. *Hebrew Bible and Ancient Versions: Selected Essays of Robert P. Gordon*. SOTSMS. 2006. Reprint, London: Routledge, 2016.

Gordis, Robert. *The Book of God and Man: A Study of Job*. Chicago: University of Chicago Press, 1965.

———. *The Book of Job: Commentary, New Translation, and Special Studies*. New York: Jewish Theological Seminary of America, 1978.

Grabbe, Lester L. *Comparative Philology and the Text of Job: A Study in Methodology*. SBLDS 34. Atlanta: Scholars, 1977.

———. *Priests, Prophets, Diviners, Sages: A Sociohistorical Study of Religious Specialists in Ancient Israel*. Harrisburg, PA: Trinity International, 1995.

Graf, David E. "Classical Text Sources in the Levant." In *Near Eastern Archaeology: A Reader*, edited by S. Richard, 440–44. Winona Lake, IN: Eisenbrauns. 2003.

Gray, George Buchanan. *A Critical Introduction to the Old Testament*. London: Duckworth, 1931.

Gray, John. "The Book of Job in the Context of Near Eastern Literature." *ZAW* 82 (1970) 251–69.

———. "Masoretic Text of the Book of Job, the Targum, and the Septuagint Version in the Light of the Qumran Targum (11QtgJob)." *ZAW* 86 (1974) 331–50.

Green, Arthur. *The Language of Truth: The Torah Commentary of the Sefat Emet*. Philadelphia: Jewish Publication Society, 1998.

Green, William Henry. *The Argument of the Book of Job Unfolded*. New York: Hurst, 1891.

Greenstein, Edward L. "Jeremiah as Inspiration to the Poet of Job." In *Inspired Speech: Prophecy in the Ancient Near East: Essays Presented to H. B. Huffmon*, edited by J. Kaltner and L. Stulman, 98–110. New York: T. & T. Clark, 2004.

———. *Job: A New Translation*. New Haven: Yale University Press, 2019.
———. "The Poem on Wisdom in Job 28 in Its Conceptual and Literary Contexts." In *Job 28: Cognition in Context*, edited by E. van Wolde, 253–80. BI 64. Leiden: Brill, 2003.
———. "The Problem of Evil in the Book of Job." *In Mishneh Todah: Studies in Deuteronomy and Its Cultural Environment in Honor of Jeffrey H. Tigay*, edited by N. S. Fox et al., 333–62. Winona Lake, IN: Eisenbrauns, 2009.
Gregory, Bradley C. *Like an Everlasting Signet Ring: Generosity in the Book of Sirach*. DCLS 2. Berlin: de Gruyter, 2010.
Gregory I. *Magna Moralia: Morals on the Book of Job*. Translated by J. H. Parker. London: F. and J. Rivington, 1847.
Grene, Clement. Review of *Job's Way through Pain: Karma, Clichés, and Questions*, by P. Hedley Jones. *RRT* 24 (2017) 309–12.
Grenz, Stanley J. *A Primer on Postmodernism*. Grand Rapids: Eerdmans, 1996.
Grimal, Nicolas. *A History of Ancient Egypt*. Oxford: Blackwell, 1992.
Groneberg, Brigitte. "Towards a Definition of Literature as Applied to Akkadian Literature." In *Mesopotamian Poetic Language: Sumerian and Akkadian*, edited by M. E. Vogelzang and H. J. L. Vanstiphout, 59–84. Groningen: Styx, 1996.
Gruber, Mayer I. "The Book of Job as Anthropodicy." *BN* 136 (2008) 59–71.
Guffy, Andrew R. "Job and the 'Mystic's Solution' to Theodicy: Philosophical Paideia and Internalized Apocalypticism in the Testament of Job." In *Pedagogy in Ancient Judaism and Early Christianity*, edited by K. M. Hogan et al., 215–40. Atlanta: SBL, 2017.
———. Review of *Job 1–21: Interpretation and Commentary*, by C. L. Seow. *JAOS* 137 (2017) 881–83.
Guillaume, Philippe. *Land, Credit, and Crisis: Agrarian Finance in the Hebrew Bible*. Sheffield: Equinox, 2012.
———, and Michael Schunck. "Job's Intercession: Antidote to Divine Folly." *Bib* 88 (2007) 457–72.
Gulaker, Cato. *Satan, the Heavenly Adversary of Man: A Narrative Analysis of the Function of Satan in the Book of Revelation*. New York: T. & T. Clark, 2021.
Gutiérrez, Gustavo. *Essential Writings*. Edited by J. B. Nickoloff. Maryknoll, NY: Orbis, 1996.
———. *On Job: God-Talk and the Suffering of the Innocent*. Maryknoll, NY: Orbis, 1987.
———. *A Theology of Liberation: History, Politics, and Salvation*. Translated by C. Inda and J. Eagleson. Maryknoll, NY: Orbis, 1973.
Haag, Ernst. *Das hellenistische Zeitalter. Israel und die Bibel im 4. bis 1. Jahrhundert vor Chr*. Stuttgart: Kohlhammer, 2003.
Haas, Cees. "Job's Perseverance in the Testament of Job." In *Studies on the Testament of Job*, edited by M. Knibb and P. van der Horst, 117–54. SNTSMS 152. Cambridge: Cambridge University Press, 1989.
Habel, Norman C. *The Book of Job: A Commentary*. OTL. Philadelphia: Westminster, 1985.
———. *Finding Wisdom in Nature: An Eco-Wisdom Reading of the Book of Job*. EBC 4. Sheffield: Sheffield Phoenix, 2014.
———. "The Narrative Art of Job." *JSOT* 27 (1983) 101–11.
———. "Only the Jackal Is My Friend." *Int* 31 (1977) 227–36.

———. "The Role of Elihu in the Design of the Book of Job." In *In the Shelter of Elyon*, edited by W. B. Barrick and J. R. Spencer, 81–98. JSOTSup 31. Sheffield: Sheffield Academic, 1984.

Hackett, Jo Ann. *The Balaam Text from Deir `Allā*. HSM 31. Chico, CA: Scholars, 1980.

Hagedorn, Anselm C. *Between Moses and Plato: Individual and Society in Deuteronomy and Ancient Greek Law*. FRLANT 204. Göttingen: Vandenhoeck und Ruprecht, 2004.

Hagedorn, Ursula, and Dieter Hagedorn. *Johannes Chrysostomos Kommentar zu Hiob*. PTS 35. Berlin: de Gruyter, 1990.

Hallo, William W. *The World's Oldest Literature: Studies in Sumerian Belles-Lettres*. CHANE 35. Leiden: Brill, 2010.

Hamilton, James E. *What Is Biblical Theology? A Guide to the Bible's Story, Symbolism, and Patterns*. Wheaton, IL: Crossway, 2014.

Hamilton, Mark W. "Deuteronomy." In *The Transforming Word: A One-Volume Commentary on the Bible*, edited by M. W. Hamilton, 207–42. Abilene, TX: Abilene Christian University Press, 2009.

———. "Elite Lives: Job 29–31 and Traditional Authority." *JSOT* 32 (2007) 69–89.

Hamilton, Victor P. "Satan." In *ABD* 5:985–89.

Handy, Lowell K. "The Authorization of Divine Power and the Guilt of God in the Book of Job: Useful Ugaritic Parallels." *JSOT* 60 (1993) 107–18.

Hankins, Davis. *The Book of Job and the Immanent Genesis of Transcendence*. Evanston, IL: Northwestern University Press, 2015.

Hanson, K. C. "When the King Crosses the Line: Royal Deviance and Restitution in Levantine Ideologies." *BTB* 26 (1996) 11–25.

Haralambakis, Maria. *The Testament of Job: Text, Narrative, and Reception History*. London: T. & T. Clark, 2012.

Haran, Menahem. "On the Diffusion of Literacy and Schools in Ancient Israel." In *Congress Volume 1986*, edited by J. Emerton, 81–95. VTSup 40. Leiden: Brill, 1988.

Harper, Robert F. *The Code of Hammurabi, King of Babylon*. Chicago: University of Chicago Press, 1904.

Harris, Thomas A. *I'm OK—You're OK*. New York: HarperCollins, 1967.

Hartley, John E. *The Book of Job*. NICOT. Grand Rapid: Eerdmans, 1988.

Hasan, Abla. *Pain and Suffering: A Qur'anic Perspective*. London: Lexington, 2022.

Hawley, Lance. "The Rhetoric of Condemnation in the Book of Job." *JBL* 139 (2020) 459–78.

Hedley Jones, Paul. *Job's Way through Pain: Karma, Clichés, and Questions*. London: Paternoster, 2014.

Hellige, Joseph B. "Interhemispheric Interaction on the Lateralized Brain." In *Concise Encyclopedia of Brain and Language*, edited by H. A. Whitaker, 248–58. Oxford: Elsevier, 2010.

Hengel, Martin. *The "Hellenization" of Judea in the First Century after Christ*. Translated by J. Bowden. 1989. Reprint, Eugene, OR: Wipf & Stock, 2003.

Herrmann, Siegfried. *Die prophetische Heilserwartungen im alten Testament. Ursprung und Gestaltwandel*. BWANT 85. Stuttgart: Kohlhammer, 1965.

———. *Untersuchungen zur Überlieferungsgestalt mittelägyptischer Literaturwerk*. Berlin: Akademie, 1957.

Hershkowitz, Debra. *The Madness of Epic: Reading Insanity from Homer to Statius*. OCM. Oxford: Clarendon, 1998.

Hesse, Franz. *Hiob*. ZBKAT 14. Zürcher: Theologischer, 1978.

Hilton, Rodney H. "The Origins of Robin Hood." In *Robin Hood: An Anthology of Scholarship and Criticism*, edited by S. T. Knight, 197–210. Cambridge: Brewer, 1999.

Hoffman, Yair. *A Blemished Perfection: The Book of Job in Context*. JSOTSup 213. Sheffield: Sheffield Academic, 1996.

———. "The Relation between the Prologue and the Speech-Cycles in Job: A Reconsideration." *VT* 31 (1981) 160–70.

Holbert, John C. "Eliphaz." In *ABD* 2:471.

———. "The Function and Significance of the '*Klage*' in the Book of Job with Special Reference to the Incidence of Formal and Verbal Irony." PhD diss., Southern Methodist University, 1975.

Hollis, Susan T. "Egyptian Literature." In *From an Antique Land: An Introduction to Ancient Near Eastern Literature*, edited by C. Ehrlich, 77–136. New York: Rowman and Littlefield, 2009.

Hölscher, Gustav. *Das Buch Hiob*. HAT 17. Tübingen: Mohr Siebeck, 1937.

Hornborg, Alf. *Global Ecology and Unequal Exchange*. London: Routledge, 2011.

Horst, Friedrich. *Hiob*. BK 16/1. Neukirchen-Vluyn: Neukirchener, 1968.

Horst, Pieter van der. "Images of Women in the Testament of Job." In *Studies on the Testament of Job*, edited by M. Knibb and P. van der Horst, 93–116. SNTSMS 152. Cambridge: Cambridge University Press, 1989.

Horwitz, William J. "The Ugaritic Scribe." *UF* 11 (1979) 389–94.

Huff, Barry G. "From Societal Scorn to Divine Delight: Job's Transformative Portrayal of Wild Animals." *Int* 73 (2019) 248–58.

Hugo, Victor. *Les Misérables*. Translated by C. Donougher. 1862. Reprint, New York: Penguin, 2015.

Hurowitz, Victor A. "ᴰNarru and ᴰZulummar in the Babylonian Theodicy (*BWL* 88.276–77)." *JAOS* 124 (2004) 777–78.

Husseini, Rana. "The Historical and Religious Seeds of 'Honor.'" In *Abraham's Children: Liberty and Tolerance in an Age of Religious Conflict*, edited by K. J. Clark, 259–77. New Haven: Yale University Press, 2012.

Hyun, Seong Whan Timothy. *Job the Unfinalizable: A Bakhtinian Reading of Job 1–11*. BI 124. Leiden: Brill, 2013.

Inouye, Stanley K. *Foundations for Asian American Ministry*. Monrovia: Iwa, 2001.

Irwin, William A. "The First Speech of Bildad." *ZAW* 51 (1933) 205–16.

Jackson, David R. "Cosmic Bully or God of Grace? The Book of Job as משל." *WTJ* 78 (2016) 65–73.

Jacobsen, Thorkild. "Primitive Democracy in Ancient Mesopotamia." *JNES* 2 (1943) 159–72.

———. *The Treasures of Darkness*. New Haven: Yale University Press, 1976.

Jacobsen, Thorkild, and Kirsten Nielsen. "Cursing the Day." *SJOT* 6 (1992) 187–204.

Jakobson, Roman. "Poetics." In *Roman Jakobson: Selected Writings*. Vol. 7, *Contributions to Comparative Mythology*, edited by S. Rudy, 341–70. Berlin: de Gruyter, 1985.

Jameson, Fredric. *Postmodernism: Or the Cultural Logic of Late Capitalism*. Durham, NC: Duke University Press, 1991.

Janzen, J. Gerald. *Job*. Interpretation. Louisville: Westminster John Knox, 1985.

———. Review of *Wisdom in Revolt*, by Leo G. Perdue. *Int* 47 (1993) 72.

Jarvik, Lissy F., and Gary W. Small. *Parentcare: A Commonsense Guide for Adult Children*. New York: Bantam, 1990.

Jasser, M. Zuhdi. *A Battle for the Soul of Islam: An American Muslim Patriot's Fight to Save His Faith*. New York: Simon and Schuster, 2012.

Jastrow, Morris. *The Book of Job*. Philadelphia: Lippincott, 1920.

Jiménez, Enrique. *The Babylonian Disputation Poems*. CHANE 87. Leiden: Brill, 2017.

Jindo, Job Y. "The Divine Courtroom Motif in the Hebrew Bible: A Holistic Perspective." In *The Divine Courtroom in Comparative Perspective*, edited by A. Mermelstein and S. E. Holtz, 76–93. BI 132. Leiden: Brill, 2014.

Johns, Anthony Hearle. "Narrative, Intertext, and Allusion in the Qur'anic Presentation of Job." *JQS* 1 (1999) 1–25.

Johns, Donald Arvid. "The Literary and Theological Function of the Elihu Speeches in the Book of Job." PhD diss., Saint Louis University, 1983.

Johnson, Benjamin J. F. *Reading David and Goliath in Greek and Hebrew: A Literary Approach*. FAT 82. Tübingen: Mohr Siebeck, 2015.

Johnson, Timothy Jay. *Now My Eye Sees You: Unveiling an Apocalyptic Job*. HBM 24. Sheffield: Sheffield Phoenix, 2009.

Jones Nelson, Alissa. "Job." In *The Old Testament and Apocrypha: Fortress Commentary on the Bible*, edited by G. Yee et al., 519–45. Minneapolis: Fortress, 2014.

Jones, Scott C. *Rumors of Wisdom: Job 28 as Poetry*. Berlin: de Gruyter, 2009.

Judd, Naomi. *River of Time: My Descent into Depression and How I Emerged with Hope*. New York: Hachette, 2016.

Jung, Carl F. *Answer to Job*. Translated by R. F. C. Hull. 1952. Reprint, London: Routledge, 2002.

Kallen, Horace M. *The Book of Job as a Greek Tragedy*. New York: Moffat, Yard, and Co., 1918.

Kalman, Jason. "Righteousness Restored: The Place of *Midrash Iyov* in the History of the Jewish Exegesis of the Biblical Book of Job." *OTE* 19 (2006) 77–100.

Kaminsky, Joel S. "Would You Impugn My Justice? A Nuanced Approach to the Hebrew Bible's Theology of Divine Recompense." *Int* 69 (2015) 299–310.

Kaplan, Robert. *The Nothing That Is: A Natural History of Zero*. New York: Oxford University Press, 2000.

Karenga, Maulana. *Ma`at: The Moral Ideal in Ancient Egypt*. London: Routledge, 2004.

Kates, Judith A. "The Cry of Redemption." In *Jewish Mysticism and the Spiritual Life*, edited by L. Fine et al., 46–50. Woodstock, VT: Jewish Lights, 2011.

Kaufmann, Yehezkel. "Job the Righteous Man and Job the Sage." In *The Dimensions of Job*, edited by N. Glatzer, 65–70. New York: Schocken, 1969.

Kautilya. *The Arthashastra*. Translated by L. N. Rangarajan. 1987. Reprint, New York: Penguin, 2016.

Kautzsch, Karl. *Die sogenannte Volksbuch von Hiob und der Ursprung von Hiob cap. I. II. XLII, 7–17.: Ein Beitrag zur Frage nach der Integrität des Buches Hiob*. Tübingen: Mohr Siebeck, 1900.

Kee, Min Suc. "The Heavenly Council and Its Type-Scene." *JSOT* 31 (2007) 259–73.

Keefe, Alice. "Hosea." In *Fortress Commentary on the Bible: The Old Testament and Apocrypha*, edited by Gale A. Yee et al., 823–35. Minneapolis: Fortress, 2014.

Kelly, Henry. *Satan in the Bible: God's Minister of Justice*. Eugene, OR: Cascade Books, 2017.

Kensky, Meira Z. *Trying God, Trying Man: The Divine Courtroom in Early Jewish and Christian Literature*. WUNT 289. Tübingen: Mohr Siebeck, 2010.

Kessler, Rainer. "'Ich weisse das mein Erlöser lebt': Sozialgeschichtlicher Hintergrund und theologische Bedeutung der Löser-Vorstellung in Hiob 19:25." *ZTK* 89 (1992) 139–58.

Kierkegaard, Søren. *Die Wiederholung*. Hamburg: Meiner, 2000.

Kinet, Dirk. "The Ambiguity of the Concepts of God and the Satan in the Book of Job." In *Job and the Silence of God*, edited by C. Duquoc and C. Floristán, 30–35. Edinburgh: T. & T. Clark, 1983.

Kissane, Edward J. *The Book of Job*. Dublin: Browne & Nolan, 1939.

Klein, Michael. הגשמת האל בתרגמים הארמים לתורה. Jerusalem: Makor, 1972.

———. *Michael Klein on the Targums: Collected Essays, 1972–2002*. Edited by A. Shinan et al. Leiden: Brill, 2011.

Klopfenstein, Martin. "חנם (*ḥinnam*) in Hiobbuch." In *Leben aus dem Wort. Beiträge zum Alten Testament*, edited by M. Klopfenstein and W. Dietrich, 117–21. BEATAJ 40. Bern: Lang, 1996.

Kluger, Rivkah Schärf. *Satan in the Old Testament*. Translated by H. Nagel. 1948. Reprint, Evanston, IL: Northwestern University Press, 1967.

Knauf, Ernst Axel. "Elihu." In *ABD* 2:463.

———. "Naamathite." In *ABD* 4:968.

———. "Shuah." In *ABD* 5:1225–26.

Knierim, Rolf. "Old Testament Form Criticism Reconsidered." *Int* 27 (1973) 435–68.

Knudtzon, Jørgen Alexander. *Assyrische Gebete an den Sonnengott für Staat und königliches Haus aus der Zeit Asarhaddons und Assurbanipals*. 2 vols. Leipzig: Hinrichs, 1893.

Koch, Klaus. "Gibt es ein Vergeltungsdogma im Alten Testament?" *ZTK* 52 (1955) 1–42. Translated as "Is There a Doctrine of Retribution in the Old Testament?" In Theodicy in the Old Testament, edited by James L. Crenshaw, 57–87. Issues in Religion and Theology 4. Philadelphia: Fortress, 1983.

———. *Was ist Formgeschichte?* Neukirchen-Vluyn: Neukirchener, 1974.

Kolenkow, Anitra. "The Literary Genre 'Testament.'" In *Early Judaism and Its Modern Interpreters*, edited by R. Kraft and G. Nickelsburg, 259–67. Atlanta: Scholars, 1986.

Komoróczy, Géza. "Work and Strike of Gods: New Light on the Divine Society in the Sumero-Akkadian Mythology." *Oikumene* 1 (1976) 9–37.

Koning, Brian M. "The Prophet and Sage: A Study on Intertextual Connections between Habakkuk and Job." PhD diss., Midwestern Baptist Theological Seminary, 2021.

Kraemer, David C. *Responses to Suffering in Classical Rabbinic Literature*. New York: Oxford University Press, 1995.

Kramer, Samuel N. "The Death of Ur-Nammu and His Descent to the Netherworld." *JCS* 21 (1967) 110–22.

Kruger, Paul A. "A World Turned on Its Head in Ancient Near Eastern Prophetic Literature: A Powerful Strategy to Depict Chaotic Scenarios." *VT* 62 (2012) 58–76.

Krüger, Thomas. "Morality and Religion in Three Babylonian Poems of Pious Sufferers." In *Teaching Morality in Antiquity: Wisdom Texts, Oral Traditions, and Images*, edited by T. Oshima and S. Kohlhaas, 182–88. Tübingen: Mohr Siebeck, 2018.

Kucicki, Janusz. *The Function of the Speeches in the Acts of the Apostles: A Key to Interpretation of Luke's Speeches in Acts*. BI 158. Leiden: Brill, 2018.

Kugel, James. *The Idea of Biblical Poetry: Parallelism and Its History*. Baltimore: Johns Hopkins Press, 1981.

Kutsko, John F. *Between Heaven and Earth: Divine Presence and Absence in the Book of Ezekiel*. BiJuSt 7. Winona Lake, IN: Eisenbrauns, 2000.

Kwon, Jiseong James. "Divergence of the Book of Job from Deuteronomic/Priestly Torah." *SJOT* 32 (2018) 49–71.

Kynes, Will. *An Obituary for "Wisdom Literature": The Birth, Death, and Intertextual Reintegration of a Biblical Corpus*. New York: Oxford University Press, 2019.

———. *My Psalm Has Turned Into Weeping: Job's Dialogue with the Psalms*. BZAW 437. Berlin: de Gruyter, 2012.

Labahn, Michael. "The Dangerous Loser: The Narrative and Rhetorical Function of the Devil as Character in the Book of Revelation." In *Evil and the Devil*, edited by I. Fröhlich and E. Koskenniemi, 156–79. LNTS 481. London: T. & T. Clark, 2013.

Lambert, David A. "The Book of Job in Ritual Perspective." *JBL* 134 (2015) 557–75.

Lambert, Wilfrid G. *Babylonian Creation Myths*. Winona Lake, IN: Eisenbrauns, 2013.

———. *The Babylonian Wisdom Literature*. Oxford: Clarendon, 1960.

———. "Some New Babylonian Wisdom Literature." In *Wisdom in Ancient Israel: Essays in Honour of J. A. Emerton*, edited by J. Day et al., 30–42. Cambridge: Cambridge University Press, 1995.

Lambert, Wilfrid G., and Alan R. Millard. *Atra-ḫasīs: The Babylonian Story of the Flood*. 1969. Reprint, Winona Lake, IN: Eisenbrauns, 1999.

Landsberger, Bruno. "Die babylonische Theodizee (akrostichisches Zwiegespräch; sog. 'Kohelet')." *ZA* 43 (1936) 32–76.

Larrimore, Mark. *The Book of Job: A Biography*. Princeton: Princeton University Press, 2013.

Lasine, Stuart. *Knowing Kings: Knowledge, Power, and Narcissism in the Hebrew Bible*. SBLSS 40. Atlanta: SBL, 2001.

LaSor, William S., et al. *Survey of the Old Testament*. 2nd ed. Grand Rapids: Eerdmans, 1996.

Launderville, Dale. *Piety and Politics: The Dynamics of Royal Authority in Homeric Greece, Biblical Israel, and Old Babylonian Mesopotamia*. Grand Rapids: Eerdmans, 2003.

Legaspi, Michael C. "Job's Wives in the Testament of Job: A Note on the Synthesis of Two Traditions." *JBL* 127 (2008) 71–79.

Leick, Gwendolyn. *Mesopotamia: The Invention of the City*. New York: Penguin, 2001.

Lemaire, André. *Les écoles et la formation de la Bible dans l'ancien Israël*. OBO 39. Göttingen: Vandenhoeck und Ruprecht, 1981.

Lemke, Werner E. "Synoptic Studies in the Chronicler's History." PhD diss. Harvard University, 1963.

Lenzi, Alan. "A Hymn to Marduk: *Ludlul bēl nēmeqi* 1.1–40." In *Akkadian Hymns and Prayers: A Reader*, edited by A. Lenzi, 483–501. SBLANEM 3. Atlanta: SBL, 2011.

———. "Scribal Hermeneutics and the Twelve Gates of *Ludlul bēl nēmeqi*." *JAOS* 135 (2015) 733–49.

———. *Secrecy and the Gods: Secret Knowledge in Ancient Mesopotamia and Biblical Israel*. SAAS 19. Helsinki: Neo-Assyrian Text Corpus Project, Institute for Asian and African Studies, 2008.

Leveen, Adriane. "Revisiting Edward Greenstein's 'The Problem of Evil in the Book of Job.'" In ואד יאלה *(Gen 2:6): Essays in Biblical and Ancient Near Eastern Studies*

Presented to Edward L. Greenstein, edited by P. Machinist et al., 2:833–50. Atlanta: SBL, 2021.

Levison, John R. "The Two Spirits in Qumran Theology." In *The Bible and the Dead Sea Scrolls*. Vol. 2, *The Dead Sea Scrolls and the Qumran Community*, edited by J. Charlesworth, 169–94. Waco, TX: Baylor University Press, 2006.

Lewis, C. S. *The Problem of Pain*, 1940. Reprint, New York: HarperCollins, 2000.

———. *Reflections on the Psalms*. New York: Harcourt, 1958.

Lewis, Theodore J. *The Origin and Character of God: Ancient Israelite Religion through the Lens of Divinity*. New York: Oxford University Press, 2020.

Lie, Arthur G. *The Annals of Sargon II, King of Assyria*. Paris: Geuthner, 1929.

Liebman, Charles. "Extremism as a Religious Norm." *JSSR* 22 (1983) 75–86.

Linafelt, Tod. "'Paint It Black': Job 3 and the Lyrical Repurposing of Prophetic Discourse." *Academia Letters* 37 (2020). https://doi.org/10.20935/AL37.

Linafelt, Tod, and Andrew R. Davis. "Translating חנם in Job 1:9 and 2:3: On the Relationship between Job's Piety and His Interiority." *VT* 63 (2013) 627–39.

Linebaugh, Jonathan A. *God, Grace, and Righteousness in Wisdom of Solomon and Paul's Letter to the Romans*. Leiden: Brill, 2013.

Litfin, Duane. "Revisiting the Unpardonable Sin: Insight from an Unexpected Source." *JETS* 60 (2017) 713–32.

Litwiller, Brett J., and Amy M. Brausch. "Cyber Bullying and Physical Bullying in Adolescent Suicide: The Role of Violent Behavior and Substance Abuse." *JYA* 42 (2013) 675–84.

Livingstone, Alasdair. *Court Poetry and Literary Miscellanea*. SAA 3. Helsinki: Neo-Assyrian Text Corpus Project, 1989.

Lo, Alison. *Job 28 as Rhetoric: An Analysis of Job 28 in the Context of Job 21–31*. Leiden: Brill, 2003.

Loader, James A. "Job's Sister: Undermining an Unnatural Religiosity." *OTE* 6 (1993) 312–29.

Lods, Adolphe. "Les Origines de la figure de Satan: ses functions à la cour celéste." In *Mélanges Syriens offerts à Monsieur René Dussaud*, edited by the Académie des Inscriptions and Belles-Lettres, 2.649–60. Paris: Librairie Orientaliste Paul Geuthner, 1939.

Lohmann, Katharina. "Das Gespräch eines Mannes mit seinem Ba." *SAK* 25 (1998) 207–36.

Longenecker, Richard N. *Biblical Exegesis in the Apostolic Period*. Grand Rapids: Eerdmans, 1999.

Longman, Tremper. "Disputation." In *DOTW* 282–92.

———. *Job*. Grand Rapids: Baker Academic, 2012.

———, and John H. Walton. *The Lost World of the Flood: Mythology, Theology, and the Deluge Debate*. Downers Grove, IL: InterVarsity, 2018.

Lopes, Maria Helena. "Tale of the Eloquent Peasant." In *REAMR* 922.

Loretz, Oswald. "Ugaritisch-Hebräisch in Job 3:3–26." *UF* 8 (1976) 123–27.

Low, Katherine. *The Bible, Gender, and Reception History: The Case of Job's Wife*. LHBOTS 586. London: T. & T. Clark, 2013.

Lowth, Robert. *De Sacra Poesi Hebraeorum: Praelectiones Academiae Oxonii Habitae*. Oxford: Clarendon, 1753.

Luiselli, Maria Michela. "Religion und Literatur: Überlegungen zur Funktion der 'persönlichen Frommigkeit' in der Literatur des Mittleren und Neuen Reiches." *SAK* 36 (2007) 157–72.

Lundbom, Jack R. "The Double Curse in Jeremiah 20:14–18." *JBL* 104 (1985) 589–600.

Magdalene, F. Rachel. "The ANE Legal Origins of Impairment as Theological Disability and the Book of Job." *PRSt* 34 (2007) 23–59.

———. *On the Scales of Righteousness: Neo-Babylonian Trial Law and the Book of Job*. BJS 348. Providence, RI: Brown Judaic Studies, 2007.

Maiberger, Paul. *Das Manna. Eine literarische, etymologische, und naturkundliche Untersuchung*. Wiesbaden: Harrassowitz, 1983.

Maimonides (Moses ben Maimon). دلالة الحايرين *(The Guide for the Perplexed)*. Translated by S. Pines. Chicago: University of Chicago Press, 1963.

Mangan, Céline. "The Attitude to Women in the Prologue to Targum Job." In *Targumic and Cognate Studies: Essays in Honour of Martin McNamara*, edited by K. Cathcart and M. Maher, 100–110. JSOTSup 230. Sheffield: Sheffield Academic, 1996.

———. "Blessing and Cursing in the Prologue of Targum Job." In *Targum and Scripture: Studies in Aramaic Translations and Interpretation in Memory of Ernest G. Clarke*, edited by P. M. Fleischer, 225–30. SAIS 2. Leiden: Brill, 2002.

———. *The Targum of Job*. ArBib 15. Edinburgh: T. & T. Clark, 1991.

Marcel, Gabriel. *Philosophy of Existentialism*. 1956. Reprint, New York: Citadel, 2002.

Markter, Florian. *Transformationen. Zur Anthropologie des Propheten Ezechiel unter besonderer Berücksichtigung des Motivs "Herz."* FB 127. Würzburg: Echter, 2013.

Marlow, Hilary. "The Lament over the River Nile: Isaiah 19:5–10 in Its Wider Context." *VT* 57 (2007) 229–42.

Martin, Troy W. "Concluding the Book of Job and YHWH: Reading Job from the End to the Beginning." *JBL* 137 (2018) 299–318.

Mathew, Geevarughese. "The Role of the Epilogue in the Book of Job." PhD diss., Drew University, 1995.

Mathewson, Dan. *Death and Survival in the Book of Job: Desymbolization and Traumatic Experience*. LHBOTS 450. London: T. & T. Clark, 2006.

Mayer, Günter. "יכח." In *TDOT* 6:64–71.

McCabe, Robert V. "The Significance of the Elihu Speeches in the Context of the Book of Job." ThD diss., Grace Theological Seminary, 1985.

McCarter, P. Kyle. "When the Gods Lose Their Temper: Divine Rage in Ugaritic Myth and the Hypostasis of Anger in Iron Age Religion." In *Divine Wrath and Divine Mercy in the World of Antiquity*, edited by R. Kratz and H. Spieckermann, 78–91. Tübingen: Mohr Siebeck, 2008.

McGilchrist, Iain. *The Master and His Emissary: The Divided Brain and the Making of the Western World*. New Haven: Yale University Press, 2019.

McKeating, Henry. "The Central Issue of the Book of Job." *ExpTim* 82 (1971) 244–45.

Mende, Theresia. *Durch Leiden zur Vollendung. Die Elihureden im Buch Ijob (Ijob 32–37)*. TThSt 49. Trier: Paulinus, 1990.

Merton, Thomas. *New Seeds of Contemplation*. New York: New Directions, 1962.

Metaxas, Eric. *Letter to the American Church*. Washington, DC: Salem, 2022.

Mewburn, Inger. *Becoming an Academic: How to Get Through Grad School and Beyond*. Baltimore: Johns Hopkins University Press, 2019.

Meyers, Eric M. "Israel and Its Neighbors, Then and Now: Revisionist History and the Quest for History." In *Confronting the Past: Archaeological and Historical Essays in Honor of William G. Dever*, edited by S. Gitin et al., 255–64. State College, PA: Eisenbrauns, 2006.

Michalowski, Piotr. *The Lamentation over the Destruction of Sumer and Ur*. Winona Lake, IN: Eisenbrauns, 1989.

Michel, Walter E. *Job in the Light of Northwest Semitic*. BibOr 1. Rome: Biblical Institute Press, 1987.

Miller, Patrick D. "Moses, My Servant: The Deuteronomic Portrait of Moses." *Int* 41 (1987) 245–55.

Miscall, Peter D. "Isaiah: New Heavens, New Earth, New Book." In *Reading between Texts: Intertextuality and the Hebrew Bible*, edited by D. N. Fewell, 41–56. Louisville: Westminster John Knox, 1992.

———. "Texts, More Texts, a Textual Reader, and a Textual Writer." *Sem* 69–70 (1995) 247–60.

Mishna, Faye. *Bullying: A Guide to Research, Intervention, and Prevention*. Oxford: Oxford University Press, 2012.

Mittleman, Alan. "The Job of Judaism and the Job of Kant." *HTR* 102 (2009) 25–50.

Moberly, R. Walter L. *The Bible, Theology, and Faith: A Study of Abraham and Jesus*. Cambridge: Cambridge University Press, 2000.

Moore, George Foot. *The Literature of the Old Testament*. New York: Holt and Company, 1913.

Moore, Michael S. "Abraham." In *EHJ* 2–3.

———. *The Balaam Traditions: Their Character and Development*. SBLDS 113. Atlanta: Scholars, 1988.

———. "Civic and Voluntary Associations in the Greco-Roman World." In *The World of the New Testament: Cultural, Social, and Historical Contexts*, edited by J. Green and L. McDonald, 149–55. Grand Rapids: Baker Academic, 2013.

———. "הגאל: The Cultural Gyroscope of Ancient Hebrew Society." *ResQ* 23 (1980) 27–35.

———. "Divine Presence." In *Dictionary of Old Testament Prophets*, edited by M. Boda and J. McConville, 166–70. Downers Grove, IL: InterVarsity, 2012.

———. *Faith under Pressure: A Study of Biblical Leaders in Conflict*. Abilene, TX: Abilene Christian University Press, 2003.

———. "Human Suffering in Lamentations." *RB* 90 (1983) 534–55.

———. "Introduction to the Wisdom and Lyric Literature." In *The Transforming Word*, edited by M. Hamilton, 9–15. Abilene, TX: Abilene Christian University Press, 2009.

———. "Job's Texts of Terror." *CBQ* 55 (1993) 662–75.

———. *Reconciliation: A Study of Biblical Families in Conflict*. Joplin, MO: College Press, 1994.

———. Review of *Abiding Astonishment: Psalms, Modernity, and the Making of History*, by W. Brueggemann. *CBQ* 54 (1992) 740–41.

———. Review of *An Adversary in Heaven:* sāṭān *in the Hebrew Bible*, by Peggy Day. *JBL* 109 (1990) 508–10.

———. Review of *The Bible and the Comic Vision*, by J. William Whedbee, *RBL* (2003).

———. Review of *The Book of Job: A Contest of Moral Imaginations*, by C. Newsom. *RBL* (2004).

———. Review of *The Book of Job: A Biography*, by M. Larrimore. *RBL* (2014).

———. Review of *Ethical God-Talk in the Book of Job: Speaking to the Almighty*, by W. C. Pohl. *CBQ* 84 (2022) 119–20.
———. Review of *Job*, by L. Wilson. *CBQ* 78 (2016) 539–40.
———. Review of *Knowing Kings*, by S. Lasine. *CBQ* 64 (2002) 355–57.
———. Review of *The Jehu Revolution: A Royal Tradition of the Northern Kingdom and Its Ramifications*, by Jonathan Miles Robker. *CBQ* 77 (2015) 151–53.
———. Review of *Now My Eye Sees You: Unveiling an Apocalyptic Job*, by Timothy Jay Johnson, *RBL* (2012).
———. "Ruth." In *Joshua, Judges, Ruth*, 293–373. UBCS 5. Grand Rapids: Baker, 2000.
———. "Sacrifice, Tithes, Offerings." In *EHJ* 533–36.
———. "Two Textual Anomalies in Ruth." *CBQ* 59 (1997) 324–43.
———. *WealthWarn: A Study of Socioeconomic Conflict in Hebrew Prophecy*. Eugene, OR: Pickwick, 2019.
———. *WealthWatch: A Study of Socioeconomic Conflict in the Bible*. Eugene, OR: Pickwick, 2011.
———. *WealthWise: A Study of Socioeconomic Conflict in Hebrew Wisdom*. Eugene, OR: Pickwick, 2021.
———. *What Is This Babbler Trying to Say? Essays on Biblical Interpretation*. Eugene, OR: Pickwick, 2016.
———. "Wise Women in the Bible: Identifying a Trajectory." In *Essays on Women in Earliest Christianity*, edited by C. Osburn, 2.87–103. Joplin, MO: College Press, 1995.
Moore, Rick. "The Integrity of the Book of Job." *CBQ* 42 (1983) 17–31.
Morales, L. Michael. *Exodus Old and New: A Biblical Theology of Redemption*. Downers Grove, IL: InterVarsity, 2020.
Moran, William L. "Notes on the Hymn to Marduk in *Ludlul bēl nēmeqi*." *JAOS* 103 (1983) 255–60.
Morris, David B. *Illness and Culture in the Postmodern Age*. Berkeley, CA: University of California Press, 1998.
Morrison, Martha A. "The Jacob and Laban Narrative in Light of Near Eastern Sources." *BAR* 46 (1983) 155–64.
Morrow, William S. *Protest against God: The Eclipse of a Biblical Tradition*. HBM 4. Sheffield: Sheffield Phoenix, 2007.
Mowinckel, Sigmund. *He That Cometh: The Messiah Concept in the Old Testament and Later Judaism*. Translated by G. W. Anderson. 1951. Reprint, Grand Rapids: Eerdmans, 2005.
———. "Hiobs גאל und Zeuge im Himmel." In *Vom Alten Testament: FS Karl Marti*, edited by K. Budde, 207–12. BZAW 41. Giessen: Töpelmann, 1925.
Muenchow, Charles. "Dust and Dirt in Job 42:6." *JBL* 108 (1989) 597–611.
Mullen, E. Theodore. *The Assembly of the Gods: The Divine Council in Canaanite and Early Hebrew Literature*. HSM 24. Chico, CA: Scholars, 1980.
Müller, Hans-Peter. *Das Hiobproblem. Seine Stellung und Entstehung im Alten Orient und im Alten Testament*. EdF 84. 1978. Reprint, Darmstadt: Wissenschaftliche Buchgesellschaft, 1995.
———. "Theodizee? Anschlußerörterungen zum Buch Hiob." *ZTK* 89 (1992) 249–79.
Muraoka, Takamitsu. "The Aramaic of the Old Targum of Job from Qumran Cave 11." *JJS* 25 (1974) 425–43.

Murphy, Roland E. "A Consideration of the Classification Wisdom Psalms." *VTSup* 9. Leiden: Brill, 156–67.

———. "The Personification of Wisdom." In *Wisdom in Ancient Israel: Essays in Honour of John Emerton*, edited by J. Day et al., 222–33. Cambridge: Cambridge University Press, 1995.

———. "Wisdom in the OT." In *ABD* 6:920–31.

———. *Wisdom Literature: Job, Proverbs, Ruth, Canticles, Ecclesiastes, and Esther.* FOTL 13. Grand Rapids: Eerdmans, 1981.

Murphy-O'Connor, Jerome. "Demetrius I and the Teacher of Righteousness (1 Macc 10:25–45). *RB* 83 (1976) 400–20.

Myhrman, David W. *Babylonian Hymns and Prayers*. Philadelphia: University Museum, 1911.

Nam, Duk-Woo. *Talking about God: Job 42:7–9 and the Nature of God in the Book of Job.* StBibLit 49. Brussels: Lang, 2003.

Nef Ulloa, Boris Agustín. "Os pobres no livro de Job: de teologia da retribução para e economia de retribução." *Cam* 24 (2019) 93–102.

Neumann, Hans. "Zum Problem der Erhebung von Gebühren im Rahmen der mesopotamischen Gerichtsorganisation in altakkadischer Zeit." In *"Gerechtigkeit und Recht zu üben" (Gen 18,19): Studien zur altorientalischen und biblischen Rechtsgeschichte, zur Religionsgeschichte Israels und zur Religionssoziologie. Festschrift für Eckart Otto zum 65 Geburtstag*, edited by R. Achenbach and M. Arneth, 1–6. BZABR 13. Wiesbaden: Harrassowitz, 2009.

Neville, Richard. "A Reassessment of the Radical Nature of Job's Ethic in Job 31:13–15." *VT* 53 (2003) 181–200.

Newsom, Carol A. *The Book of Job: A Contest of Moral Imaginations*. New York: Oxford University Press, 2003.

———. "The Invention of the Divine Courtroom in the Book of Job." In *The Divine Courtroom in Comparative Perspective*, edited by A. Memelstein and S. E. Holtzand, 246–59. Leiden: Brill, 2014.

———. "Job." In *ER* 4930–33.

———. "Job." In *Women's Bible Commentary*, edited by C. Newsom et al., 208–15. Louisville: Westminster John Knox, 2012.

Nicholson, Ernest W. "The Limits of Theodicy as a Theme of the Book of Job." In *Wisdom in Ancient Israel: Essays in Honour of J. A. Emerton*, edited by J. Day et al., 71–82. Cambridge: Cambridge University Press, 1995.

Nickelsburg, George E. "Seeking the Origin of the Two Ways Tradition in Jewish and Christian Ethical Texts." In *A Multiform Heritage: Studies on Early Judaism and Christianity in Honor of Robert A. Kraft*, edited by B. G. Wright. SPHS 24. Atlanta: Scholars, 1999.

Nicol, Neal, and Harry Wylie. *Between the Dying and the Dead: Dr. Jack Kevorkian's Life and the Battle to Legalize Euthanasia*. Madison, WI: University of Wisconsin Press, 2006.

Niebuhr, Reinhold. *The Nature and Destiny of Man*. 2 vols. 1945. Reprint, Oxford: Oxford University Press, 1964.

Nielsen, Kirsten. "שטן." In *TDOT* 14:73–78.

Noam, Vered. *Shifting Images of the Hasmoneans: Second Temple Legends and Their Reception in Josephus and Rabbinic Literature*. Translated by D. Ordan. Oxford: Oxford University Press, 2018.

Noegel, Scott B. "Janus Parallelism in Job and Its Literary Significance." *JBL* 115 (1996) 313–20.

Nolan, Patrick, and Gerhard Lenski. *Human Societies: An Introduction to Macrosociology*. New York: Oxford University Press, 2014.

Nurse, Anne M. *Confronting Child Sexual Abuse: Knowledge to Action*. Ann Arbor, MI: Lever, 2020.

O'Connor, Kathleen M. *Job*. NCBC 19. Collegeville, MN: Liturgical, 2012.

O'Connor, Michael. *Hebrew Verse Structure*. Winona Lake, IN: Eisenbrauns, 1980.

Olyan, Saul. *Social Inequality in the World of the Text: The Significance of Ritual and Social Distinctions in the Hebrew Bible*. Göttingen: Vandenhoeck & Ruprecht, 2011.

Oorschot, Jürgen van. "Tendenzen der Hiobforschung." *TRu* 60 (1995) 351–88.

Oshima, Takayoshi. *Babylonian Poems of Pious Sufferers: Ludlul bēl nēmeqi and the Babylonian Theodicy*. ORA 14. Tübingen: Mohr Siebeck, 2014.

———. *The Babylonian Theodicy*. SAACT 9. Helsinki: Neo-Assyrian Text Corpus Project, 2013.

Osing, Jürgen. "Gespräch des Lebensmüden." *LÄ* 2 (1977) 571–73.

Otto, Eberhard. *Der Vorwurf an Gott. Zur Entstehung der ägyptischen Auseinandersetzungsliteratur*. Hildesheim: Gerstenberg, 1951.

Otto, Rudolf. *The Idea of the Holy*. Translated by J. W. Harvey. 1917. Reprint, Eugene, OR: Wipf & Stock, 2021.

Otzen, Benedikt. "עמל." In *TDOT* 11:196–202.

Pagels, Elaine. *The Origin of Satan*. New York: Random House, 1995.

Pallis, Svend Aage. *The Babylonian* Akītu *Festival*. Copenhagen: Andr. Fred Host and Son, 1926.

Parkinson, Richard B. "The Dialogue of Ipuuer and the Lord of All." In *The Tale of Sinuhe and Other Ancient Egyptian Poems, 1940–1640 BC*, 166–99. OWC. Oxford: Oxford University Press, 1998.

———. "The Dialogue of a Man and His Soul." In *The Tale of Sinuhe and Other Ancient Egyptian Poems, 1940–1640 BC*, 151–65. OWC. Oxford: Oxford University Press, 1998.

———. "Literary Form and *The Tale of the Eloquent Peasant*." *JEA* 78 (1992) 163–78.

———. *The Tale of the Eloquent Peasant*. Oxford: Griffith Institute, 1988.

———. "The Tale of the Eloquent Peasant." In *The Tale of Sinuhe and Other Ancient Egyptian Poems, 1940–1640 BC*, 58–75. OWC. Oxford: Oxford University Press, 1998.

———. "Types of Literature in the Middle Kingdom." In *Ancient Egyptian Literature: History and Forms*, edited by A. Loprieno, 297–312. Leiden: Brill, 1996.

Parmentier, Martien F. G. "Job the Rebel: From the Rabbis to the Church Fathers." In *Saints and Role Models in Judaism and Christianity*, edited by M. Poorthuis and J. Schwartz, 227–42. Leiden: Brill, 2004.

Parpola, Simo, and Kazoko Watanabe. *Neo-Assyrian Treaties and Loyalty Oaths*. SAA 2. Helsinki: University of Helsinki Press, 1988.

Paul, Shalom M. "Vain Imprecations on Having Been Born in Job 3 and Mesopotamian Literature." In *Marbeh Ḥokmah: Studies in the Bible and the Ancient Near East in Loving Memory of Victor Avigdor Hurowitz*, edited by S. Yona et al., 401–6. Winona Lake, IN: Eisenbrauns, 2015.

Paulus, Jean. "Le thème du Juste Souffrant dans la pensée grecque et israélite." *RHR* 121 (1940) 18–66.

Peake, Arthur S. *Job*. NCB. Edinburgh: T. C. and E .C. Jack, 1905.

Pecchioli Daddi, Francesca. "A Song of Release from Hattic Tradition." In *Akten des IV Internationalen Kongresses für Hethitologie*, edited by G. Wilhelm, 552–60. Wiesbaden: Harrassowitz, 2001.

Pelham, Abigail. *Contested Creations in the Book of Job: The-World-as-It-Ought-and-Ought-Not-to-Be*. BibInt 113. Leiden: Brill, 2012.

Pemberton, Glenn. *Hurting with God: Learning to Lament with the Psalms*. Abilene, TX: Abilene Christian University, 2012.

Penchansky, David. "Job's Wife: The Satan's Handmaid." In *Shall Not the Judge of All the Earth Do What Is Right? Studies on the Nature of God in Tribute to James L. Crenshaw*, edited by D. Penchansky and P. L. Redditt, 223–28. Winona Lake, IN: Eisenbrauns, 2000.

———. *Understanding Wisdom Literature: Conflict and Dissonance in the Hebrew Text*. Grand Rapids: Eerdmans, 2012.

Perdue, Leo G. *Wisdom and Creation: The Theology of Wisdom Literature*. 1994. Reprint, Eugene, OR: Wipf & Stock, 2009.

———. *Wisdom in Revolt: Metaphorical Theology in the Book of Job*. JSOTSup 112. Sheffield: Sheffield Academic, 1991.

Perrin, Norman. *What Is Redaction Criticism?* Philadelphia: Fortress, 1973.

Pettys, Valerie Forstman. "Let There Be Darkness: Continuity and Discontinuity in the 'Curse' of Job 3." *JSOT* 98 (2002) 89–104.

Phillips, Elaine A. "Speaking Truthfully: Job's Friends and Job." *BBR* 18 (2008) 31–43.

Pilch, John J. *A Cultural Handbook to the Bible*. Grand Rapids: Eerdmans, 2012.

Pinker, Aron. "Bildad's Contribution to the Debate: A New Interpretation of Job 8:17–19." *VT* 66 (2016) 406–32.

Pleins, J. David. *The Social Visions of the Hebrew Bible: A Theological Introduction*. Louisville: Westminster John Knox, 2001.

Pohl, William C. *Ethical God-Talk in the Book of Job: Speaking to the Almighty*. LHB/OTS 698. New York: T. & T. Clark, 2020.

———. Review of *Friendship and Virtue Ethics in the Book of Job*, by P. Vesely. *BBR* 30 (2020) 309–11.

Polaski, Donald. *Authorizing an End: The Isaiah Apocalypse and Intertextuality*. Leiden: Brill, 2000.

Polzin, Robert. "The Framework of the Book of Job." *Int* 28 (1974) 182–200.

Pope, Marvin H. *El in the Ugaritic Texts*. Leiden: Brill, 1955.

———. *Job: A New Translation with Introduction and Commentary*. AB 15. Garden City, NY: Doubleday, 1973.

Pope, Nicole. *Honor Killings in the Twenty-First Century*. New York: Palgrave Macmillan, 2012.

Porter, Barbara N. *Trees, Kings, and Politics: Studies in Assyrian Iconography*. OBO 197. Göttingen: Vandenhoeck & Ruprecht, 2003.

Porter, Stanley E., and Beth M. Stovell, eds. *Biblical Hermeneutics: Five Views*. Downers Grove, IL: InterVarsity, 2012.

Portier-Young, Anathea. "'Eyes to the Blind': A Dialogue between Tobit and Job." In *Intertextual Studies in Ben Sira and Tobit: Essays in Honor of Alexander Di Lella*, 14–27. CBQMS 38. Washington, DC, 2005.

Poser, Ruth. *Das Ezechielbuch als Trauma-Literatur*. VTSup 154. Leiden: Brill, 2012.

Puech, Emile. "Les écoles dans l'Israël préexilique. Données épigraphiques." In *Congress Volume 1986*, edited by J. Emerton, 189–203. VTSup 40. Leiden: Brill, 1988.

Pyper, Hugh. "The Reader in Pain: Job as Text and Pretext." In *Text as Pretext*, edited by R. P. Carroll, 234–55. Sheffield: Sheffield Academic, 1992.

Qimron, Elisha. "Dualism in the Essene Communities." In *The Bible and the Dead Sea Scrolls*. Vol. 2, *The Dead Sea Scrolls and the Qumran Community*, edited by J. Charlesworth, 195–202. Waco, TX: Baylor University Press, 2006.

Rachman, Gideon. *Zero-Sum Future: American Power in an Age of Anxiety*. New York: Simon & Schuster, 2011.

Rad, Gerhard von. "διάβολος." In *TDNT* 2:73–74.

———. *Old Testament Theology*. Translated by D. M. G. Stalker. 2 vols. New York: Harper & Row, 1962–65.

———. *Wisdom in Israel*. Translated by J. D. Martin. Harrisburg, PA: Trinity Press International, 1972.

Rahman, Fazlur. *Major Themes of the Qur'an*. Chicago: University of Chicago Press, 2018.

Rahnenführer, Dankwart. "Das Testament des Hiob und das Neue Testament." *ZNW* 62 (1971) 68–93.

Rashi (רבי שלמה יצחקי, Rabbi Shlomo Yitzchaqi). *Midrash on Job*. Edited by Avraham Shoshana. Jerusalem: Machon Ofek, 2000.

Rast, Walter E. "Bible and Archaeology." In *Near Eastern Archaeology: A Reader*, edited by S. Richard, 48–53. Winona Lake, IN: Eisenbrauns, 2003.

Raz, Yosefa. "Reading Pain in the Book of Job." In *The Book of Job: Aesthetics, Ethics, Hermeneutics*, edited by L. Batnitzky and I. Pardes, 77–98. Berlin: de Gruyter, 2015.

Redfield, J. *Nature and Culture in the Iliad: The Tragedy of Hector*. Chicago: University of Chicago Press, 1975.

Redford, Donald B. "Ancient Egyptian Literature: An Overview." In *CANE* 2223–41.

Reichert, Victor A. *Job*. 1946. Reprint, New York: Soncino, 1965.

Reiner, Erica. "Die akkadische Literatur." In *Neues Handbuch der Literatur-Wissenschaft: Altorientalische Literature*, edited by W. Röllig, 115–210. Wiesbaden: Athenaion, 1978.

Renz, Johannes, and Wolfgang Röllig. *Handbuch der althebräischen Epigraphik*. 3 vols. Darmstadt: Wissenschaftliche Buchgesellschaft, 1995.

Richards, Janet. "Modified Order, Responsible Legitimacy, and Redistributed Wealth: Egypt, 2260–1650 BC." In *Order, Legitimacy, and Wealth in Ancient States*, edited by J. Richards and M. van Buren, 36–45. Cambridge: Cambridge University Press, 2000.

Richardson, Mervyn E. J. *Hammurabi's Laws: Text, Translation, and Glossary*. 2000. Reprint, London: T. & T. Clark, 2004.

Richter, Heinz. *Studien zum Hiob. Die Aufbau des Hiobbuches, dargestellt an den Gattungen des Rechtslebens*. ThA 11. Berlin: Evangelistische Verlaganstalt, 1955.

Ricoeur, Paul. "Myth: Myth and History." In *ER* 6373–80.

Ringgren, Helmer. "גאל." In *TDOT* 2:350–55.

Roberts, J. J. M. "Job and the Israelite Religious Tradition." In *The Bible and the Ancient Near East: Collected Essays*, 110–16. Winona Lake, IN: Eisenbrauns, 2002.

———. "Job's Summons to Yahweh: The Exploitation of a Legal Metaphor." *ResQ* 16 (1973) 159–65.
———. "The Motif of the Weeping God in Jeremiah and Its Background in the Lament Tradition of the Ancient Near East." In *The Bible and the Ancient Near East: Collected Essays*, 132–42. Winona Lake, IN: Eisenbrauns, 2002.
Ross, James F. "Job 33.14–30: The Phenomenology of Lament." *JBL* 94 (1975) 38–46.
Roy, Ranjan. *Chronic Pain and Family: A Clinical Perspective*. New York: Springer, 2006.
Rudolph, Kurt. "Gnosticism." In *ABD* 2:1033–40.
Russell, Jeffrey Burton. *The Devil: Perceptions of Evil from Antiquity to Primitive Christianity*. Ithaca, NY: Cornell University Press, 1987.
Ryan, Garrett. *Greek Cities and Roman Governors: Placing Power in Imperial Asia Minor*. London: Routledge, 2021.
Sadler, Rodney. "Genesis." In *Fortress Commentary on the Bible: The Old Testament and Apocrypha*, edited by Gale Yee et al., 89–136. Minneapolis: Fortress, 2014.
Sakenfeld, Katharine D. *The Meaning of* Ḥesed *in the Hebrew Bible: A New Inquiry*. 1978. Reprint, Eugene, OR: Wipf & Stock, 2002.
Salakpi, Alexander G. K. "Social Alienation as a Consequence of Human Suffering in the Book of Job: A Study of Job 19:13–22." PhD diss., Catholic University of America, 2009.
Salisbury, Joyce E. "Naomi." In *EWAW* 245–46.
Salters, Robert B. "Acrostics and Lamentations." In *On Stone and Scroll: Essays in Honour of Graham Ivor Davies*, edited by J. K. Aitken et al., 425–40. Berlin: de Gruyter, 2011.
Sandoval, Timothy J. "Introduction to Wisdom and Worship: Themes and Perspectives in the Poetic Writings." In *The Old Testament and Apocrypha: Fortress Commentary on the Bible*, edited by G. Yee et al., 495–517. Minneapolis: Fortress, 2014.
Sasson, Jack. *Ruth: A New Translation with a Philological Commentary and a Formalist-Folkloristic Interpretation*. Baltimore: Johns Hopkins University Press, 1979.
Sasson, Victor. "The Literary and Theological Function of Job's Wife in the Book of Job." *Bib* 79 (1998) 86–90.
Sawyer, John F. A. "The Authorship and Structure of the Book of Job." *Studia Biblica 1978*. Vol. 1, *Papers on Old Testament and Related Themes*, edited by E. Livingstone, 253–57. JSOTSup 11. Sheffield: JSOT Press, 1979.
Scarlata, Mark W. *Outside of Eden: Cain in the Ancient Versions of Genesis 4:1–16*. New York: T. & T. Clark, 2012.
Schäfer, Peter. *Two Gods in Heaven: Jewish Concepts of God in Antiquity*. Translated by A. Brown. Princeton: Princeton University Press, 2020.
Schaller, Berndt. "Das Testament Hiobs und die Septuaginta-Übersetzung des Buches Hiob." *Bib* 61 (1980) 377–406.
Scher, Richard K. "Academic Macho." *EH* 61 (1983) 83–87.
Schifferdecker, Kathryn. *Out of the Whirlwind: Creation Theology in the Book of Job*. HTS 61. Cambridge: Harvard University Press, 2008.
Schiffman, Lawrence H. *Qumran and Jerusalem: Studies in the Dead Sea Scrolls and the History of Judaism*. Grand Rapids: Eerdmans, 2010.
———. *Texts and Traditions: A Source Reader for the Study of Second Temple and Rabbinic Judaism*. Hoboken, NJ: KTAV, 1998.
Schindler, Audrey. "One Who Has Borne Most: The *Cri de Coeur* of Job's Wife." *ABR* 54 (2006) 24–36.

Schmid, Konrad. "God as Defendant, Advocate, and Judge in the Book of Job." In ואד יעלה (*Gen 2:6*): *Essays in Biblical and Ancient Near Eastern Studies Presented to Edward L. Greenstein*, edited by P. Machinist et al., 889–912. WAW 5–6. Atlanta: SBL, 2021.

Schniedewind, William. *How the Bible Became a Book: The Textualization of Ancient Israel*. Cambridge: Cambridge University Press, 2004.

Scholnick, Sylvia H. "The Meaning of משפט in the Book of Job." *JBL* 101 (1982) 521–29.

Schöplin, Karin. Review of *Transformationen: Zur Anthropologie des Propheten Ezechiel unter besonderer Berücksichtigung des Motivs "Herz,"* by F. Markter. *BZ* 58 (2014) 318–20.

Schüpphaus, Joachim. "כסל." In *TDOT* 7:264–69.

Schüssler Fiorenza, Elisabeth. *But She Said: Feminist Practices of Biblical Interpretation*. Boston: Beacon, 1992.

Secunda, Shai. *The Iranian Talmud: Reading the Bavli in its Sassanian Context*. Philadelphia: University of Pennsylvania Press, 2014,

Selmier, W. Travis, and Chang Hoon Oh. "The Power of Major Trade Languages in Trade and Foreign Direct Investment." *RIPE* 20 (2013) 586–614.

Seow, Choon Leong. *Job 1–21: Interpretation and Commentary*. Illuminations. Grand Rapids: Eerdmans, 2013.

Seri, Andrea. "The Fifty Names of Marduk in *Enūma eliš*." *JAOS* 126 (2006) 507–19.

Sessions, William Lad. "Honor and God." *JR* 87 (2007) 206–24.

Shah, Nirvi. "Safety Plan for Schools: No Guns." *EW*, April 2, 2013.

Sheldon, Linda Jean. "The Book of Job as Hebrew Theodicy: An Ancient Near Eastern Intertextual Conflict between Law and Cosmology." PhD diss., University of California, 2002.

Shelley, Trevor, and Jacob Seigler. "Is Pain a Problem? J. J. Rousseau and C. S. Lewis on Suffering and Human Nature." *Sehnsucht* 4 (2010) 19–42.

Shepherd, David. "מן קדם: Deferential Treatment in Biblical Aramaic and the Qumran Targum of Job." *VT* 50 (2000) 401–4.

———. *Targum and Translation: A Reconsideration of the Qumran Aramaic Version of Job*. Assen: Royal Van Gorcum, 2004.

Sherwood, Ian. "Job's 'Restoration': An Ascetic Misinterpretation of the Epilogue of the Book of Job." PhD diss., Memorial University of Newfoundland, 2004.

Shipp, Jan. *Mormonism: The Story of a New Religious Tradition*. Chicago: University of Illinois Press, 1987.

Shipp, R. Mark. *Of Dead Kings and Dirges: Myth and Meaning in Isaiah 14:4b-21*. AcBib 11. Leiden: Brill, 2002.

Shoro, Shahnaz. *Honour Killing in the Second Decade of the 21st Century*. Cambridge: Cambridge Scholars, 2017.

Shupak, Nili. "The Contribution of Egyptian Wisdom to the Study of the Biblical Wisdom Literature." In *Was There a Wisdom Tradition? New Prospects in Israelite Wisdom Studies*, edited by M. Sneed, 265–304. AIL 23. Atlanta: SBL, 2015.

———. "A New Source for the Study of the Judiciary and Law in Ancient Egypt: 'The Tale of the Eloquent Peasant.'" *JNES* 51 (1992) 1–18.

———. "The Tale of the Eloquent Peasant." In *COS* 1.98–104.

Shurter, Edwin DuBois. *The Science and Art of Effective Debating: A Text Book for High Schools and Colleges*. New York: Noble and Noble, 1925.

Sidursky, Michael. "A Tablet of Prayers for a King? (K. 2279)." *JRAS* 37 (1920) 565–72.

Signer, Michael. *Demagogue: The Fight to Save America from Its Worst Enemies*. New York: Macmillan, 2009.

Simonetti, Cristina. "When the Trial Does Not Work: Pathological Elements in the Judicial Procedure in the Old Babylonian Period." In *Law And (Dis)order in the Ancient Near East: Proceedings of the 59th Rencontre Assyriologique International Held at Ghent, Belgium, 14–19 July 2013*, edited by K. de Graef and A. Goddeeris, 284–90. University Park, PA: Eisenbrauns, 2021.

Simundson, Daniel J. "Suffering." In *ABD* 6:219–25.

Sinnott, Alice M. *The Personification of Wisdom*. SOTSMS. 2005. Reprint, New York: Routledge, 2017.

Sitzler, Dorothea. *"Vorwurf gegen Gott." Ein religiöses Motiv im Alten Orient (Ägypten und Mesopotamien)*. SOR 32. Wiesbaden: Harrassowitz, 1995.

Slack, Jeremy. *Deported to Death: How Drug Violence Is Changing Migration on the US-Mexico Border*. Oakland: University of California Press, 2019.

Sloan, Robert B., and Carey C. Newman. "Ancient Jewish Hermeneutics." In *Biblical Hermeneutics: A Comprehensive Introduction to Interpreting Scripture*, edited by B. Corley et al., 56–71. Nashville: Broadman, 2002.

Smelik, Klaas. "Ma`at." In *DDD* 534–35.

Smith, Cooper. "'I Have Heard the Sound of Your Words': Allusion in the Elihu Speeches of Job 32–37." PhD diss., Wheaton College, 2019.

Smith, Mark S. "The Ba`al Cycle." In *UNP* 81–180.

———. *The Origins of Biblical Monotheism: Israel's Polytheistic Background and the Ugaritic Texts*. Oxford: Oxford University Press, 2003.

———. *The Ugaritic Ba`al Cycle*. Vol. 1, *Introduction with Text, Translation, and Commentary on KTU 1.1–1.2*. Leiden: Brill, 1994.

Smith, Mark S., and Wayne Pitard. *The Ugaritic Ba`al Cycle*. Vol. 2, *Introduction with Text, Translation and Commentary of KTU/CAT 1.3–1.4*. Leiden: Brill, 2009.

Smith, Wesley J. "'Rational Suicide' as the New Jim Crow." In *Contemporary Perspectives on Rational Suicide*, edited by J. L. Werth Jr., 54–62. Philadelphia: Taylor & Francis, 1999.

Sneed, Mark R. "'Grasping after the Wind': The Elusive Attempt to Define and Delimit Wisdom." In *Was There a Wisdom Tradition? New Prospects in Israelite Wisdom Studies*, edited by M. Sneed, 39–68. AIL 23. Atlanta: SBL, 2015.

———. "Methods, Muddles, and Modes of Literature: The Question of Influence between Wisdom and Prophecy." *In Riddles and Revelations: Explorations into the Relationship between Wisdom and Prophecy in the Hebrew Bible*, edited by M. J. Boda et al., 30–44. LHBOTS 634. London: T. & T. Clark, 2018.

———. *The Politics of Pessimism in Ecclesiastes: A Social-Science Perspective*. AIL 12. Atlanta: SBL, 2012.

Soards, Marion L. *The Speeches in Acts: Their Content, Context, and Concerns*. Louisville: Westminster John Knox, 1994.

Soden, Wolfram von. "'Weisheitstexte' in akkadischer Sprache." In *Texte aus der Umwelt des Alten Testaments Band III. Weisheitstexte, Mythen und Epen*, 110–88. Gütersloh: Gerd Mohn, 1990.

Sommerfeld, Walter. *Der Aufstieg Marduks. Der Stellung Marduks in der babylonischen Religion des Zweiten Jahrtausends v. Chr.* AOAT 213. Kevelaer: Butzon & Bercker, 1982.

Sorge, Bob. *Pain, Perplexity, and Promotion: A Prophetic Interpretation of the Book of Job*. Grandview. MO: Oasis House, 1999.

Sorlin, Henri, and Louis Neyrand, eds. *Jean Chrysostom, Commentaire sur Job*. SC 348. Paris: Cerf, 1988.

Spieckermann, Hermann. *Gottes Liebe zu Israel: Studien zur Theologie des Alten Testaments*. FAT 33. Tübingen: Mohr Siebeck, 2004.

———. "Wrath and Mercy as Crucial Terms of Theological Hermeneutics." In *Divine Wrath and Mercy in the World of Antiquity*, edited by R. Kratz and H. Spieckermann, 3–16. FAT 33. Tübingen: Mohr Siebeck, 2008.

Spittler, Russell P. "Testament of Job." In *OTP* 1:829–68.

Stamm, J. J. "Die Theodizee in Babylon und Israel." *JEOL* 9 (1944) 99–107.

Staubli, Thomas. "Cultural and Religious Impacts of Long-Term Cross-Cultural Migration between Egypt and the Levant." *JAEI* 12 (2016) 50–88.

Stokes, Ryan R. *Satan: How God's Executioner Became the Enemy*. Grand Rapids: Eerdmans, 2019.

Stuckenbruck, Loren T. "The Interiorization of Dualism within the Human Being in Second Temple Judaism: The Treatise of the Two Spirits (1QS 3.13–4.26)." In *Light against Darkness: Dualism in Ancient Mediterranean Religion and the Contemporary World*, edited by A. Lange et al., 145–68. Göttingen: Vandenhoeck und Ruprecht, 2011.

Stull, Bradford T. *Religious Dialectics of Pain and Imagination*. Albany, NY: State University of New York Press, 1994.

Stump, Eleonore. *Wandering in Darkness: Narrative and the Problem of Suffering*. Oxford: Clarendon, 2010.

Suriano, Matthew J. "Death, Disinheritance, and Job's Kinsman-Redeemer." *JBL* 129 (2010) 49–66.

Susman, Margarete. *Das Buch Hiob und das Schicksal des jüdischen Volkes*. Zürich: Steinberg, 1948.

Sweeney, Marvin A. *Isaiah 1–39, with an Introduction to Prophetic Literature*. FOTL 16. Grand Rapids: Eerdmans, 1996.

Syring, Wolf Dieter. *Hiob und seine Anwalt. Die Prosatext des Hiobbuches und ihre Rolle in seiner Redaktions—und Rezeptionsgeschichte*. BZAW 336. Berlin: de Gruyter, 2004.

Tate, W. Randolph. *Biblical Interpretation: An Integrated Approach*. Peabody, MA: Hendrickson, 2008.

Terrien, Samuel. "The Book of Job: Introduction and Exegesis." In *IB* 3 (1954) 877–1198.

———. *The Elusive Presence: Toward a New Biblical Theology*. New York: Harper and Row, 1978.

———. *Job*. CAT 13. Neuchatel: Delachaux et Niestlé, 1963.

———. *Job: Poet of Existence*. Indianapolis: Bobbs-Merrill, 1957.

Thornton, Dillon T. "Satan, Yhwh's Executioner." *JBL* 133 (2014) 251–70.

Tropper, Amram. *Simeon the Righteous in Rabbinic Literature*. AJEC 84. Leiden: Brill, 2013.

Thurow, Lester. *The Zero-Sum Society: Distribution and the Possibilities for Change*. New York: Basic, 1980.

Ticciati, Susannah. *Job and the Disruption of Identity: Reading beyond Barth*. London: T. & T. Clark, 2005.

Tilley, Terence W. *The Evils of Theodicy*. Eugene, OR: Wipf & Stock, 2000.

Toorn, Karel van der. "In the Lions' Den: the Babylonian Background of a Biblical Motif." *CBQ* 60 (1998) 626–40.

———. "Theodicy in Akkadian Literature." In *Theodicy in the World of the Bible: The Goodness of God and the Problem of Evil*, edited by A. Laato and J. de Moor, 57–89. Leiden: Brill, 2003.

———. "Why Wisdom Became a Secret: On Wisdom as a Written Genre." In *Wisdom Literature in Mesopotamia and Israel*, edited by R. J. Clifford, 21–32. SBLSymS 36. Atlanta: SBL, 2007.

Tsevat, Matitiahu. "The Meaning of the Book of Job." *HUCA* 37 (1966) 73–106.

Trotter, Jonathan R. "The Developing Narrative of the Life of Job: The Implications of Some Shared Elements of the Book of Tobit and the Testament of Job." *CBQ* 77 (2015) 449–66.

Tugendhaft, Aaron. "Unsettling Sovereignty: Politics and Poetics in the Ba`al Cycle." *JAOS* 132 (2012) 367–84.

Ulloa, Karl G. "Los susurros de Satán: el mensaje de la visión de Elifaz (Job 4, 17–21) y su vinculación con el resto del libro." *EstBib* 78 (2020) 39–65.

Van Seters, John. "Jacob's Marriage and Ancient Near East Customs: A Reexamination." *HTR* 62 (1969) 377–95.

Vermeylen, Jacques. *Métamorphoses: Les rédactions successives du livre de Job*. Leuven: Peeters, 2015.

Vesely, Patricia. *Friendship and Virtue Ethics in the Book of Job*. Cambridge: Cambridge University Press, 2019.

Viano, Samantha, et al. "Kindergarten Cop: A Case Study of How a Coalition between School Districts and Law Enforcement Led to School Resource Officers in Elementary Schools." *EEPA* 43 (2021) 253–79.

Vicchio, Stephen J. *Biblical Figures in the Islamic Faith*. Eugene, OR: Wipf & Stock, 2008.

———. *The Book of Job: A History of Interpretation and a Commentary*. Eugene, OR: Wipf & Stock, 2020.

Volf, Miroslav. *Free of Charge: Giving and Forgiving in a Culture Stripped of Grace*. Grand Rapids: Zondervan, 2005.

Wahl, Harald Martin. "Elihu, Frevler oder Frommer? Die Auslegung die Hiobbuches (Job 32–37) durch ein Psedepigraphon (TJob 41–43)." *JSJ* 25 (1994) 1–17.

———. "Das 'Evangelium' Elihus." In *The Book of Job*, edited by W. M. Beuken, 356–61. Leuven: Leuven University Press, 1994.

———. *Der gerechte Schöpfer: Eine redaktions—und theologiegeschichtliche Untersuchung der Elihureden —Hiob 32–37*. BZAW 207. Berlin: de Gruyter, 1993.

Walker, Christopher, and Michael Dick. *The Induction of the Cult Image in Ancient Mesopotamia: The Mesopotamian Mis Pî Ritual*. SAALT 1. Helsinki: Neo-Assyrian Text Corpus Project, 2001.

Wallace, Howard N. "Adam." In *ABD* 1:63–64.

Waltke, Bruce K. *An Old Testament Theology: An Exegetical, Canonical, and Thematic Approach*. Grand Rapids: Zondervan, 2007.

Walton, John. "Retribution." In *DOTW* 648–56.

———, and Tremper Longman. *How to Read Job*. Downers Grove, IL: InterVarsity, 2015.

Ward, Michael R. *Abundance: Creating a Culture of Generosity*. Minneapolis: Fortress, 2020.

Washburn, Jennifer. *University, Inc.: The Corporate Corruption of American Higher Education*. New York: Basic, 2005.

Waters, Larry J. "Elihu's View of Suffering in Job 32–37." PhD diss., Dallas Theological Seminary, 1998.

Watson, Wilfrid G. E. *Traditional Techniques in Classical Hebrew Verse*. Sheffield: Sheffield Academic, 1994.

Waugh, Linda R. "Preface." In *Roman Jakobson: Selected Writings*. Vol. 7, *Contributions to Comparative Mythology*, edited by S. Rudy, ix–xxiii. Berlin: de Gruyter, 1985.

Weeks, Stuart. *An Introduction to the Study of Wisdom Literature*. New York: T. & T. Clark, 2010.

Weill, Raimond. "Le livre des 'désespéré.' Le sens. L'intention et la composition litteraire de l'ouvrage." *BIFAO* 45 (1947) 89–154.

Weinfeld, Moshe. "Job and Its Mesopotamian Parallels—A Typological Analysis." In *Text and Context: Old Testament and Semitic Studies for F. C. Fensham*, edited by W. Claasen, 217–26. JSOTSup 48. Sheffield: JSOT Press, 1988.

Weiser, Artur. *Das Buch Hiob übersetzt und erklärt*. ATD 13. Göttingen: Vandenhoeck und Ruprecht, 1951.

Weiss, Dov. "The Sin of Protesting God in Rabbinic and Patristic Literature." *AJSR* 39 (2015) 367–92.

Weiss, Meir. *The Story of Job's Beginning, Job 1–2: A Literary Analysis*. Jerusalem: Magnes, 1983.

Weiss, Raphael. התרגום הארמי לספר איוב. Tel Aviv: Tel Aviv University, 1979.

Welz, Claudia. *Love's Transcendence and the Problem of Theodicy*. RPT 30. Tübingen: Mohr Siebeck, 2008.

Westbrook, Raymond. "The Character of Ancient Near Eastern Law." In *A History of Ancient Near Eastern Law*, edited by R. Westbrook et al., 1.1–2. HdO 72/1. Leiden: Brill, 2003.

Westermann, Claus. *Praise and Lament in the Psalms*, 1961. Translated by K. Crim. Atlanta: John Knox, 1965.

———. *The Structure of the Book of Job: A Form-Critical Analysis*. Translated by C. Muenchow. Philadelphia: Fortress, 1981.

———. "Struktur und Geschichte der Klage im Alten Testament." *ZAW* 66 (1954) 44–80.

Wharton, James A. *Job*. Westminster Bible Companion. Louisville: Westminster John Knox, 1999.

Whedbee, J. William. "The Comedy of Job." *Sem* 7 (1977) 1–39.

White, Ellen. *Yahweh's Council: Its Structure and Membership*. FAT 65. Tübingen: Mohr Siebeck, 2014.

Whybray, Norman. *Job*. Sheffield: Sheffield Phoenix, 2008.

———. *Introduction to the Pentateuch*. Grand Rapids: Eerdmans, 1995.

———. "Shall Not the Judge of All the Earth Do What Is Just? God's Oppression of the Innocent in the Old Testament." In *Shall Not the Judge of All the Earth Do What Is Right? Studies on the Nature of God in Tribute to James L. Crenshaw*, edited by D. Penchansky and P. Redditt, 1–19. Winona Lake, IN: Eisenbrauns, 2000.

Wiggins, Nosson. *The Tannaim and Amoraim*. Brooklyn, NY: Judaica, 2019.

Wilcke, Claus. *Early Ancient Near Eastern Law: A History of Its Beginnings: The Early Dynastic and Sargonic Periods*. Winona Lake, IN: Eisenbrauns, 2007.

Wilcox, Karl G. "Job, His Daughters, and His Wife." *JSOT* 42 (2018) 303–15.

Williams, Linda Verlee. *Teaching for the Two-Sided Mind: A Guide to Right Brain/Left Brain Education*. New York: Simon and Schuster, 1983.

Wilson, Gerald H. *Job*. UBCS. Grand Rapids: Baker, 2007.

Wilson, John A. "The Admonitions of Ipu-Wer." In *ANET* 441–46.

———. *The Culture of Ancient Egypt*. Chicago: University of Chicago Press, 1951.

———. "A Dispute over Suicide." In *ANET* 405–7.

———. "Protests of the Eloquent Peasant." In *ANET* 407–10.

Wilson, Lindsay. *Job*. THOTC. Grand Rapids: Eerdmans, 2015.

Winnington-Ingram, Reginald P. "Tragedy and Greek Archaic Thought." In *Greek Drama*, edited by H. Bloom, 115–30. Philadelphia: Chelsea, 2004.

Wiseman, Donald J. "Books in the Ancient Near East and in the Old Testament." In *CHB* 1.30–47.

Witte, Markus. "Does the Torah Keep Its Promise? Job's Critical Intertextual Dialogue with Deuteronomy." In *Reading Job Intertextually*, edited by K. Dell and W. Kynes, 54–65. LHBOTS 574. London: Bloomsbury T. & T. Clark, 2013.

Wolde, Ellen van. "'Wisdom—Who Can Find It?' A Non-Cognitive and Cognitive Study of Job 28:1–11." In *Job 28: Cognition in Context*, edited by E. van Wolde, 1–36. Leiden: Brill, 2003.

Wolfson, Elliott R. "Shekinah." In *ER* 12:8312–16.

Wong, Fook-Kong. "Manna Revisited: A Study of the Mythological and Interpretative Contexts of Manna." PhD diss., Harvard University, 1998.

Wood, Michael. *In Search of Myths and Heroes: Exploring Four Epic Legends of the World*. Berkeley, CA: University of California Press, 2005.

Wright, David P. *Inventing God's Law: How the Covenant Code of the Bible Used and Revised the Laws of Hammurabi*. Oxford: Oxford University Press, 2009.

Yancey, Philip, and Paul A. Brand. *The Gift of Pain*. Grand Rapids: Zondervan, 1997.

Yaron, Reuven. "The Coptos Decree and 2 Sam 12:14." *VT* 9 (1959) 89–91.

Yoder, Christine. "The 'Woman of Substance' (אשת חיל): A Socioeconomic Reading of Proverbs 31:10–31." *JBL* 122 (2003) 427–47.

Yu, Charles. "To Comfort Job: The Speeches in the Book of Job as Rhetorical Discourse." PhD diss., University of Wisconsin, 2011.

———. "A Ridiculous God: Job Uses Psalm 8.5 to Respond to Eliphaz." In *Inner Biblical Allusion in the Poetry of Wisdom and Psalms*, edited by M. Boda et al., 84–102. London: T. & T. Clark, 2019.

Zuckerman, Bruce. *Job the Silent: A Study in Historical Counterpoint*. New York: Oxford University Press, 1991.

Subject Index

A/Ibraham, 3n12, 21n84, 121
Al Aša`ri, 58n166

Ba`al, 20, 21, 21n82
Babylon(ian), 3n15, 11, 20, 21n88, 22n90, 73n10, 79n52, 84n94, 91, 96n190, 115n121, 120
Boaz, 16n47, 46n77
BT, 11, 19, 19n66, 69n245, 84, 84n94, 84n95, 84n97, 85n97, 88n123, 90n142, 91, 94n174, 123

compensation, 4, 4n18, 4n19, 7, 7n46, 10, 10n16, 17n53, 25, 25n111, 25n114, 26, 27n123, 48n88, 55n140, 55n143, 59n171, 59n172, 60, 63, 65, 65n213, 65n214, 66, 66n226, 67n226, 70, 71, 74, 74n21, 79, 79n50, 79n56, 81, 87, 87n120, 87n121, 95, 97, 101, 101n22, 104, 105, 105n47, 106, 109, 113, 122

DILA, 18, 66n221, 73n17, 74n21, 80, 80n66, 81, 81n67, 81n68, 81n70, 82n75, 82n76, 82n77, 82n78, 82n79, 82n80, 82n82, 90n146, 105n50, 122n45
DMS, 18, 34n167, 73n12, 80n63, 83, 83n86, 83n87, 83n91, 84n92, 120, 120n33, 123

Ee, 20, 20n78, 20n79, 85n99, 85n104
Egypt(ian), 3n13, 3n15, 7, 11, 19, 19n71, 20n79, 26, 56n148, 71, 71n2, 72, 73n12, 73n18, 73n20, 74n24, 76, 78n48, 79n53, 80, 80n59, 80n61, 82n81, 83, 83n84, 96, 103n36, 105n50, 104n41, 111, 111n92, 120
Erra, 2n8, 19n67, 22n90, 86n110, 95n180

Hammurabi, 1n2, 32n157, 74n25, 96n184, 96n190
honor, 13n32, 17, 33n164, 43n61, 65, 65n212, 65n215, 74n25, 79, 95n181, 103, 105, 113

integrity, 2n4, 2n8, 9n6, 13n33, 14n37, 16n51, 23, 24, 31, 33, 34, 39, 39n19, 42, 42n44, 42n47, 51n114, 69, 101, 105, 116n125, 123
Islam(ic), 10n12, 23n100, 44n63, 44n64

justice, 9n5, 16n49, 17n53, 31n149, 31n150, 38, 38n16, 39n19, 48, 51n112, 52, 52n125, 53n126, 59, 62, 63n198, 65, 65n215, 66, 66n221, 68n239, 69, 70, 70n247, 73, 74, 75, 75n30, 75n32, 77n42, 78, 79n54, 80, 80n59, 82, 82n80, 89n131, 104, 115, 116n125,

122, 122n45, 122n47, 125n58
justification, 9, 12, 45, 46n76, 47, 50, 50n108, 51, 52, 56, 67, 99, 114

Lud, 11n20, 19, 46n75, 84n97, 87, 91, 91n153, 91n155, 92n157, 92n159, 93n160, 93n161, 93n163, 93n164, 93n165, 94n167, 94n168, 94n170, 94n171, 94n172, 94n173, 94n174, 95n175, 95n176, 95n177, 95n178, 95n179, 95n180, 95n181, 96, 96n184, 96n185, 96n186, 96n187, 96n188, 115n121

Marduk, 3n15, 11, 20, 20n79, 74n25, 85n99, 85n104, 86n107, 86n113, 91, 91n154, 91n155, 92n156, 93, 94n173, 95, 95n179, 95n181, 96, 96n188, 96n190
Mesopotamia(n), 19, 19n71, 20n73, 46n75, 80, 80n59, 84, 92n158, 95n183, 96
Moses, 1n1, 1n3, 16n46, 26, 31n152

pain, 3n13, 39, 64n199, 75, 88, 110, 118, 118n4, 118n6, 118n8, 118n9, 119, 119n19, 119n20, 121n40, 121n42, 122, 123
Paul of Tarsus, 42n49, 48n93, 57n160, 64n199, 118, 118n13
piety, 2, 2n4, 3n12, 3n15, 9, 9n7, 10, 11, 11n18, 12, 14n37, 14n39, 16n49, 17, 22n94, 28, 29, 30, 31, 32, 33, 33n164, 36, 42, 42n43, 47, 47n82, 48, 51, 53n133, 60, 64, 67n230, 70, 71, 79, 97, 101, 102n30, 107, 108, 114, 122, 125n61
(pious) sufferer, 3, 3n15, 11, 15, 19, 46n75, 74, 84, 86, 87, 87n109, 88, 88n123, 88n124, 89, 89n131, 90, 91, 92n158, 97, 124
prosper(ity), 2, 2n5, 3n12, 3n15, 10, 11, 11n18, 11n22, 28, 29, 30, 54n139, 59, 85, 87n118, 88, 88n124, 92, 92n158, 94, 94n172, 94n173, 125n61
punishment, 1, 5n29, 10, 17n53, 24, 45n70, 50n110, 55n140, 55n143, 70n247, 76, 77, 79n54, 97, 98, 118, 122, 125n61

Qumran, 6n40, 45n73, 79n50, 99n12
Qur'an, 3n12, 4n18, 7n46, 11n22, 13n33, 21n88, 23n99, 24n103, 24n104, 25n110, 25n113, 25n114, 26n119, 26n122, 36n2, 37n6, 37n12, 38n14, 42n48, 43n52, 43n62, 45n73, 47n83, 47n86, 48n87, 50n110, 55n140, 75n31, 75n33, 76n36, 78n49, 95n181, 103n40, 115n121, 118n13

redemption, 8, 26, 63, 64, 64n201, 92, 92n157, 93n160, 95, 96, 118
retribution, 4, 4n18, 4n19, 6n40, 7, 7n46, 8, 8n3, 10, 12, 16n46, 17n53, 17n55, 18n59, 23n98, 24, 34, 38n16, 41n42, 43n51, 45n70, 52, 53, 53n133, 54, 54n139, 55, 55n143, 60, 63, 70, 70n247, 71, 74, 74n21, 81, 97, 102, 105n47, 106, 109, 122, 122n45, 124, 125n61
reward, 4n18, 4n19, 10, 10n12, 11n17, 12, 25n113, 25n114, 26n119, 45n70, 70, 70n247, 79n56, 98, 118
Ruth, 15, 16, 16n46

S/satan, 4n19, 6n40, 10n12, 11n17, 15n43, 16, 17n52, 22n90,

23, 23n99, 23n101, 24n102, 24n103, 24n104, 29n139, 30, 30n140, 33, 33n162, 34, 46n75, 46n76, 61n184, 90n138, 101, 107, 107n58, 108, 108n67, 108n68, 108n69, 109, 109n79, 110, 110n80, 111, 112, 112n96, 112n98
suffering, 1n3, 2n5, 2n6, 6n40, 8n2, 15n43, 17, 21, 32, 33, 33n162, 34, 38n18, 39n18, 43, 43n51, 45n73, 53, 54n138, 55n143, 57, 57n160, 59, 60, 60n175, 62, 63, 64, 64n212, 69, 81, 85, 88, 91, 92n157, 101, 107, 110, 117, 118, 118n13, 122, 122n47, 123, 124, 124n56, 125n61

Talmud, 1n1, 1n3, 4n18, 15n42, 16n46, 40n29, 42n44, 46n75, 48n93, 53n133, 64n207, 98n3, 100, 100n17, 100n18, 100n19, 101n22, 111n87
TEP, 11, 18, 18n62, 66n218, 72, 72n7, 72n9, 73, 73n10, 73n12, 73n16, 73n17, 74, 74n21, 74n22, 74n23, 74n24, 74n25, 74n26, 75n27, 75n28, 75n30, 75n31, 75n32, 75n34, 76n35, 76n36, 77n45, 78, 78n45, 78n46, 78n49, 79n50, 79n54, 79n55, 79n57, 80n58, 80n59, 80n64, 90n145, 105n50, 122n45
theodicy, 9, 9n4, 10, 10n11, 12, 19n66, 21n87, 22n90, 42n49, 70n247, 84n95, 85n97, 87n108, 87n109, 87n112, 87n119, 89n131, 89n135, 90n142, 90n146, 93n160, 108n63, 114

wager, 1, 2n4, 22n94, 23n101
wealth, 1n2, 2, 2n7, 26n120, 29, 59, 66, 69n245, 73n10, 80, 81n72, 85, 85n105, 87, 87n118, 88, 90, 90n141, 91, 91n149, 95n178, 96, 104, 104n42, 114
wisdom, 8n1, 18n59, 19, 21n83, 31, 32n156, 45n70, 46n75, 47n82, 48, 48n94, 49, 51n111, 53n133, 54n137, 55n143, 58, 58n163, 64n199, 68n239, 70n247, 71, 71n1, 72, 72n4, 72n9, 74n24, 81, 84n95, 88n125, 91n152, 91n154, 93n166, 94n174, 95n183, 97, 105n50, 108n66

Author Index

Adams, J. W., 53n127
Adams, S. L., 71, 72n4
Aimers, G. J., 2n4, 22n94, 23n101
Albertz, R., 89n135, 92n156
Albright, A., 123n50
Albright, W. F., 85n102
Allen, J. P., 72n6, 72n9, 73n12, 83n84, 83n88
Alonso Schökel, L., 8n3
Al-Rawi, F. N. H., 96n190
Alster, B., 20n79, 87n119
Alt, A., 32n156
Alter, R., 13n30, 14, 14n41, 41n40, 107n62
Alter, Y. L., 64n203
Andersen, F. I., 16n48, 22n95, 34, 34n171
Anderson, J. S., 33n165
Andrew, C., 30n146
Annus, A., 19n65, 91n152, 93n165, 95n178
Apt, N., 7n46
Aquinas, T., 6n40
Aristotle, 44n66, 81n68, 114n117
Assmann, J., 84n92, 88n125
Audet, J. P., 32n156
Augustine, A., 6n40, 17n52
Avrahami, Y., 31n152

Baines, J., 73n10
Baines, S. E., 125n58
Bakhtin, M., 5, 5n29, 41n40, 98n2
Bakon, S., 2n4, 3n17, 53, 53n130, 69n241
Baldwin, S., 4n18, 60, 60n177
Balentine, S. E., 48, 48n91
Bales, K., 43n62
Ball, C. J., 19n68
Balla, I., 34n172
Barbalet, J., 96, 96n191
Barclay, J. M. G., 78n49
Barnett, R., 48n98
Barone, D., 43n56
Barré, M., 2n8
Barth, K., 100n16
Bartlett, A., 30n145, 103n33
Barton, J., 119n24
Bauer, H., 28n134
Beaulieu, P.-A., 95n183
Beckerath, J. von, 73n20
Beckman, G, 20n75
Beilby, J. K., 46n76
Bellos, D., 76n38
Bengsten, S. S. E., 49n98
Benjamin, D. E., 19n70
Ben Zvi, E., 113n110
Bergant, D., 43n54, 110n80, 110n83, 111, 111n88
Berge, K., 19n70
Berges, U., 82n74
Berne, E., 38n18
Beuken, W., 18n58
Bewer, J. A., 61n183
Bingöl, T. Y., 43n59
Birzer, M. L., 32n160
Black, E., 53n127
Black, S., 43n56
Blenkinsopp, J., 32n155

Bloch, R., 108n65
Bloom, A., 75n42
Boda, M., 125n58
Bodner, K., 25n115
Bömer, F., 121n39
Borger, R., 87n118
Bottéro, J., 73n10, 85n99
Botterweck, J. G., 49n98
Bowler, K., 95n174
Boyd, J. O., 9n7
Brand, P., 64n199, 118, 118n5
Brausch, A. M., 43n59
Breitkopf, A. W., 29n137, 49n101, 60n176
Brock, S. P., 107n57
Brockelmann, C., 28n134
Brooke, G. J., 57n152
Brown, D., 107n62
Brown, K., 37n6, 46n78, 54n136
Brown, W., 72n4
Brunner, H., 72n9
Budde, K., 18n58, 63n198
Burnight, J., 5, 5n35, 41, 41n41
Butler, C., 7n47
Buttenweiser, M., 10n12, 38n16

Cahana-Blum, J., 24n105
Cagni, L., 2n8
Calmet, A., 28n135
Carenga, M., 74n24
Carr, D. M., 61n180
Carson, D. A., 52n120
Ceresko, A. R., 15n44
Cernucan, M., 15n43, 19, 19n72, 61n181
Chaitow, L., 118n9
Charlesworth, J. H., 106n54
Chavalas, M., 1n2
Chaviv, Ya`akov ibn, 100
Childs, B. S., 44n65
Cho, P. K.-K., 69n243
Chrysostom, J., 48n93
Churnai, V., 70, 70n249
Civil, M., 90n143
Clines, D. J. A., 1n2, 3n12, 4, 4n21, 10, 10n17, 15n44, 18n58, 22n95, 24n102, 28n135, 30n146, 31n150, 37n5, 39n22, 40, 40n24, 41n36, 53n133, 54n134, 55, 55n142, 62, 63n193, 81n72
Cohen, Y., 9n4, 93n166, 95n181
Cole, D. S., 118n9
Collins, B. J., 92n156, 96n185
Collins, J. J., 107, 107n58, 108n64
Coogan, M. D., 28n131
Cook, D. T., 43n58
Cook, E., 101n23
Cornill, C. H., 61n183
Couturier, G., 32n155
Crenshaw, J. A., 2n6, 5, 5n28, 8n2, 9n4, 10, 10n11, 10n13, 24, 24n107, 39n19, 48n89, 55, 55n140, 64n212, 68n239, 105n46, 108n66
Cross, F. M., 3n14, 20n77, 44n64
Curtis, J. B., 125n61

Dahood, M., 15n44, 19n70
D'Andrade, K., 74n25
Davidson, A., 40, 40n28
Davies, E. W., 28n130
Davis, A., 27, 27n128, 28n129
Dawson, K., 120n129
Day, P. L., 2n4, 2n6, 12n28, 13n29, 18n58, 21n89, 24n103, 42n47, 61n180
de Jong, I. K. F., 44n63
Delekat, L., 29n136
Delitzsch, F., 57n158
Dell, K., 3n17, 5, 5n36, 9n4, 12n27, 18n59
Denning Bolle, S., 73n10
Dever, W. G., 18n61, 20n77
Dhorme, E., 18n58, 28n135
Dick, M., 5n32, 75n175
Diewert, D. A., 38n17
Dillman, A., 120n27
Dion, P., 19n67, 22n95
Dostoevsky, F., 5, 5n29, 41n40
Drinkard, J. F., 47n85
Driver, S. R., 55n141, 62n188
Duhaime, J., 107n58
Duhm, B., 18n58, 28n135, 61n180
Dunham, K. C., 3n17, 19n72, 39n20, 39n22, 40n29, 41,

41n37, 42n49, 43n51, 44, 44n64, 44n66, 46n75, 47n82, 48, 48n92, 48n98, 51n112, 69n241, 69n245, 103n39

Eagleton, T., 7n47
Eaton, J., 12n26, 65, 66n217
Ebach, J., 10, 10n16, 28, 28n130, 28n133
Ebeling, E., 84n94
Eddy, P. R., 46n76
Eisen, R., 6, 6n40, 60n176
Eissfeldt, O., 15n44, 19n67, 29n138, 61n183
Eller, J. D., 45n69
Ellis, N., 21n84
Emerton, J., 24n105
Endo, Y., 49n97
Erman, A., 18n62, 72n5, 83, 83n86
Ernst, C. W., 4n22
Eshel, H., 56n146
Espak, P., 80n62
Ewald, G. H. A. von, 28n135

Farber Flügge, G., 89n130
Farook, M. O., 44n64
Faulkner, R. O., 83n86
Fee, G. D., 11n21, 95n174
Finkel, A. Y., 100n15, 100n17
Finn, J., 96n190
Fishbane, M., 20n75, 98n2
Fohrer, G., 5, 5n26, 5n36, 19n71, 27n127, 40n28, 63n198
Fokkelman, J. P., 15n44
Foley, H., 121n35, 121n41
Fontaine, C. A., 5, 5n31, 9n8, 125n61
Forsyth, N., 23n101
Foster, B., 4n17, 11n21, 14n41, 91n152, 91n153, 92n156, 96n192
Fox, M. V., 4n19, 71n1
Franke, J., 18n61
Fredriksen, P., 16n49
Freedman, D. N., 62, 62n192
Frey, J., 107n58
Fried, R. M., 22n92
Frisch, A., 41n40
Frost, R., 97, 97n197
Frow, J., 71n1
Frymer-Kensky, T., 39n19
Fuchs, G., 22n95, 120n30
Fullerton, K., 40, 40n29
Fyall, R. S., 3n12, 8n1, 12n25

Gabriel, G., 20n79
Gabriel, J. M., 38n18
Gammie, J. G., 99n13
Gamper, A., 21n90
Gardiner, A. H., 22n91, 80n59, 81n69, 82n74, 82n76, 82n80
Garrett, S., 29n139, 107, 107n60, 109, 110, 110n80, 110n82, 112, 112n100
Gaster, T. H., 23n102
Gately, M., 123n53
Gault, B., 23, 23n98
Geiger, A., 14n38
Geller, S. A., 17n56, 58n163
Gemser, B., 5n32, 19n66
George, A., 89n136, 96n190
Gerhards, M., 5n28
Gerleman, G., 55n143, 99n13
Gersonides, 1n3, 6, 58, 58n167, 60, 60n176
Gerstenberger, E. S., 15n45, 75n40
Gese, H., 9n5, 47n82, 54n138
Geyer, N., 117n3
Ghantous, H., 55n143
Gibson, J. C. L., 42n43
Gilkey, L., 64n201
Ginzberg, L., 103, 103n38, 105n49
Giovino, M., 87n118
Goedicke, H., 72n9
Goldingay, J., 26n122, 53, 53n132, 70n252
Goldsmith, R. H., 57n157
Good, E. M., 2n4, 15n43, 18n58, 33, 34n166, 123n53, 125n61
Gordis, R., 51n116, 55, 55n143, 57n156, 105n45
Gordon, C. H., 25n112
Gordon, R. P., 106n53
Grabbe, L. L., 19n69, 56n146
Graf, D. E., 18n61

Gray, J., 19n70, 55n141, 62n188, 62n192, 99n14
Green, A., 64n203
Green, W. H., 39, 39n21
Greenstein, E. L., 6, 6n38, 7n45, 9n4, 18n57, 58n163, 120n27
Gregory I, 6n40, 30, 30n141
Gregory, B., 108n70
Grene, C., 70, 70n251
Grimal, N., 73n20
Groneberg, B., 4n17, 18n61
Gruber, M., 9n4
Guffy, A. R., 9n8, 108n63
Guillaume, P., 70n248, 89n135
Gutiérrez, G., 10, 10n11, 10n12, 70, 70n252

Haag, E., 99n14
Haas, C., 99n14
Habel, N. C., 3n17, 4, 4n21, 12n27, 13n29, 15n44, 18n58, 39n22, 40, 40n32, 41, 41n39, 42n47, 46n80, 51n112, 55n141, 61n179, 62, 62n190, 62n191
Hackett, J. A., 81n70
Hagedorn, A. C., 31n152, 48n93
Hallo, W. W., 18n61
Hamilton, J. E., 12n25
Hamilton, M. W., 97, 97n196, 98n3
Handy, L. K., 23n99
Hankins, D., 6, 6n42
Hanson, K. C., 60n173
Haralambakis, M., 106n54, 107n59
Haran, M., 19n69
Harris, T. A., 38n18
Hartley, J., 3n13, 4, 4n21, 14n37, 22n95, 27n127, 30, 30n144, 36n3, 40, 40n33, 43n53, 47n86, 52, 52n120, 55n142
Hasan, A., 118n13
Hawley, L., 123n49
Hellige, J. B., 42n46
Hengel, M., 99n14
Herodotus, 109n72
Herrmann, S., 72n7
Hershkowitz, D., 121n35
Hilton, R. H., 90n138
Hoffman, Y., 10n16, 13n29, 15n42, 17n56
Holbert, J. C., 43n53, 119n24
Hollis, S. T., 84n92
Homer, 50n107
Hornborg, A., 94n174
Horst, P. van der, 106, 106n55, 110, 110n81
Horwitz, W. J., 19n70
Huff, B. G., 56n145
Hugo, V., 76, 76n39, 110n84
Hurowitz, V. A., 90, 90n140, 90n142
Husseini, R., 43n61
Hyun, S. W. T., 13n29, 55n144

Inouye, S. K., 45n69
Irwin, W. A., 54n139

Jacobsen, T., 3n13, 3n14, 20n74, 120n31
Jackson, D. R., 78n47
Jakobson, R., 18n61
Jameson, F., 7n47
Janzen, J. G., 3n14, 5, 5n27, 7n44, 10, 10n14, 18n59, 22n95, 32, 32n158, 46n76
Jarvik, L. F., 118n7
Jasser, Z., 44n64
Jastrow, M., 44n67
Jiménez, E., 87n118
Jindo, J., 20n74, 30n147
Johns, D., 62, 62n186
Johnson, T. J., 5, 5n32
Jones, S. C., 58n163
Jones Nelson, A., 4n18, 21n83, 23n98, 61n179
Josephus, 1n2, 26n120
Joüon, P., 46n76
Judd, N., 122n46
Jung, C. F., 41n39

Kallen, H., 5, 5n33
Kalman, J., 70, 70n250, 99n7
Kaminsky, J. S., 97, 97n199
Kaplan, R., 25n109
Kates, J. A., 64, 64n204
Kaufmann, Y., 6n40
Kautilya, 78n48

Kautzsch, K., 18n58
Keefe, A., 15n43
Kensky, M. Z., 21n90
Kessler, R., 28, 28n135, 63n199
Kierkegaard, S., 9n7, 70n247
Kinet, D., 107n58
Kissane, E. J., 4n18
Kelly, H., 23n99
Klein, M., 99n12, 101n23
Klopfenstein, M., 25n108
Kluger, R., 4n19
Knauff, E. A., 3n16, 37n7, 37n10
Knierim, R., 119n24
Knutdtzon, J. A., 21n88
Koch, K., 37n6, 97n198
Kolenkow, A., 108n64
Komoróczy, G., 20n75
Koning, B. M., 45n7
Kraemer, D. C., 60n175
Kramer, S. N., 3n15
Kruger, P. A., 88n125
Krüger, T., 90n140, 91n154
Kucicki, J., 74n23
Kugel, J., 17n56, 83n85
Kutsko, J. F., 75n28
Kwon, J. J., 97, 97n200
Kynes, W., 71n1, 119n22

Labahn, M., 23n100
Ladin, K., 123n53
Lamartine, A. de, 120, 120n34
Lambert, W. G., 20n73, 20n78, 20n80, 22n92, 84, 84n97, 85n97, 85n105, 86n108, 86n109, 86n112, 88n125, 89n130, 89n131, 90n141, 90n146, 91n152, 91n153
Landsberger, B., 85n97
Lane, E. W., 4n18, 66n224
Larrimore, M., 3n17, 6, 6n39, 12n25, 98, 98n1
Lasine, S., 30n143, 41n39
LaSor, W. S., 33, 33n161
Launderville, D., 22n92
Leander, P., 28n134
Legaspi, M. C., 111n87
Leick, G., 91n154
Lemaire, A., 19n69
Lemke, W. E., 23n102
Lenski, G., 91n153
Lenzi, A., 19n65, 20n73, 91n152, 91n155, 93n165, 95n178, 95n182
Leveen, A., 2n4, 57, 57n155
Levison, J. R., 6n40
Lewis, C. S., 22, 23n97, 110, 110n86, 119, 119n19, 122, 122n43, 122n46, 122n47, 122n48
Lewis, T. J., 20n74
Lichtheim, M., 73n10, 80n66, 83
Lie, A. G., 87n118
Liebman, C., 121n41
Linafelt, T., 27, 27n128, 28n129, 99n10
Linebaugh, J., 64n199
Litfin, D., 53n129
Litwiller, B. J., 43n59
Livingstone, A., 87n118
Lo, A., 58n163
Loader, J. A., 16n46
Lods, A., 23n99
Lohmann, K., 83, 83n87
Longenecker, R. N., 56n149
Longman, T., 12, 12n24, 38n17, 40, 40n30, 43n51, 108n69
Lopes, M. H., 74n24
Loretz, O., 19n69
Low, K., 14n37, 15n43
Lowth, R., 17n56
Luiselli, M. M., 3n15
Lundbom, J., 120n26

Magdalene, F. R., 23n99, 98n3
Maiberger, P., 26n118
Maimonides, 1n3, 3n17, 6, 40, 40n27, 57, 57n160, 58n166
Mangan, C., 17n52, 20n73, 99n12, 101n21, 101n23, 102n28, 103n37, 104n41, 104n44, 106n51
Markter, F., 95n176
Marlow, H., 81n70
Martin, T. W., 49n101
Mathew, G., 18n58
Mathewson, D., 7n47
Mayer, G., 51n116

McCabe, R., 69, 69n241, 70
McCarter, P. K., 101n26
McGilchrist, I., 45n68
McKeating, H., 107n55
Mende, T., 64n206
Merton, T., 119n20
Metaxas, E., 124n55
Mewburn, I., 37n5
Meyers, E. M., 20n77
Michalowski, P., 120n25
Michel, W. E., 53n126
Millard, A., 20n80
Miller, A., 22n92
Miller, P. D., 1n3
Miscall, P., 7n46
Mishna, F., 43n59
Mittleman, A., 98n3, 99n6
Mngomezulu, T., 117n3
Moberly, W., 9, 9n6, 24, 24n106
Moore, G. F., 3n17
Moore, M. S., 3n12, 3n13, 3n15, 5n30, 5n32, 5n34, 6n39, 6n42, 11n20, 11n22, 12n23, 12n24, 15n45, 16n46, 18n59, 20n74, 20n79, 20n81, 22n92, 24n105, 28n131, 28n133, 37n6, 40n23, 43n55, 46n74, 47n86, 49n97, 52n125, 55n144, 56n147, 61n180, 63n195, 63n198, 65n209, 68n234, 73n18, 73n19, 76n34, 80n63, 80n65, 81n68, 81n72, 82n75, 82n78, 84n95, 84n97, 87n116, 89n130, 89n137, 92n156, 95n177, 98n4, 110n84, 114n112, 118n10, 120n26, 121n38, 121n39
Moore, R., 42n47
Morales, L. M., 8n2
Moran. W. L., 92n156
Morris, D. B., 119n20
Morrison, M. A., 25n112
Morrow, W. S., 36n4
Mowinckel, S., 3n13, 80n65
Muenchow, C., 125n61
Mullen, E. T., 20n73, 21n82
Müller, H.-P., 4n21, 7n45, 9n4, 22n94, 119, 119n17
Muraoka, T., 99n12
Murphy, R. E., 15n45, 24n105, 55n141, 84n95
Murphy-O'Connor, J., 45n73
Myhrman, D. W., 21n88

Nam, D.-W., 69n246
Nef Ulloa, B. A., 23n101, 41n42
Neumann, H., 20n75
Neville, R., 91n151
Newman, C. C., 56n149
Newsom, C., 5, 5n30, 9, 9n4, 9n9, 12n27, 15n43, 21n90, 24n104, 27n127, 41, 41n38, 41n40, 42n50, 59, 60n174, 61, 61n181, 61n183, 61n184, 64, 64n202, 97n195, 98n2
Neyrand, L., 48n93
Nicholson, E., 9n4
Nickelsburg, G. W. E., 6n40
Nicol, N., 123n50
Niebuhr, R., 44n62
Nielsen, K., 3n13, 22n90, 120n31
Noam, V., 103n38
Noegel, S., 102n28
Nolan, P., 91n153
Nurse, A. M., 43n57

O'Connor, K. M., 124n56
O'Connor, M., 17n56
Oh, C. H., 45n69
Olyan, S., 96n189
Oorschot, 7n45
Oshima, T., 19n66, 84n95, 84n96, 87n108, 86n109, 86n112, 87n119, 89n131, 90, 90n141, 90n146, 91n149, 91n152, 92n157, 93n161, 93n164, 94n167, 97n194
Osing, J., 83n86
Otto, E., 71n2
Otto, R., 46n74
Otzen, B., 46n80

Pagels, E., 24n103
Pallis, S. A., 20n79

Parkinson, R., 7, 7n43, 11n19, 12n27, 18n62, 18n63, 72, 72n6, 72n7, 72n8, 72n9, 73n12, 74, 74n21, 74n23, 75, 75n29, 75n30, 78, 78n45, 78n47, 80n63, 81n71, 83n89
Parmentier, M. F. G., 67n227
Parpola, S., 57n154
Paul, S. M., 3n14
Paulus, J., 5n33
Peake, A. S., 40n28
Pecchioli Daddi, F., 94n169
Pelham, A., 7n44, 10n17, 46n78
Pemberton, G., 119n22
Penchansky, D., 17n52, 18n58, 68, 69n240
Perdue, L., 8n1, 45n70, 48, 48n90, 48n94, 58n162, 70n247
Perrin, N., 61n180
Pettys, V., 118, 118n11
Phillips, E., 52, 52n121, 60, 60n178
Philo, 112n99
Pilch, J. J., 23n99
Pinker, A., 54n139
Pitard, W., 20n82
Plato, 31n148
Pleins, J. D., 22n94
Pohl, W., 3n14, 3n16, 5, 5n32, 17n55, 31n154, 36n4, 37n6, 63n193, 99, 99n11, 119, 119n23
Polanski, D., 22n95
Polzin, R., 40n29, 61n180
Pope, M., 2n4, 4, 4n22, 22n95, 23n98, 37n8, 40, 40n26, 40n34, 42n43, 51n112, 62, 62n188, 80n63
Pope, N., 43n55
Porter, B. N., 87n118
Poser, R., 68n233
Porter, S. E., 22n96
Portier-Young, A., 109n74
Puech, E., 19n69
Pyper, H., 119n15

Qimron, E., 107n58

Rachman, G., 95n174
Rad, G. von, 45n70, 94n174
Rahman, F., 24n103
Rahnenführer, D., 107n59
Rashi, 1n2, 1n3, 2n11, 6, 13n30, 23n99, 36n2, 38, 38n16, 42n44, 42n45, 46n75, 54n135
Rast, W. E., 20n77
Raz, Y., 4n20, 119, 119n16
Redfield, J., 44n63
Redford, D., 71, 71n2, 80n66, 83n83
Reichert, V. A., 57n159
Renz, J., 20n77
Reiner, E., 4n17, 18n61
Richards, J., 73n10
Richardson, M., 89n132
Richter, H., 5, 5n32, 8n3, 26n87, 32n156
Ricoeur, P., 22n92
Ringgren, H., 80n65
Roberts, J. J. M., 21n90, 22n95, 120n25
Röllig, W., 20n77
Ross, J. F., 8n2
Roy, R., 118n9
Rudolph, K., 23n100
Ryan, G., 31, 31n148

Saadiah Gaon, 21n89, 24n103
Sakenfeld, K. D., 110n84
Salakpi, A. G. K., 55n144
Salisbury, J. E., 16n47
Salters, R. B., 84n95
Sandoval, T., 9, 10n10
Sasson, V., 2, 2n6, 2n9, 15n43, 20n73, 34, 34n167
Sawyer, J. F., 15n44
Scarlata, M. W., 106n53
Schäfer, P., 107n58
Schaller, B., 99n14, 107, 107n61
Scher, R. K., 37n5
Schifferdecker, K., 48n89, 90n147
Schiffman, L., 45n73, 98n4
Scholnick, S. H., 21n86, 51n117
Schussler Fiorenza, E., 15n43
Schindler, A., 2n10, 17n52
Schmid, K., 14n35
Schniedewind, W., 98n2

Schöplin, K., 68n233
Schunck, M., 70n248
Schüpphaus, J., 42n44
Seigler, J., 118n9
Selmier, W. T., 45n69
Seow, C. L., 3n17, 5, 5n25, 9, 9n8, 10n12, 14n39, 17n52, 17n57, 21n87, 22n95, 23n99, 23n100, 24, 24n104, 24n105, 37n5, 40, 40n31, 42n45, 44, 44n67, 46n76, 47n81, 50n103, 50n104, 53n126, 53n131, 56n146, 62, 62n189, 80n65
Seri, A., 86n107
Sessions, W. L., 65n212
Sethe, K., 81n69
Shah, N., 43n58
Sheldon, L. J., 21n90
Shelley, T., 118n9
Shepherd, D., 99n12, 101n23, 102n28, 102n30
Sherwood, I., 11n18, 125n61
Shipp, J., 20n76
Shipp, R. M., 79n52
Shoro, S., 43n61
Shupak, N., 72, 72n3, 72n5, 72n6
Shurter, E. D., 14n40
Sidursky, M., 86n108, 95n178
Signer, M., 47n83
Simonetti, C., 32n157
Simundson, D., 119, 119n14
Sinnott, A. M., 24n105
Sitzler, D., 84n97, 96n192
Slack, J., 43n60
Sloan, R. B., 56n149
Small, G., 118n7
Smelik, K., 74n24, 79n53
Smith, C., 63, 63n194, 67n231
Smith, M., 21n82
Smith, W. J., 123n50
Sneed, M., 71n1, 84n94
Soards, M., 74n23
Soden, W. von, 85n107, 90n141
Sommerfeld, W., 20n79, 96n190
Sophocles, 3n15
Sorge, B., 2n11, 118n6
Sorlin, H., 48n93
Spieckermann, H., 91, 92n156, 95n182, 115n121
Spittler, R., 99n14, 108n64, 108n70, 111, 111n89
Stamm, J. J., 19n66, 21n87
Staubli, T., 73n13
Stokes, R. R., 23n99
Stovell, B. M., 22n96
Stuckenbruck, L. T., 107n58
Stull, B. T., 119n20
Stump, E., 13n31, 14n35, 30, 30n143
Šubši-mešre-šakkan, 3n15
Suriano, M. J., 21n89
Susman, M., 5, 5n24
Sweeney, M. A., 18n60
Syring, W. D., 18n58

Tate, W. R., 7n46
Terrien, S., 4, 5n23, 40, 40n25, 63n198, 97n197, 118n4
Thornton, D. T., 23n99
Thurow, L., 94n174
Ticciati, S., 9n6
Tilley, T. W., 10n11
Toorn, K. van der, 93n160, 93n162
Tropper, A., 103n38
Trotter, J. R., 107n61
Tsevat, M., 122n45
Tugendhaft, A., 20, 20n75

Van Seters, J., 25n112
Vermeylen, J., 61n180
Vesely, P., 9n9, 31, 31n149, 31n154, 51n114
Viano, S., 23n58
Vicchio, S., 1n3, 6, 6n40, 10n12, 21n89, 22n96, 23n100, 24n103, 34n169
Volf, M., 110, 110n85

Wahl, H., 61, 62n185
Walker, C., 75n175
Wallace, H. N., 48n93
Waltke, B., 9, 9n7, 24, 24n106
Walton, J., 17n55, 108n69
Ward, M. R., 59n170
Washburn, J., 77n42

Watanabe, K., 57n154
Waters, L., 62, 62n187
Watson, W. G., 15n44
Waugh, L. R., 18n61
Weeks, S., 71n1
Wehr, H., 4n18, 47n83, 87n121, 93n160
Weill, R., 22n93
Weinfeld, M., 92n157
Weiser, A., 63n198
Weiss, D., 99, 99n8, 99n9
Weiss, M., 21n85, 24n105
Welz, C., 70n247
Westbrook, R., 32, 32n156
Westermann, C., 5, 5n33, 37n6, 119n22, 119n24
Wharton, J. A., 2n8
Whedbee, J. W., 5, 5n34, 22n94
White, E., 13n30, 25n115
Whybray, R., 14n41, 30, 30n142, 30n143
Wiggins, N., 99n7
Wilcke, C., 32n155
Wilcox, K. G., 15n43
Williams, L. V., 45n68
Wilson, G. H., 6n41, 8n3
Wilson, J. A., 72n6, 79n54, 79n56, 82n80
Wilson, L., 6, 7n47, 17n53, 119n18
Winnington-Ingram, R. P., 3n15
Wiseman, D., 19n71
Witte, M., 116n125
Wolde, E. van, 58n163
Wolfson, E. R., 105n49
Wong, F.-K., 26n118
Wood, M., 121n36
Wright, D. P., 26n117
Wylie, H., 123n50

Xenophon, 31n153

Yancey, P., 64n199, 118n5
Yaron, R., 14n38
Yoder, C., 113n110
Yoffee, N., 73n10
Yu, C., 47n83, 50n108

Zuckerman, B., 6, 6n37

Printed in the USA
CPSIA information can be obtained
at www.ICGtesting.com
LVHW021746290124
770238LV00003B/109

9 781666 707342